THEY NEARLY REACHED THE SKY

WEST HAM UNITED IN EUROPE

BRIAN BELTON

FONTHILL

Fonthill Media Language Policy

Fonthill Media publishes in the international English language market. One language edition is published worldwide. As there are minor differences in spelling and presentation, especially with regard to American English and British English, a policy is necessary to define which form of English to use. The Fonthill Policy is to use the form of English native to the author. Brian Belton was born and educated in East London; therefore British English has been adopted in this publication.

Fonthill Media Limited
Fonthill Media LLC
www.fonthillmedia.com
office@fonthillmedia.com

First published in the United Kingdom and the United States of America 2017

British Library Cataloguing in Publication Data:
A catalogue record for this book is available from the British Library

Typeset in Minion Pro 10pt on 13pt
Printed and bound by CPI Group (UK) Ltd, Croydon, CR0 4YY

CONTENTS

FOREWORD

This book might be misunderstood as a record of the achievements and failures of a football club in European football. However, putting aside the consideration that to achieve anything, one needs to accept failure as part of the learning process by which any accomplishment is realised, Brian Belton has written something that is more than a mere documentation of events.

The pages he has filled are a reflection on probably the most international of sports, how people relate to each other through the game, and what it is to identify with a club in the context of a continental perspective. As such, Brian has indeed written about football, but also culture and identity. He has told a tale of people, players, fans, managers, and so on—those that literally 'made' (and continue to generate) matches, competitions, tournaments, and the game itself. It is this collection of facts, viewpoints, and insights that makes this book able to satisfy a number of tastes and outlooks on football and its history. However, it also says something about our global society. This is quite poignant at a time when the UK has decided to leave its place within an inter-reliant, mutually-supportive European community, and become something of a lone wolf in a dog-eat-dog world.

When Brian asked me to write this foreword, he did so as a 'football person'— someone who had watched me as a part and member of the Hammers' side, playing for the club he has been intrinsically linked with all his life. Brian's family have been part of what West Ham is (or rather, it has been part of them) for generations. Like many of the supporters of the East London 'Irons', he regarded, and still regards me, as a 'Hammer'. I guess, at least in part, that I am; those claret and blue days of my life remain important and had an influence on making me who I am today.

The relationship between fans and players has always been co-dependent—one defines the other. Professional players would not exist without supporters, and without players, there is nothing for the fan to support. Sometimes, it seems that the synergy and interdependence that (for me) is inherent in the game has almost been forgotten over the last few decades. Often, it seems the association between professionals and the crowds that pay to see them perform has become more of an 'us' and 'them' thing—the 'we' of football has become a bit lost.

However, I readily agreed to contribute to Brian's work precisely because I was, and remain, conscious that football is, in the last analysis, a collaborative exercise.

The team and the club are organic things—an expression of symbiosis the like of which it is hard to find elsewhere in our evermore individualised society. A good or useful team member will always want to contribute to the whole. We continually remake our world in this way.

When I played, I was very conscious of the solidarity that existed between everyone involved with West Ham. I played and trained with some of the great players mentioned in this book, including Billy Bonds, Trevor Brooking, Tommy Taylor, Alvin Martin, and Frank Lampard Sr, and under arguably the best and most successful manager the club has ever had: John Lyall. However, wherever we went as a club, whatever we did, that 'we' was the means that enabled us to achieve anything and everything, and of course this 'usness' included the fans.

It is such sentiment that football is crafted out of, and I am glad to continue to be part of this. I suspect, because you have picked up this book and have read thus far, you are involved in much the same endeavour. At some level, we are all aware we are stronger together. As Muhammad Ali had it in his 'shortest poem ever'—holding up one finger: 'Me', making a fist: 'We'.

Anton Otulakowski

West Ham United 1976–1979 (Up the 'Ammers!)

Born in Thornhill near Dewsbury, West Yorkshire, in January 1956, Anton Otulakowski got into football after gaining a deal of success as a young gymnast. While playing for Ossett Town, Otulakowski's talent was noticed when Barnsley scouts invited him to take a trial. He was taken on as youth player, and ultimately broke into the first team as a midfielder during 1975.

A season later, the then twenty-one-year-old was brought to Upton Park by John Lyall, just after the club had been beaten by RSC Anderlecht in the European Cup Winners' Cup final in Belgium. In what seemed like no time, Otulakowski had moved from Fourth Division football to the top flight of the English game.

One of Otulakowski's first outings as a Hammer was Les Barrett's testimonial, playing alongside the likes of Bobby Moore, George Best, and Rodney Marsh. From the get-go, he was, in his own words, 'awe-struck'. However, as the game went on, he settled and scored with a skillful chip over the goalkeeper.

The following Friday, the team sheet was posted for West Ham's match at Old Trafford, and Otulakowski saw his name in the starting line-up. When he got to Manchester, he had transformed from a player who turned out in front of a gate of, say, 3,000, to someone who lined up in the presence of 55,000 fans.

West Ham won the game 0–2 (Trevor Brooking and Billy Jennings scored for the Irons) and Otulakowski was man-of-the-match. Everything had happened at a breathtaking pace. Oddly, given our contemporary view of top professionals today, Otulakowski had been obliged to work his notice for the gas board before he was able to play.

Otulakowski remained at the Boleyn Ground for the best part of three years. After 1970, he would turn out for Southend United, Millwall, and Crystal Palace, before leaving football in 1987 with nearly 350 league appearances under his belt.

Otulakowski's Polish father, Jan, came to the UK as a refugee following the Second World War. John (as Otulakowski Sr became almost as soon as he got to Britain) found himself in Lincolnshire. Having been a dairy farmer in Poland, he turned down the option of moving into English agriculture, choosing instead to get work in the textile industry.

Not wanting to return to Poland as Communism began to take a grip there, John was sponsored to go to the USA, but three weeks before his proposed departure, he met Anton's mother, Winnie. Ultimately, the couple would have four children together.

Dewsbury had a strong Polish community after the Second World War, and as a child, Anton appeared in the footballing ranks of Dewsbury Polish Club. This gave his dad the pleasurable opportunity to both support his son and interact with his fellow Poles. However, Anton's name and identity caused him to standout, and John remembered, 'Michael Parkinson doing a story for *The Times* on how a team like Barnsley, which he was suggesting was a very flat-cap-and-fish-and-chips kind of place, [could] have a player called Otulakowski play for them.'

While Anton was amused by this, some of his extended family took umbrage at this kind of opinion voiced by one of the Tykes' most famous supporters.

Currently, Anton Otulakowski runs his own property portfolio and continues to see himself first and foremost as a Yorkshireman. However, while residing in the idyllic Yorkshire Dales with his nearest neighbour a mile away, part of him is and will forever be a Hammer.

When he came to Upton Park, Otulakowski's Polish roots (like later Hammer Paul Konchesky) took me back to being an eight-year-old. I was taken to the USA by family members making a holiday of West Ham's adventure in the American International Soccer League during the summer of 1963. We were having breakfast in a diner in New York when several members of the Górnik Zabrze team came in. My cousin, who was much older than me, immediately approached them for autographs, which they all provided with a deal of bonhomie and good humour.

West Ham, a club that won its first two major trophies by the efforts of local players only (see Belton, 2005), have from the late 1960s drawn on the talents of players from all over Europe and the world. Anton, with his background, continued a tradition at West Ham of bringing together a diverse cultural mix and melding it into a team. This always fascinated me and was probably part of the basis for my lifelong interest in identity, which has encompassed a doctorate, several books, and tens of thousands of miles travelled.

Before that encounter in the USA, the Hammers had not had much contact with Polish sides. In fact, the club had only met the one team.

L.S.K. Lodz (POL)	Upton Park	18/11/1957	W 4–1	Dick 2, Bond, Brown

West Ham United: Ernie Gregory, John Bond, Noel Cantwell, Andy Malcolm, Ken Brown, Bill Lansdowne, Billy Dare, John Smith, Vic Keeble, John Dick, Malcolm Musgrove

Since the encounter in New York, West Ham have met a few Polish sides.

American International Soccer League 1963				
Klub Sportowy Gornik (POL)	Randalls Island Stadium, New York	Group 1 play-off, 1st leg. 31/07/1963	D 1–1	Byrne

West Ham United: Jim Standen, Joe Kirkup, Jack Burkett, Martin Peters, Ken Brown, Bobby Moore, Alan Sealey, Ronnie Boyce, Johnny Byrne, Geoff Hurst, Peter Brabrook. Manager: Ron Greenwood.

Klub Sportowy Gornik (POL)	Randalls Island Stadium: New York	Group 1 play-off, 2nd leg. 04/08/1963	W 1–0	Hurst

West Ham United: Jim Standen, Joe Kirkup, Jack Burkett, Martin Peters, Ken Brown, Ronnie Boyce, Peter Brabrook, Alan Sealey, Geoff Hurst, Johnny Sissons, Tony Scott

SPN Widzew Lodz (POL)	Chadwell Heath	16/02/1999	D 0–0	

West Ham United: Stephen Bywater, Andy Harris (Southend Player), Lee Hodges, Steve Potts, Chris Coyne, David Partridge, Marc Keller (Grant McCann), Marc-Vivien Foé, Samassi Abou, Joe Cole, Scott Minto

Arka Gdynia (POL)	Stadion GOSiR	29/10/2009	D 2–2	Dixon, Daprela

West Ham United: Marek Štěch, Tony Brookes, Jordon Brown, Bondz N'Gala, Fabio Daprelà, Nigel Quashie, Georg Grasser, Eoin Wearen, Dan Kearns, Frank Nouble, Terry Dixon

I asked Anton Otulakowski to write the foreword for this book for a number of reasons. Firstly, because I admired the way he played as part of the team. He was one of those professionals who would give his all for the greater whole—pretty much a rarity in more selfish times. Previously, I have been lucky enough to have been a recipient of the kindness of Sir Geoff Hurst, Jimmy Ruffell, Martin Peters, Frank O'Farrell, Ken Brown, Phil Parkes, and other Hammers stars who have generously written forewords for my books. Former England captain Gerry Francis and Scottish international Pat Nevin have done the same when I have written about QPR and Chelsea.

I asked Anton because he was a foot-soldier of the game—the kind of player without whom there would be no professional football. His voice, view, and presence are pertinent for that reason in that he represents the boyhood dream of many of us—to be 'discovered' and play for a top side, even if just for a limited time.

Anton was with West Ham during what I see as the last romantic period of football history, a time that is unlikely to be repeated. It is through players like him, connected to that precious folklore of football, that many of his generation (people like me) became adherents of the game. Anton is a patron saint of this mythology—one that actually lived it. I am grateful to him for writing the foreword but also for what he represents in the game that for so many of us is part of our background—the ticks and tocks of our lives.

INTRODUCTION

In the history of the club, West Ham have played more than 350 games against European opposition right across the continent, some from countries that no longer exist. These contests can be used to map the development and trajectory of West Ham as an institution, but also as a social phenomenon, playing a part in breaking down political and social barriers in a romantic spirit of curiosity and adventure. It was the latter that attracted me to write this book and what I hope to convey via the names of players, clubs, times, incidents, experiences, regrets, and the continued hunt for glory—but not, as is the case so often in football fandom, just for its own sake.

I attempt to paint a picture with facts and reflections. However, both these media are imprecise tools. Reports on games, the further back in time they were played, are often inaccurate or end up (annoyingly) lost or forgotten.

Over the pages that follow, I have gathered together what I could of each encounter the Hammers have had with European competition, both within and outside the confines of the continental borders. I would like to think it is a complete compendium, but I doubt that. Professional teams, certainly before the Second World War, appear at times (especially while touring) to have played games at something close to the drop of a hat. At the same time, I would be willing to bet that the Boleyn Ground has played host to some visiting sides that might have initially turned up to train or meet a club that had let them down or simply disappeared. Someone will come across a report or meet a supporter, perhaps even a former player, who will reminisce about such games, which I suppose is frustrating, but it is also part of the archaeology of football history; by its very nature, it is a work in progress.

I have only headed up matches played in organised tournaments and tours. Others I detail without an unnecessary epithet. I have tried to avoid labelling any encounter as a 'friendly' as I do not believe that any football game played by professionals is anything but competitive; too much relies on performance and the result for this not to be the case. That, of course, could also be said for the 100-a-side matches I played in Greengate Park, Plaistow, during my days at the esteemed academy of learning and football, Burke Secondary Modern School. 'Jumpers for goalposts' they may have been (kits being Sta-Prest and DMs), but 'friendly' they were not. I still have the scars to prove it.

Personal pride, bragging rights, and integrity honed by competitive instinct apart, one only needs to ask a professional player if they take any match frivolously—a situation where they and their career are under scrutiny. Malcolm Allison told me some years ago:

> Every game is serious. Training games are serious. As a professional you have to ask if you are not going to take it seriously why play? Yeah, maybe there is not much at stake in a wider sense, but at a personal level it comes down to you against the other guy; them against us!
>
> We had a game against AC Milan at Upton Park. That was quite something in the early 1950s. They walked all over us; it was embarrassing. West Ham didn't play badly, we just played the way we normally played. We got no real coaching then, we worked it out for ourselves. But I didn't come away thinking 'Oh well, it don't [sic] matter because it was a friendly'. I didn't sleep for days! I was angry with myself and others, probably the whole system.

A Hammer of the same era, Noel Cantwell, confirmed Allison's outlook:

> I've known players to get into stand-up fights kicking a tennis ball around a car park while waiting for the team coach! You want to win. It's planted in your head every minute of every day from when you are a kid. Yes, friendly or exhibition games might be a chance to experiment, try someone or something new, but to an extent every game has elements of that, if you're an inventive player or coach. True, there's no reason to try and hold on to a draw in such games, but there's every reason to try and get one if it's the best you can hope for, say if you're 1–0 down with three minutes to go. You try, of course you do!

Where I have been reasonably certain about the composition of West Ham teams and goal scorers, I have included the names of the players. I have applied the same rule to opposing sides, attendances, match officials, managers, and the like. Where I have been uncertain, I have not included details. I have pretty much stuck to the data put together either at, during, or shortly after games as I think this does something to capture the spirit of support. For this reason, not all the matches detailed capture exactly the same information—and yes, I might have trawled through the net, but if the reader is so inclinded they can do that for themselves. This aside, programmes, press reports, and therefore the books and websites that rely on them are not always dependable guides, even though they are sometimes all we have. That said, I have tried not to call on the latter. I did not want to present just a mega-list overly drawn from faceless sources; I wanted something closer to home and from the perspective of supporters.

With this in mind, I have followed the records made by myself, my father, and my grandfather (a sort of hereditary asperser's trait perhaps?). Between us, I think we have watched most of the games played against European clubs at Upton Park and a fair few elsewhere. Other relatives and friends have also added to this collection over the years, particularly for the less 'iconic' pre-season tours—anyone I could remind, persuade, blackmail, or beg in fact.

I would not claim these records are infallible. No record is, but my own handwriting seems to have deteriorated from the point I began to use keyboards for study and work, and the fossil remains of East London raindrops from the 1920s, 1930s, and 1940s have taken their toll, but at least any errors can be personally owned and corrected.

While accuracy has been striven for, the point is more about an evocation of context and ethos. Names mean things to us; they conjure up a face, a person, a time, perhaps when we were young and everything was new. A time when the evening games at Upton Park were pure magic, the grass was greener and the world much bigger. That is the enchantment of history, it can take us back to a past we knew—once once lived and now remembered.

However, via the mention of Len Goulden, Vic Watson, or Syd Puddefoot, we are transported to places that existed maybe long before we were born, that perhaps, like these men, are long gone. Nevertheless, we are connected by the game; players live once more and we recognise the shirt, the crossed hammers over the heart, the sound of the whistle blown, and a ball being kicked.

In the face of death is life, and in the game there is living. 'We' continue forever blowing bubbles; the 'me' is maintained by the continuance of 'usness' in claret and blue... 'Go on you Irons!'

1

WHAT WE HOPE FOR IN EUROPE

On Friday 7 August 2015, I went to a restless sleep with the news that West Ham had been knocked out of the Europa League by Astra Giurgiu after losing 2–1 at the Stadionul Marin Anastasovici in Giurgiu, which, as everyone knows, is the capital city of Giurgiu County in southern Romania, Muntenia.

I have better memories of facing Romanian opposition. In the winter of 1980, the Hammers had met and defeated another Romanian side, Politehnica Timişoara, over two legs in the European Cup Winners' Cup—winning the home leg and losing away. Timişoara is one of Romania's largest cities, situated in the far west of the country close to the Serbian and Hungarian borders. Giurgiu, on the other hand, can be found amid mudflats and marshes on the left bank of the Danube, which is a pretty suitable place to be humiliated.

The Black Devils (Astra Giurgiu) have a somewhat sketchy history, but in its current incarnation, the club has been in the top flight of Romanian football for half a dozen years. This was their third season in Europe, having been knocked out of the same competition in 2013–14 by Israeli club Maccabi Haifa. In the 2014-15 season, they finished bottom of their group and were eliminated, winning just one game.

West Ham's road to Romania had been consistently painful. A 3–0 victory over FC Lusitanos from Andorra (a side founded in 1999) hardly constituted a moment of glory, and the single goal in the away win was frankly pathetic. This brought Birkirkara to the Boleyn Ground, where the Mediterranean minnows limited the home side to another solitary goal win. The result was reversed in central Malta, but the Hammers scraped though on penalties. These latter ties were firsts in that the Hammers had never played teams from either Andorra or Malta.

The Irons had qualified for the competition via the Premier League Fair Play Table, which looked ironic after James Collins was sent off in the home game with the Black Devils following Diafra Sakho's dismissal in Andorra, and James Tomkins seeing red in Malta. The record indicates West Ham had pretty much been a bunch of flat-footed cloggers, kicking their way around something less than Conference-level European football.

UFEA Europa League 2015–16				
FC Lusitans (AND) Ref: Vadims Direktorenko	Upton Park, att: 34,699	First qualifying round, 1st leg 02/07/2015	W 3–0	Sakho 2, Tomkins

West Ham United: Darren Randolph, James Tomkins, Matt Jarvis, Mauro Zárate (Djair Parfitt-Williams), Diafra Sakho (Elliot Lee), Joey O'Brien (Josh Cullen), Nicky Morgan, Morgan Amalfitano, Diego Poyet, Reece Burke, Reece Oxford, Lewis Page. Manager: *Slaven Bilić.*

FC Lusitans: Rubio, Crespo, Moi, Peter, Romero, Reis, Aguilar (Conteh), Molina, Nicolas (Moya), Franclim (Sonajee), Maciel

| FC Lusitans (AND) Ref: Anders Poulsen | Estadi Comunal d'Andorra la Vella, att: 1,300 | First qualifying round, 2nd leg 09/07/2015 | W 0-1 | Lee |

FC Lusitans: Gerardo, Acosta (Moya), Nicolas, Munoz, Romero, Dos Reis, Aguilar, Molina, Nicolas, Soares, Maciel

West Ham United: Darren Randolph, Joey O'Brien (Reece Burke), James Tomkins, Reece Oxford, Lewis Page, Diego Poyet, Josh Cullen (Amos Nasha). Matt Jarvis, Nicky Morgan, Morgan Amalfitano (Djair Parfitt-Williams), Diafra Sakho, Elliot Lee. Manager: *Slaven Bilić.*

| Birkirkara FC (MLT) Ref: Markus Hameter | Upton Park, att: 33,048 | Second qualifying round, 1st leg 16/07/2015 | W 1–0 | Tomkins |

West Ham United: Adrián, Joey O'Brien, James Tomkins, Winston Reid, Aaron Cresswell, Kevin Nolan (Diego Poyet) Mark Noble, Matt Jarvis, Nicky Morgan, Morgan Amalfitano (Martin Samuelsen), Mauro Zárate, Modibo Maïga (Elliot Lee). Manager: *Slaven Bilić.*

Birkirkara FC; Haber, Mazzetti, Camenzuli, Fenech (Zammit), Miccoli, Vukanac, Murga (Agius), Liliu (Plut), Zerafa, Z. Muscat, R. Muscat

| Birkirkara FC (MLT) Ref: Enea Jorgi | National Stadium Ta'Qali, att: 1,300 | Second qualifying round, 2nd leg 23/07/2015 | L 0–1 (D 1–1, W 3–5 pens) | *Miccoli* |

Birkirkara FC: Haber, Z. Muscat, Marcelina (Zammit), Vukanac, Mazzetti, Fenech, Camenzuli, Zerafa, R. Muscat (Agius), Liliu, Miccoli (Plut)

West Ham United: Adrián, Joey O'Brien, James Tomkins, James Collins, Aaron Cresswell, Cheikhou Kouyaté, Mark Noble, Kevin Nolan (Diego Poyet), Matt Jarvis (Martin Samuelsen), Nicky Morgan, Morgan Amalfitano (Modibo Maïga), Mauro Zárate. Manager: *Slaven Bilić.*

| AFC Astra Giurgiu (ROM) Ref: Adrien Jaccottet | Upton Park, att: 33,838 | Third qualifying round, 1st leg 30/07/2015 | D 2–2 | Valencia, Zárate *Boldrin, Ogbonna (o.g.)* |

West Ham United: Adrián, Joey O'Brien (Reece Burke), Angelo Ogbonna, James Collins, Aaron Cresswell, Reece Oxford. Mark Noble, Cheikhou Kouyaté, Dimitri Payet, Enner Valencia (Modibo Maïga), Mauro Zárate (Matt Jarvis). Manager: *Slaven Bilić.*

AFC Astra Giurgiu: Lung, Alves, Seto, Enache, Budescu (Lovin), Morais, Boldrin (Dandea), Gaman, Teixeira, Quieros, De Amorim (Florea)

AFC Astra Giurgiu (ROM)	Stadionul Marin Anastasovici, att: 6,300	Third qualifying round, 2nd leg 06/08/2015	L 2–1 (L 4–3)	Budescu 2 Lanzini
Ref: Paolo Valeri				

FC Astra Giurgiu: Lung, Alves, Seto, Enache, Budescu, Morais, Boldrin, Gaman, Teixeira, Queiros, Amorim
West Ham United: Darren Randolph, Kevin Nolan, Carl Jenkinson, Modibo Maïga, Diego Poyet, Doneil Henry, Manuel Lanzini, Elliot Lee (Jordon Brown), Lewis Page (Alex Pike), Josh Cullen, Kyle Knoyle. Manager: *Slaven Bilić.*

While this was not the greatest performance by West Ham, it was a vast improvement on the club's most recent showing in the same tournament. At the end of the 2004–05 season, the Hammers had just about made the top half-dozen in the Championship, but did manage to achieve Premiership status by way of the play-offs. As such, survival seemed to be the most realistic target for the Irons the following season. However, the club exceeded the expectations of most people. Seven successive victories in January and February (the 2–3 triumph over Arsenal being perhaps the most notable as it made West Ham the last club to defeat the Gunners at Highbury) slotted Alan Pardew's side into sixth spot. It also secured the February 'Manager of the Month' award for the 'dangerous and distant animal', as the media once dubbed the Wimbledon-born, one-time cab driver.

Beating Spurs 2–1 at Upton Park in the final Premiership game of the season (so sweetly denying them a Champions League place) meant that West Ham finished in ninth place. This, alongside reaching the FA Cup final for the first time in a quarter of a century, made it a pretty good season for the East Londoners.

West Ham lost to Liverpool at Wembley, but they pushed the reigning Champions of Europe (who had finished third in the Premiership) to penalties after squandering a two-goal lead. However, Rafa Benítez's boys had qualified for the Champions League because of their league position, and as suc,h West Ham had pushed themselves into the UEFA Cup. They were drawn to meet Palermo in the opening stage of the competition.

Palermo had concluded their Serie A schedule in eighth place, and as such looked to the prospect of playing the UEFA Intertoto Cup. However, the 2006 match-rigging scandal in Italian football led to a number of clubs being penalised and Palermo being promoted into fifth place in Serie A, thus qualifying for the UEFA Cup. Beefing up the side during the transfer window, Palermo splurged millions of Euros on quality players like Aimo Diana, Mark Bresciano, Fábio Simplício, and Amauri, which lead to something of a consensus in Italian football that *Rosanero* ('the pink-blacks') would have a good season.

West Ham had a pretty ignominious history of meetings with Italian clubs going back to, what was then, an innovative friendly in 1954.

AC Milan (ITA)	Upton Park, att: 35,000	14/12/1954	L 0–6	
West Ham United: George Taylor, John Bond, Harry Kinsell (Noel Cantwell) Andy Malcolm, Ken Brown, Malcolm Allison, Harry Hooper, Jim Barrett Jnr, Tommy Dixon, John Dick. Malcolm Musgrove				

International Soccer League 1963				
Mantova (ITA)	Soldier Field, Chicago	05/06/1963	L 2–4	Hurst, Sealey
West Ham United: Jim Standen, Joe Kirkup, Jack Burkett, Martin Peters, Ken Brown, Ronnie Boyce, Peter Brabrook, Alan Sealey, Geoff Hurst, Johnny Sissons, Tony Scott. Manager: Ron Greenwood.				

Varese (ITA)	Randalls Island Stadium, New York	08/07/1965	D 2–2	Bovington, Brown
West Ham United: Jim Standen, Eddie Bovington, Jack Burkett, Ronnie Boyce, Ken Brown, Bobby Moore, Tony Scott, Martin Peters, Johnny Byrne, Geoff Hurst, Johnny Sissons				

Bologna (ITA)	Varsity Stadium, Toronto, Canada	18/06/1971	L 0–1	
West Ham United: Bobby Ferguson, John McDowell, Frank Lampard Sr, Bobby Howe, Tommy Taylor, Pat Holland, Harry Redknapp, Ronnie Boyce, Clyde Best, Trevor Brooking, Bryan Robson				
Bologna (ITA)	Roosevelt Stadium, New York, att: 4,000	20/06/1971	L 1–2	Hurst (pen)
West Ham United: Bobby Ferguson, John McDowell, Frank Lampard Sr, Bobby Howe, Tommy Taylor, Pat Holland (Kevin Lock), Harry Redknapp (Johnny Aryis), Ronnie Boyce, Geoff Hurst, Bryan Robson (Clyde Best)				

The 'Anglo-Italian' experiences (1975 and 1992) saw the Hammers yet again fail to impress against Italian opposition, while in the Makita Tournament of 1991, West Ham were once more humbled.

Makita Tournament 1991				
Sampdoria (ITA)	Highbury	03/08/1991	L 1–6	Parris *Buso 4, Cerezo, Lombardo*
West Ham United: Ludo Mikloško, Kenny Brown, Ray Houghton, Tim Breacker, Colin Foster, George Parris, Ian Bishop, Frank McAvennie, Martin Allen, Stuart Slater, Trevor Morely. Playing sub: Leroy Rosenior. Manager: Billy Bonds.				

Given the above, West Ham's fate in September 2006 was probably not surprising:

UEFA Europa Cup 2006–07				
Palermo (ITA) Ref: S. Johannesson	Upton Park, att: 32,222	First round, 1st leg 14/09/2006	L 0–1	*Caracciolo*
West Ham United: Roy Carroll, Anton Ferdinand, Gabbidon, Paul Konchesky, Tyrone Mears, Yossi Benayoun, Lee Bowyer (Matthew Ethrington), Javier Mascherano, Nigel Reo-Coker, Carlos Tevez (Marlon Harewood). Bobby Zamora (Carlton Cole). Manager: Alan Pardew.				
Palermo (ITA) Ref: G. Kasnaferis	Stadio Renzo Barbera, att: 19,284	First round, 2nd leg 28/09/2006	L 3–0 (L 4–0)	*Simplicio 2, Di Michele*
West Ham United: Roy Carroll, James Collins, Danny Gabbidon, Paul Konchesky, Jon Spector, Lee Bowyer, Javier Mascherano (Yossi Benayoun), Nigel Reo-Coker, Carlton Cole (Bobby Zamora), Marlon Harewood (Teddy Sheringham), Carlos Tevez. Manager: Alan Pardew.				

The group stage proved to be too much for Palermo; they finished last in a group that contained Celta Vigo, Eintracht Frankfurt, Fenerbahçe, and Newcastle United.

Subsequent meetings with Italian sides have mostly been unrewarding occasions for the Hammers.

Lazio (ITA)	Libring	21/07/2007	L 0–2	
West Ham United: Rob Green, Jon Spector (James Collins), Calum Davenport (Matthew Upson), Anton Ferdinand (Christian Dailly), George McCartney (Daniel Gabbidon), Lee Bowyer (Jack Collison), Heyden Mullins (Luís Boa Morte), Scott Parker, Matthew Ethrington (Kyel Reid), Dean Ashton (Carlton Cole), Craig Bellamy				

A.S. Roma (ITA) Ref: H. Webb	Upton Park, att: 26,425	4/8/07	W 2–1	McCartney, Ashton
West Ham United: Rob Green (Richard Wright), Lucus Neill, George McCartney, Anton Ferdinand (Daniel Gabbidon), Matthew Upson, Fredric Ljungberg (John Pantsil), Lee Bowyer (Carlton Cole), Mark Noble, Luís Boa Morte (Matthew Ethrington), Bobby Zamora (Dean Ashton), Craig Bellamy (Heyden Mullins)				

Bobby Moore Cup 2009				
SSC Napoli (ITA)	Upton Park, att: 21,364	08/08/2009	L 0–1	*Maggio*
West Ham United: Rob Green, Julian Faubert (Jon Spector), James Tomkins (James Collins), Matthew Upson (Daniel Gabbidon), Hérita Ilunga, Mark Noble, Scott Parker, Jack Collison (Zavron Hines), Luis Jiménez (Junior Stanislas), Kieron Dyer (Savio Nsereko), Carlton Cole. Manager: Gianfranco Zola.				

In 2014, West Ham got their only their fourth win over an Italian club in eighteen attempts.

Marathonbet Cup 2014				
Sampdoria (ITA)	Upton Park, att: 13,693	09/08/2014	W 3–2	Noble (pen), Diamé, Burke *Okaka, Éder*

West Ham United: Adrián, James Tomkins, James Collins (Reece Burke), Winston Reid, Aaron Cresswell, (Dan Potts), Cheikhou Kouyaté (Mo Diamé), Mark Noble, Kevin Nolan (c), Ray Stewart Downing, Mauro Zárate (Ricardo Vaz Tê), Carlton Cole (Elliot Lee). Subs: Jussi Jääskeläinen, Josh Cullen, Diego Poyet. Manager: Sam Allardyce.

Sampdoria: Da Costa; De Silvestri, Salamon, Gastaldello (Costa), Cacciatore; Soriano (Campana), Palombo (Rizzo), Krsticic (Obiang); Gabbiadini (Fedato), Okaka (Sansone), Éder (Bergessio).

West Ham's Foreign Legion

In 2013, it was reported that players from fifty different countries had pulled on the West Ham jersey while the club have been in the Premier League. Of course, over the club's history (certainly from the late 1960s on), the Hammers have fielded many more non-British players than are detailed here. Nevertheless, in 2013, the international roster was thus:

England: 98 (Number of players)

France: 13

Australia: 7

Northern Ireland: 7

Portugal: 7

Wales: 7

Republic of Ireland: 6

Israel: 4

Argentina: 3

Croatia: 3

Czech Republic: 3

Italy: 3

Scotland: 3

Senegal: 3

USA: 3

Cameroon: 2

Chile: 2

Denmark: 2

Finland: 2

Germany: 2

Guinea: 2

Mali: 2

Mexico: 2

Netherlands: 2

Romania: 2

Spain: 2

Switzerland: 2

Austria: 1 (Emanuel Pogatetz)

Belgium: 1 (Ruud Boffin)

Brazil: 1 (Ilan)

Bulgaria: 1 (Svetoslav Todorov)

Canada: 1 (Craig Forrest)

Costa Rica: 1 (Paulo Wanchope)

Côte d'Ivoire: 1 (Guy Demel)

DR Congo: 1 (Hérita Ilunga)

Egypt: 1 (Mido)

Ghana: 1 (John Pantsil)

Hungary: 1 (Péter Kurucz)

Morocco: 1 (Marouane Chamakh)

New Zealand: 1 (Winston Reid)

Nigeria: 1 (Victor Obinna)

Norway: 1 (Ragnvald Soma)

Peru: 1 (Nolberto Solano)

Serbia: 1 (Saša Ilić)

Slovakia: 1 (Vladimír Labant)

South Africa: 1 (Benni McCarthy)

St Kitts and Nevis: 1 (Adam Newton)

Sweden: 1 (Freddie Ljungberg)

Trinidad and Tobago: 1 (Shaka Hislop)

Uruguay: 1 (Walter López)

It is noticeable that most of these players have not been much more than transient, which I guess tells us something about West Ham and the contemporary at Premiership level. Goalkeeper Péter Kurucz is pretty typical of this type of player. At twenty-three, he departed Upton Park, having made one first-team appearance for the Hammers as a second-half substitute in the 0–4 home Premier League defeat by Manchester United on 5 December 2009. West Ham have only played two games against Hungarian (of sorts) clubs:

Club tour of Austria-Hungary 1923				
Buda (Austria-Hungary)	Budapest	21/05/1923	W 3–2	Brown 2, Ruffell
West Ham United: West Ham United: Ted Hufton, Billy Henderson, George Horler, George Carter, George Kay, Syd Bishop, Dick Richards, Bill Brown, Vic Watson, Bert Fletcher and Jimmy Ruffell. Manager: Syd King.				
Sparta Budapest (Austria-Hungary)	Prague	24/05/1923	D 1–1	Watson
West Ham United: West Ham United: Tommy Hampson, Billy Henderson, Jack Hebden, George Carter, George Kay, Syd Bishop, Dick Richards, Bill Brown, Vic Watson, Bert Fletcher and Jimmy Ruffell. Manager: Syd King.				

West Ham have had seven Portuguese players on their roster, among them: Hugo Porfirio, Daniel Da Cruz Carvalho 'Dani', Paulo Futre, Luís Boa Morte, and Paulo Alves. The Hammers have some form against clubs from this country.

Prince Felipe Tournament 1976				
Belenenses (POR)	Estadio El Sardinero	11/08/1976	D 1–1	Jennings
West Ham United: Mervyn Day, John McDowell, Keith Coleman, Pat Holland, Bill Green, Billy Bonds, Tommy Taylor, Graham Paddon, Billy Jennings, Trevor Brooking, Keith Robson. Manager: John Lyall.				

Centenary Match 1996				
Sporting Lisbon (POR)	Upton Park	07/05/1996	L 1–4	Dicks
West Ham United: Ludo Mikloško (Steve Mautone), Tim Breacker, Julian Dicks, Steve Potts, Alvin Martin, Iain Dowie (Tony Cottee), Daniel Da Cruz Carvalho Dani, Roger Boli, Danny Williamson (Lee Hodges), Frank Lampard Jr (Manny Omoyinmi), Slaven Bilic (Michael Hughes). Manager: Harry Redknapp.				

SC Braga (POR)	Estadio AXA	10/08/2012	D 1–1	Reid
West Ham United: Jussi Jääskeläinen, Guy Demel (Dan Potts), Winstone Reid, James Collins (Gary O'Neil), Joey O'Brien, James Tomkins, Mo Diamé (George Moncur), Mark Noble, RicardoVaz Tê, Modibo Maïga, Carlton Cole (Matthew Taylor)				

Torneio do Guadiana 2013				
Sporting Clube de Portugal (POR)	Estadio Municipal de Portugal	05/08/2013	W 3–2	Morrison 2, Nolan
West Ham United: Jussi Jääskeläinen, Joey O'Brien, Matthew Taylor (Răzvan Rat), James Tomkins (Pelly Ruddock), Winstone Reid, Mark Noble, Ravel Morrison, Kevin Nolan, Carlton Cole, Matt Jarvis, Modibo Maïga (Elliot Lee)				
SC Braga (POR)	Estadio Municipal de Portugal	06/08/2013	L 0–1	
West Ham United: Adrián, Guy Demel, Răzvan Rat, James Collins, James Tomkins (Pelly Ruddock), Alou Diarra, Mo Diamé, Matthew Taylor (Kevin Nolan), RicardoVaz Tê, Jack Collison, Modibo Maïga (Ravel Morrison). Manager: Sam Allardyce.				

Bobby Moore Cup 2013				
Pacos de Ferreira (POR)	Upton Park	10/08/2013	2–1	Morrison, Maïga
West Ham United: Jussi Jääskeläinen (Adrián), Guy Demel, Winstone Reid, James Tomkins (James Collins), Joey O'Brien (Răzvan Rat), Kevin Nolan (Matthew Taylor), Mark Noble, Ravel Morrison (Mo Diamé), Carlton Cole (Ricardo), Modibo Maïga, Matt Jarvis. Manager: Sam Allardyce.				

West Ham's one Bulgarian player was Svetoslav Todorov. The Hammers have only ever played one game against a club from his nation.

Ciudad De Zaragoza: III Trofeo Internacional De Futbol 1973				
CSKA Bulgaria (BUL)	Zaragoza	Semi-final 30/05/1973	L 3–0	
West Ham United: Bobby Ferguson, Clive Charles, Frank Lampard Sr, Billy Bonds, Dave Llewelyn, Bert Lutton, Clyde Best (Johnny Ayris), Ronnie Boyce, Ted MacDougall, Trevor Brooking, Bryan Robson. Manager: Ron Greenwood.				

Likewise, the Irons have faced Ukrainian and Turkish sides just once each.

Absolute Sports Travel Cup 2014				
Shakhtar Donetsk (UKR)	R Costings Abbey Stadium, Cambridge	19/07/2014	D 0–0	
West Ham United: Tim Brown (Danny Boness 77'), Sam Westley (Kyle Knoyle 62'), Reece Burke (Harney 62'), Reece Oxford (Emmanuel Onariase 62'), Lewis Page (Nathan Mavila 62'), Kieren Bywater (Amos Nasha 62'), Josh Cullen (Moses Makasi 62'), Blair Turgott (Jaanai Gordon 62'), Sebastian Lletget (Djair Parfitt-Williams 62'), Kieran Sadlier (Alex Pike 46') (Jeremiah Amoo 77'), Elliot Lee (Paul McCallum '62). Manager: Sam Allardyce.				

Bursaspor (TUR)	Thermenarena, Bad Radkersburg	22/07/2009	D 1–1	Dyer

West Ham United: Rob Green (Marek Štěch), Julian Faubert, James Collins (Bondz N'Gala), Matthew Upson (Elliot Lee), Hérita Ilunga, Jack Collison (Georg Grasser), Luis Jiménez (Jordan Spence), Luís Boa Morte (Anthony Edgar), Kieron Dyer (Josh Payne), Junior Stanislas (Savi Nsereko), Carlton Cole (Zavron Hines)

The mixture of ups and downs will be all too familiar for followers of the fickle and mercurial Irons. There is a familiar, almost cultural pattern in terms of what the club does. The game, as a business, peddles expectation and sentiment—this is the commodity base of football. West Ham's unique selling point is tantalisation: what might or might not happen, a heady mix of disappointment and euphoria, and in the words of Sammy Cahn and Jimmy Van Heusen—not the duel strikers of Ajax *c.* 1973, but the writers of the 1955 song, 'Love and Marriage'—'You can't have one without the other'.

2

GOING LOCO IN THE INTERTOTO

As a supporter, the farce staged at the start of the 2015–16 season reminded me of being led into continental football by Harry Redknapp in the last season of the twentieth century. It was another July start for the Intertoto competition, which some of us long-in-the-tooth doyens of the Hammers dubbed the 'inter-two-bob-cup', which seemed very apt given 'H's' desultory stewardship.

West Ham had qualified for European competition for the first time since the 1980–81 season, having climbed to the heady heights of fifth-spot in the seventh season of the Premier League—their second best placing in the top flight of the English game since they had finished third in 1985–86.

Three new names had been brought to Upton Park. At a cost of £1.75 million, Paolo Di Canio was, in retrospect, a bargain—certainly compared to the then-club-record fee (£4.5 million) that was needed to bring Cameroonian midfielder Marc-Vivien Foé, as well as the £1 million Scott Minto (wing-back) to East London.

Never a prolific goalscorer (four in thirteen outings that season), Di Canio was nevertheless a force of nature and the dynamo that drove West Ham to seven victories in their last fourteen matches of the 1998–99 schedule. The Italian was to say he thought he had entered a 'lunatic asylum' when he got to the Boleyn Ground (try being around there for fifty-five years). This was understandable, in retrospect, given the Harry Redknapp regime where the *laissez-faire* approach ruled. The manager divided his time between strolls around the Irons' Chadwell Heath training ground, the racecourse, and the golf course. Thus, while Redknapp named the team's qualification for the Intertoto Cup 'a tremendous achievement', it was closer to a miracle—one that likely had more to do with Paolo Di Canio's presence and inspiration than anything the manager had done or failed to do.

West Ham started their European odyssey in the third-round against FC Jokerit, a team founded that season as the sort of outcrop of a local ice-hockey club. The first leg brought the Finnish part-timers to Upton Park on 17 July, some three weeks before the Premier League kicked off.

Not including the Cup Winners' Cup of 1975–76, the Irons' previous results against Finnish sides had been 'interesting'.

End of season tour 1967				
HJK Helsinki (FIN)	Sonera Stadium, att: 10,000 +	06/06/1967	W 6–3	Dear 2, Hurst 2, Boyce, Peters
West Ham United: Bobby Ferguson, Billy Bonds, John Charles, Martin Peters, Paul Heffer, Bobby Moore, Peter Brabrook, Ronnie Boyce, Brian Dear, Geoff Hurst, Johnny Sissons. Manager: Ron Greenwood.				

FC Haka (FIN)	Tehtaan Kentta	16/07/1987	D 0–0	
West Ham United: Tom McAlister, Ray Stewart (Steve Potts), Tommy McQueen, Steve Walford, Alvin Martin (Paul Ince), Alan Devonshire (Kevin Keen), Mark Ward, Frank McAvennie, George Parris, Tony Cottee, Stewart Robson				

GBK Kokkola (FIN)	The Central Ground	Kokkola Cup, 18/07/1987	W 0–2	Stewart (pen), Cottee
West Ham United: Tom McAlister, Ray Stewart, Tommy McQueen, Steve Walford (Steve Potts), Alvin Martin, Alan Dickens, Mark Ward, Frank McAvennie, George Parris, Tony Cottee, Stewart Robson				

Riihimaeki (FIN)	Riihimaen Pallokentta, att: 1,500	02/08/1988	W 1–2	Slater, Rosenior
West Ham United: Allen McKnight (Tom McAlister), Ray Stewart, Julien Dicks, Alan Dickens, Alvin Martin, Tony Gale, Mark Ward, Stuart Slater, Leroy Rosenior, Kevin Keen, Steve Potts. Playing subs: Liam Brady, Gary Strodder, Eamonn Dolon.				

Finnair Tournament, 4–5 August 1988				
Ilves Tampere (FIN)	Tampere, att: 1,183	04/08/1988	L 1–0	
West Ham United: Allen McKnight, Ray Stewart, Julien Dicks, Alan Dickens, Tony Gale, Gary Strodder, Mark Ward, Leroy Rosenior, Stuart Slater, Kevin Keen, Steve Potts. Playing sub: Liam Brady. Manager: John Lyall.				

In 1999, a narrow victory in East London was followed a week later at the Olympiastadion (Helsinki), where a second-half goal gave the travelling Hammers a 1–1 draw. It was a close-run thing, and really nothing at all to write home about; I certainly did not.

Intertoto Cup 1999–2000				
FC Jokerit (FIN)	Upton Park, att: 11,908	Third round, 1st leg 17/07/1999	W 1–0	Kitson
West Ham United: Craig Forrest, Neil Ruddock, Rio Ferdinand, Steve Potts (Marc Keller), Scott Minto, Steve Lomas, Trevor Sinclair (Ian Wright), Frank Lampard Jr, Joe Cole, Paul Kitson, Paolo Di Canio. Manager: Harry Redknapp.				

FC Jokerit (FIN)	Olympiastadion, Helsinki, att: 7,667	Third round, 2nd leg 24/07/1999	D 1–1	Lampard *Koskela*

West Ham United: Shaka Hislop, Rob Jones (Steve Potts), Neil Ruddock, Rio Ferdinand, Scott Minto, Trevor Sinclair, Frank Lampard Jr, Steve Lomas, Marc Keller (Stan Lazaridis), Paolo Di Canio (Michael Carrick), Paul Kitson. Manager: Harry Redknapp.

Dear Old Dutch

Just four days had passed before another scrappy, single-goal win in front of a meagre turnout against Heerenveen. Paulo Wanchope scored his debut goal for West Ham in the Netherlands, providing hope that the new signing might at some point prove to be money well spent.

Intertoto Cup 1999–00				
SC Heerenveen (NED)	Upton Park, att: 7,485	Semi-final, 1st leg 28/07/1999	W 1–0	Lampard

West Ham United: Shaka Hislop, Steve Potts, Neil Ruddock (Stuart Pearce), Rio Ferdinand, Scott Minto, Trevor Sinclair, Frank Lampard Jr, Steve Lomas, Marc Keller (John Moncur), Paolo Di Canio (Michael Carrick), Paulo Wanchope. Manager: Harry Redknapp.

SC Heerenveen (NED)	Abe Lenstra Stadium, att: 13,500	Semi-final, 2nd leg 04/08/1999	W 0–1 (W 0–2)	Wanchope

West Ham United: Shaka Hislop, Steve Lomas, Stuart Pearce, Rio Ferdinand, Scott Minto, Frank Lampard Jr, Marc-Vivien Foé, John Moncur (Joe Cole), Paolo Di Canio (Paul Kitson), Trevor Sinclair, Paulo Wanchope. Manager: Harry Redknapp

West Ham have a long history of competition against Dutch clubs, including the first serious game against overseas opposition at Upton Park.

Haaarlem (NED)	Upton Park	27/12/1922	W 4–2	Hodges 2, Burgess, Leafe

West Ham United: Tommy Hampson, Bill Henderson, George Horler, Percy Allen, George Carter, Syd Bishop, Alf Leafe, Dick Burgess, Harry Hodges, Charlie Crossley, Jimmy Ruffell

Club tour of the Netherlands 1925				
Ajax Amsterdam (NED)	The Stadium, Amsterdam	14/05/1925	W 0–2	Vic Watson 2

West Ham United: Bob Dixon, Stan Earl, Cyril Norrington, Archie Hull, Jim Barrett, Albert Cadwell, Tom Yews, George Robson, Vic Watson, Viv Gibbins, Jimmy Ruffell. Manager: Syd King

Arnhem (NED)	Vitesse	17/05/1925	L 3–2	Campbell 2

West Ham United: Ted Hufton, Tom Hodgson, George Eastman, Jim Collins, George Kay, Jim Barrett, Bill Edwards, Billy Moore, John Campbell, Bert Fletcher, Jimmy Ruffell. Manager: Syd King.

Swallows (NED)	Utrecht	21/05/1925	D 1–1	Watson

West Ham United: Ted Hufton, Tom Hodgson, Bill Henderson, Jim Collins, George Kay, Jim Barrett, Tom Yews, Billy Moore, Vic Watson, Bert Fletcher, Jimmy Ruffell. Manager: Syd King.

On Tuesday 28 December 1926, the Dutch side Helder played a Hammers' reserve side at Upton Park (while the first-team were losing 3–0 at Derby) that included one of the great pre-War Irons, Jimmy Ruffell. The game, which kicked off at 2.30 p.m., finished in a 7–5 win for the home side.

Helder
(NED)
Upton Park
28/12/1928
W 7–5
Bishop, Moore, Payne, Williams 2, Dowsley 2

West Ham United: Dave Ballie, Bill Henderson, George Horler, Archie Hull, Bill Cox, Albert Cadwell, John Payne, John Dowsley, Syd Bishop, Billy Moore, Bill Williams

Club tour of the Netherlands 1929

Ajax Amsterdam (NED)	The Stadium, Amsterdam	18/05/1929	W 0–6	Robson 3, Gibbins 2, Yews

West Ham United: Bob Dixon, Stan Earl, Cyril Norrington, Fred Norris, Jim Barrett, Archie Hull, Tom Yews, George Robson, Vic Watson, Viv Gibbins, Jimmy Ruffell. Manager: Syd King.

Enschede (NED)	Enschede	20/05/1929	D 3–3	Robson, Barrett 2

West Ham United: Bob Dixon, Reg Goodacre, Cyril Norrington, Fred Norris, Wally St Pier, Albert Cadwell, Tom Yews, George Robson, Jim Barrett, Viv Gibbins, Jimmy Ruffell. Manager: Syd King.

Swallows Rotterdam (NED)	Rotterdam	22/05/1929	W 2–3	Yews 2, Gibbins

West Ham United: Bob Dixon, Stan Earl, Cyril Norrington, Fred Norris, Wally St Pier, Archie Hull, Tom Yews, George Robson, Jim Barrett, Viv Gibbins, Albert Cadwell. Manager: Syd King.

Hague (NED)	Hague	24/05/1929	L 2–1	Watson

West Ham United: Bob Dixon, Stan Earl, Reg Goodacre, Fred Norris, Wally St Pier, Archie Hull, Tom Yews, George Robson, Vic Watson, Albert Cadwell, Jimmy Ruffell. Manager: Syd King.

Tour the Netherlands, Denmark, and Sweden 1930

Rotterdam (NED)
Rotterdam
31/05/1930
W 2–0
Morris, Cribb

West Ham United: Ted Hufton, Stan Earl, Bill Cox, Jim Collins, Wally St Pier, George Parkin, Tom Yews, Les Wilkins, Arthur Morris, Walter Pollard, Stan Cribb. Manager: Syd King.

Club tour in the Netherlands 1937

Dutch FA Select XI (NED)	Arnhem	06/05/1937	D 1–1	Green

West Ham United: Jack Weare, Charlie Bicknell, Albert Walker, Norman Corbett, Dick Walker, Joe Cockroft, Jack Kirkcaldie, Tom Green, Sam Small, Jim Mike Marshall, John Morton. Manager: Charlie Paynter.

Dutch FA Select XI (NED)	Leeuwarden	08/05/1937	W 2–3	Morton 2, Small

West Ham United: Jack Weare, Alf Chalkley, Albert Walker, Ted Fenton, Dick Walker, Joe Cockroft, Stan Foxall, Tom Green, Sam Small, Jim Mike Marshall, John Morton. Manager: Charlie Paynter.

Dutch FA Select XI (NED)	Utrecht	12/05/1937	L 3–1	Green

West Ham United: Jack Weare, Alf Chalkley, Albert Walker, Ted Fenton, Jim Barrett, Joe Cockroft, Stan Foxall, Dyson, Sam Small, Tom Green, John Morton. Manager: Charlie Paynter.

Dutch FA Select XI (NED)	Eindhoven	17/05/1937	W 1–4	Small 2, Morton, Foxall

West Ham United: Jack Weare, Charlie Bicknell, Alf Chalkley, Norman Corbett, Dick Walker, Joe Cockroft, Stan Foxall, Dyson, Sam Small, Tom Green, John Morton

Holland Sports Club Rotterdam (NED)	Upton Park att: 10,000	12/03/1955	D 0–0	

West Ham United: George Taylor, George Wright, Noel Cantwell, Andy Malcolm, Malcolm Allison, Frank O'Farrell, Albert Foan, Les Bennett, Dave Sexton, Bobby Moore, Malcolm Musgrove. Manager: Charlie Paynter.

Sparta Rotterdam (NED)	Upton Park	Dick Walker Testimonial 14/10/1957	W 5–0	Keeble, Dick 3, Smith (pen)

West Ham United: Ernie Gregory, George Wright, Noel Cantwell, Andy Malcolm, Ken Brown, Bill Lansdowne, Billy Dare, John Smith, Vic Keeble, John Dick, Malcolm Musgrove. Manager: Charlie Paynter.

International *Voetbaltornoo* Ghent 1958				
Beerschot A.C. (NED)	Stadion Jules Otten, Ghent	Group Match 02/05/1958	W 2–0	Dick 2

West Ham United: Noel Dwyer, George Wright, John Bond, Andy Malcolm, Ken Brown, Harry Obeney, Doug Wragg, John Smith, Noel Cantwell, John Dick, Malcolm Musgrove. Manager: Ted Fenton.

Club tour of Belgium, Germany, and the Netherlands 1959				
Fortuna (NED)	Geelen	05/05/1959	W 2–3	Cantwell 2, Musgrove

West Ham United: Noel Dwyer, Joe Kirkup, John Bond, Andy Malcolm, Ken Brown, Harry Obeney, Doug Wragg, John Smith, Noel Cantwell, John Dick, Malcolm Musgrove. Manager: Ted Fenton.

Den Haag (NED)	Zuiderpark Stadion	09/08/1981	W 0–1	Paul Goddard

West Ham United: Phil Parkes, Ray Stewart, Frank Lampard Sr, Billy Bonds, Alvin Martin, Paul Brush, Bobby Barnes, Paul Goddard, Nicky Morgan, Paul Allen, Geoff Pike

Den Haag (NED)	Zuiderpark Stadion	15/08/1982	W 0–2	Pike, van der Elst

West Ham United: Phil Parkes, Paul Brush, Frank Lampard Sr, Billy Bonds, Alvin Martin, Jimmy Neighbour, François van der Elst, Paul Goddard, Alex Clark (Nicky Morgan), Paul Allen, Geoff Pike

Arminia Bielefeld Tournament 1983

Ajax Amsterdam (NED)	Bielefeld Alm Stadium	Semi-final 05/08/1983	L 1–3	Brooking

West Ham United: Phil Parkes, Frank Lampard Sr(Paul Allen), Paul Brush, Billy Bonds, Alvin Martin, Alan Devonshire, Steve Whitton (Tony Cottee), Paul Goddard, Dave Swindlehurst, Trevor Brooking, Geoff Pike. Manager: John Lyall.

Zeeuwsch Vlaanderen Tournament 22–23 July 1987

PSV Eindhoven (NED)	BVV Stadium	23/07/1987	L 4–0	

West Ham United: Tom McAlister, Ray Stewart, George Parris, Gary Strodder (Steve Walford), Alvin Martin, Alan Devonshire (Kevin Keen), Mark Ward, Frank McAvennie, Alan Dickens, Tony Cottee, Liam Brady. Manager: John Lyall.

FC Utrecht (NED)	Springfield Stadium, Jersey	11/08/2001	0–0 (W 4–3 on pens)	(Pens: Cole, Defoe, Kitson, Sinclair)

West Ham United: David James, Rigobert Song (Sebastian Schemmel), Nigel Winterburn, Christian Dailly, Ragnvald Soma, John Moncur (Pierre Ducrocq), Trevor Sinclair, Michael Carrick, Paul Kitson, Svetoslav Todorov (Jermaine Defoe), Joe Cole (Laurent Courtois)

Out Performance Display Cup 2002

Vitesse Arnhem (NED)	Roots Hall	09/08/2002	W 1–0	Kanouté

West Ham United: David James, Sebastian Schemmel (Gary Breen), Ian Pearce (Glen Johnson), Christian Dailly, Nigel Winterburn (Grant McCann), Joe Cole (John Moncur), Édouard Cissé (Richard Garcia), Michael Carrick, Trevor Sinclair, Jermaine Defoe (Youssef Sofiane), Frédéric Kanouté (Titi Camara). Manager: Glenn Roeder.

Out Performance Display Cup 2003

PSV Eindhoven (NED)	Upton Park	01/08/2003	L 1–2	Garcia

West Ham United: David James, Tomáš Řepka, Shaun Byrne, Anton Ferdinand, Ian Pearce (David Connolly), Robert Lee (Michael Carrick), Christian Dailly, Richard Garcia, Jermaine Defoe, Joe Cole, Frédéric Kanouté (Youssef Sofiane). Manager: Glenn Roeder.

ADO Den Haag (NED)	Zuiderpark	02/08/2005	D 1–1	Zamora

West Ham United: Shaka Hislop, Tomáš Řepka, Clive Clarke (Petr Mikolanda), James Collins (Mark Ward), Malky Mackay, Carl Fletcher (Marcel Licka), Yossi Benayoun, Mark Noble (Christian Dailly), Bobby Zamora, Marlon Harewood (Gavin Williams), Luke Chadwick (Shaun Newton)

Den Haag (NED)	Zuiderpark	Exhibition match 12/08/1986	D 1–1	Gale
West Ham United: Tom McAlister, Steve Walford, George Parris, Paul Hilton, Alvin Martin, Geoff Pike (Tony Gale), Mark Ward, Frank McAvennie (Tony Cottee), Alan Dickens, Paul Goddard, Neil Orr				

Perhaps the best game between West Ham and a Dutch club was the 1975–76 Cup Winners' Cup encounter with FC Den Haag.

French Connection

While holding their own in the 1999–2000 Premiership, the Irons seemed to grind to a halt in Europe after the 0–1 loss to Metz (Louis Saha was on target for the French side). Frank Lampard Jr missed a penalty, which did not help what appeared to be the dashing of West Ham's hopes for Intertoto triumph, although that does seem like something of a contradiction in terms.

A fortnight later, at the Stade Saint-Symphorien, first-half contributions from Trevor Sinclair and Lampard Jr revived hope in the hearts of travelling supporters. However, with twenty-two minutes left to play, Nenad Jestrović (who between 2003 and 2005 would play twelve games for his country, Serbia and Montenegro, scoring five goals) levelled the aggregate score. If the Irons were able to hold out, the two away goals would be enough to put Metz to the proverbial sword, although the latter situation began to feel decidedly doubtful when the home side began to look pre-eminent as the game entered its last stages.

Thankfully, the tension was lifted by a seventy-fourth minute goal from Paulo Wanchope. The Costa Rican scored after rounding the Metz keeper Lionel Letizi.

Intertoto Cup 1999–2000				
FC Metz (FRA)	Upton Park, att: 25,372	Final, 1st leg 10/08/1999	L 0–1	*Saha*
Shaka Hislop, Steve Potts, Scott Minto, Steve Lomas, Rio Ferdinand, Marc-Vivien Foé (Paul Kitson), Trevor Sinclair, Paolo Di Canio, Paulo Wanchope, Frank Lampard Jr, John Moncur. **Manager: Harry Redknapp.**				
FC Metz (FRA)	Saint Symphorien Stadium, att: 19,559	Final, 2nd leg 24/08/1999	W 1–3 (W 2–3)	*Jestrović* Sinclair, Wanchope, Lampard
West Ham United: Shaka Hislop, Steve Potts, Marc Keller, Steve Lomas, Rio Ferdinand, Marc-Vivien Foé, Trevor Sinclair, Paulo Wanchope, Paolo Di Canio (Joe Cole), Frank Lampard Jr, John Moncur. **Manager: Harry Redknapp.**				

This had been West Ham's first meeting with a French club for a decade, and the club's first win against French opposition for thirty-six years.

Club tour of Germany, Switzerland, and France 1924				
France	Paris	22/05/1924	L 2–1	Ruffell

West Ham United: Tommy Hampson, Bill Henderson, John Young, Syd Bishop, George Kay, Albert Cadwell, Tom Yews, Vic Watson, John Campbell, Billy Moore, Jimmy Ruffell. Manager: Syd King.

Club tour of Frace 1936				
Racing Club Lens (FRA)	Lens	27/05/1936	L 1–0	

West Ham United: Herman Conway, Charlie Bicknell, Albert Walker, Ted Fenton, Jim Barrett, Joe Cockroft, John Foreman, Jim Collins, Stan Foxall, Len Goulden. Jimmy Ruffell. Manager: Charlie Paynter.

Olympique de Marseille (FRA)	Upton Park	21/10/1936	W 4–3	Martin 3, Peters

West Ham United: Jack Weare, Alf Chalkley, Albert Walker, Bill Roberts, Jim Barrett, Joe Cockroft, Peter Peters, Jim Mike Marshall, Tudor Martin, Len Goulden, Joe Guest

International *Voetbaltornoo* Ghent 1958				
Stade de Reims (FRA)	Stadion Jules Otten	Group match 02/05/1958	W 1–3	Bond, Cantwell, Dick

West Ham United: Ernie Gregory, Bill Lansdowne, John Bond, Andy Malcolm, Ken Brown, Harry Obeney, Doug Wragg, John Smith, Noel Cantwell, John Dick, Malcolm Musgrove. Manager: Ted Fenton.

International Soccer League 1963				
Valenciennes (FRA)	Randalls Island Stadium, New York	23/06/1963	W 3–1	Hurst 3

West Ham United: Jim Standen, Joe Kirkup, Jack Burkett, Martin Peters, Ken Brown, Bobby Moore, Alan Sealey, Ronnie Boyce, Johnny Byrne, Geoff Hurst, Peter Brabrook. Manager: Ron Greenwood.

Continental Tour 8–14 August 1984				
Girondins Bordeaux (FRA)	Bordeaux	18/08/1984	L 2–0	

West Ham United: Tom McAlister, Ray Stewart, Steve Walford, Paul Allen, Alvin Martin, Tony Gale, Steve Whitton, Tony Cottee (Bobby Barnes), Paul Goddard, Alan Dickens (Warren Donald), Geoff Pike. Manager: John Lyall.

Girondins Bordeaux (FRA)	Stade Chaban Delmas	15/07/1989	L 2–1	Kelly

West Ham United: Phil Parkes, Steve Potts, Julien Dicks, Tony Gale, Gary Strodder, Alvin Martin, George Parris, Paul Ince, Liam Brady, David Kelly, Eamonn Dolon
Playing subs: Tommy McQueen, Kevin Keen, Stuart Slater, Frank McAvennie

West Ham were one of three Intertoto Cup winners, along with Montpellier and Juventus. Yes, that is right: three winners. The Irons were rewarded with a decidedly (but suitably) diminutive trophy about the size of a table cigarette lighter, which reflected the odd distinction the side had achieved. The real reward was qualification for the UEFA Cup—their first exposure to this competition.

When the Intertoto tournament came under the ambit of UEFA in 1995, the format included both group and knockout stages, which meant things started with a dozen groups of five with the sixteen best sides going on to the knockout stages comprising two-legged ties at each stage. The two finalists qualified for the more prestigious UEFA Cup.

In 1996 and 1997, the twelve group winners of the Intertoto played a knockout tournament that produced three teams to advance to the UEFA Cup.

The group stage of the Intertoto competition was scuppered for the 1998 tournament in favour of a simple knockout competition, although clubs from the more powerful soccer nations entered at a later stage (West Ham in 1999 thus did not play in the first two rounds of the Intertoto). This situation endured until 2005 after which the format changed again. There were three rounds (two less than previously). Eleven winning teams emerged from the third round, and they contested a second qualifying round of the UEFA Cup. The Intertoto qualifying clubs that advanced the furthest in the UEFA Cup were each awarded a trophy (techincally a plaque). The first club to be so rewarded was Newcastle United.

Talk about a muddle!

Anglo-Italian

West Ham have a tradition (of sorts) of playing in these type of nutty, experimental tournaments. In 1975, the Irons were nominated as England's representatives in the Anglo-Italian Cup Winners' Cup. This competition had, and was to have, an awkward and pretty mundane history, but it was competed for between the FA Cup winners and their Italian counterparts. The Football League Cup winners had previously competed in this tournament, but the Football Association decided that the FA Cup winners would participate—who knows why?

Anglo-Italian Cup Winners' Cup 1975–76				
Fiorentina (ITA)	The Stadio Communale, att: 35,000	1st leg 03/09/1975	L 1-0	Guerini 19'
West Ham United: Mervyn Day, John McDowell, Frank Lampard Sr, Billy Bonds, Tommy Taylor, Kevin Lock, Alan Taylor, Graham Paddon, Pat Holland (Billy Jennings), Trevor Brooking, Keith Robson. Manager: John Lyall.				
Fiorentina: Superchi, (Mattolini) Beatrice, Roggi, Pellegrini, Della Martira, Guerini, Caso, Merlo, Casarsa (Bresciani), Antognoni, Speggiorin.				

Fiorentina (ITA)	Upton Park, att: 14,699	2nd leg 10/12/1975	L 0–1 (L 0–2)	*Speggiorin 19'*

Fiorentina: Mattolini, Galdiolo, Tendi, Pellegrini, Della Martira, Beatrice, Desolati, Merlo, Casarsa, Antognoni, Speggiorin (Bresciani)

West Ham United: Mervyn Day, John McDowell (Keith Coleman), Frank Lampard Sr, Pat Holland, Tommy Taylor, Kevin Lock, Alan Taylor, Graham Paddon, Billy Jennings, Trevor Brooking, Ayris (Alan Curbishley). Manager: John Lyall

In 1992, a revamped version of much the same idea (although for second tier clubs) consigned the Hammers to one of eight qualifying groups composed of English sides. Group Eight played out thus:

2 September 1992	West Ham	2–2	Bristol Rovers
16 September 1992	Bristol Rovers	3–0	Southend
30 September 1992	Southend	0–3	West Ham

	P	W	D	L	F	A	Pts
West Ham United	2	1	1	0	5	2	4
Bristol Rovers	2	1	1	0	5	2	4
Southend	2	0	0	2	0	6	0

West Ham went through on the toss of a coin to contest an international section that involved the Hammers and three other qualifying English clubs (Tranmere, Bristol City, and Derby) playing four Italian clubs each. This produced two league tables: one Italian, based on their relative performances against the English clubs; the other English, established by their comparative results against the Italian sides.

Anglo-Italian Cup 1992–93				
Cremonese (ITA)	Stadio Giovanni Zini, att: 1,639	11/11/1992	L 2–0	

West Ham United: Ludo Mikloško, Kenny Brown, Julien Dicks, Steve Potts, Alvin Martin, Martin Allen, Stewart Robson, George Parris (Kevin Keen), Trevor Morely, Clive Allen, Matty Holmes. Manager: Billy Bonds.

AC Reggiana (ITA)	Upton Park	24/11/1992	W 2–0	Allen 2

West Ham United: Ludo Mikloško, Breaker, Julien Dicks, Steve Potts, Alvin Martin (Kenny Brown), Martin Allen, Stewart Robson (Ian Bishop), Matty Holmes, Trevor Morely, Clive Allen, Kevin Keen. Manager: Billy Bonds.

Cozenza (ITA)	Stadio San Vito, att: 800	08/11/1992	W 0–1	Allen

West Ham United: Ludo Mikloško, Breaker, Julien Dicks, Steve Potts, Alvin Martin, Martin Allen, Rush, George Parris, Steve Jones, Clive Allen, Kevin Keen (Kenny Brown). Manager: Billy Bonds.

AC Pisa (ITA)	Arena Garibaldi, Stadio Romeo Anconetani	16/12/92	D 0–0	
West Ham United: Ludo Mikloško, Breaker, Julien Dicks, Steve Potts, Alvin Martin, Martin Allen, Rush, Ian Bishop, Alex Bunbury, Clive Allen (Steve Jones), Kevin Keen (Stewart Robson). Manager: Billy Bonds.				

This is how the league panned out:

	P	W	D	L	F	A	Pts
Derby County	4	3	0	1	10	3	9
Tranmere Rovers	4	2	1	1	4	3	7
West Ham United	4	2	1	1	3	2	7
Bristol City	4	0	1	1	6	10	1

There were English and Italian semi-finals, which pitched the respective winners of the four leagues (two English and two Italian) against each other (home and away). So, Derby defeated Brentford while Cremonese defeated Bari. In the final, at a Wembley about two-thirds empty, the Italians beat the Rams 1–3. All in all, it had been much ado about nothing.

As of 2009, the painful process of the Intertoto Cup was put out of its misery and replaced by direct qualification for the first stages of the UEFA Europa League, which was expanded to four rounds to accommodate the change. Their triumphant Euro-crusade in the 1999–2000 Intertoto competition provided the Hammers with a passport into the Europa League.

Goals against NK Osijek from Paulo Wanchope, Paolo Di Canio, and Frank Lampard Jr gave the Irons a comfortable 3–0 lead in the first leg of the first round. This was the first time that West Ham had faced a team of Croatian nationality, although the club had previously met a side from another nation that arose out of the former Yugoslavia.

ND Mura 05 (SVN)	Fazanerija Stadium, Murska Sobota	23/07/2009	D 0–0	
West Ham United: Rob Green (Péter Kurucz), Jordan Spence, Bondz N'Gala, Danny Gabbidon (James Tomkins), Georg Grasser (James Collins), Savio Nsereko (Mark Noble), Oliver Lee (Jiménez), Josh Payne (Scott Parker), Junior Stanislas, Zavron Hines (Carlton Cole)				

Of course, Zagreb is now the capital of Croatia, and Split the second largest city in that country. Between 1945 and 1991, Croatia and Slovenia had been part of Yugoslavia.

Zagreb Gradjanski (YUG)	Upton Park	25/11/1936	W 1–0	Simpson
West Ham United: Jack Weare, Charlie Bicknell, Charlie Walker, Bill Adams, Dick Walker, Joe Cockroft, Stan Foxall, Jim Mike Marshall, Peter Simpson, Lawrence Conwell, Joe Guest				

La Gantoise Tournament 6–8 August 1982				
Hajduk Split (YUG)	Ghent	Final 08/08/1982	D 0–0 (L 5–4 pens)	(Pens: Bonds, Lampard, Goddard, Stewart)
West Ham United: Phil Parkes, Ray Stewart, Frank Lampard Sr (Paul Brush), Billy Bonds, Alvin Martin, Alan Devonshire, François Van der Elst, Paul Goddard, Alex Clark, Paul Allen, Geoff Pike. Manager: John Lyall.				

Dinamo Zagreb (YUG)	Upton Park	Geoff Pike Testimonial 10/05/1988	L 1–4	Goddard
West Ham United: Tom McAlister (Phil Parkes), Steve Potts, Julien Dicks, Geoff Pike, Paul Hilton, Tony Gale, Mark Ward, George Parris, Alan Dickens, Tony Cottee, Stewart Robson Playing subs: Frank Lampard Sr, Paul Ince, Gary Strodder, Paul Goddard, David Cross, Kevin Keen				

Croatian defender Igor Štimac made his second appearance for the Irons in the game against Osijek. He had been brought to Upton Park from Derby County for a fee of £600,000. Back in the land of his birth for the away leg of the tie, he was greeted with a booking. However, goals from Paul Kitson, Neil Ruddock, and Marc-Vivien Foé assured the Hammers a 1–3 victory.

It transpired that Štimac should not have been playing in European competition. He had been due to serve a two-game ban during his time with Hajduk Split. Fortunately for the Irons, UEFA put their hands up for having failed to make either club aware of the situation, and as such, rejected Osijek's demand to be given the tie and take West Ham's place in the competition. For all this, Štimac was obliged to serve his ban and as such was unavailable for the second-round ties against Steaua Bucharest.

Europa League 1999–2000				
NK Osijek (HRV)	Upton Park, att: 25,331	First round, first leg 16/09/1999	W 3–0	Di Canio, Wanchope, Lampard
West Ham United: Shaka Hislop, Steve Potts, Javier Margas, Steve Lomas, Igor Štimac, John Moncur (Marc-Vivien Foé), Trevor Sinclair, Marc Keller, Paolo Di Canio (Paul Kitson), Frank Lampard Jr, Paulo Wanchope. Manager: Harry Redknapp.				
NK Osijek Croatia	Gradski Vrt att: 15,000	First round, 2nd leg 30/09/1999	W 1–3 (W 1–6)	Bubalo Kitson, Ruddock, Foé
West Ham United: Shaka Hislop, Steve Potts, Rio Ferdinand (Neil Ruddock), Steve Lomas, Igor Štimac, Marc-Vivien Foé, Trevor Sinclair (Adam Newton), Paul Kitson, Paolo Di Canio (Paulo Wanchope), Frank Lampard Jr, Marc Keller. Manager: Harry Redknapp.				

Viteziştii ('the speedsters') were the strongest side West Ham came up against in 1999. Laurenţiu Roşu and Sabin Ile scored for the home side in the first leg at the Stadionul Steaua, leaving West Ham with the metaphoric mountain to climb at the Boleyn Ground a couple of weeks later. They got nowhere near to accomplishing the feat; the game ended goalless.

Europa League 1999–00				
Steaua Bucharest (ROM)	Stadion Steaua, att: 12,500	Second round, 1st leg 21/10/1999	L 2–0	Roşu, Ile
West Ham United: Shaka Hislop, Steve Potts (Javier Margas), Neil Ruddock, Steve Lomas, Rio Ferdinand, Marc-Vivien Foé, Trevor Sinclair, John Moncur, Paolo Di Canio (Joe Cole), Frank Lampard Jr, Paulo Wanchope. Manager: Harry Redknapp.				
Steaua Bucharest (ROM)	Upton Park, att: 24,514	Second round, 2nd leg 04/11/1999	D 0–0	
West Ham United: Shaka Hislop, Javier Margas, Rio Ferdinand, Neil Ruddock, Trevor Sinclair, Steve Lomas, Frank Lampard Jr, Marc Keller (Paul Kitson), Joe Cole, Paulo Wanchope, Paolo Di Canio. Manager: Harry Redknapp.				

The experience was a far cry from my earliest recollections of the side's history of European glory during my second visit to Wembley. My first occasion at the famous stadium, in my last month as an eight-year-old, had been the Hammers' first FA Cup final victory against Preston North End a year earlier.

The European Cup Winners' Cup Final that took place on 19 May 1965 had one of the biggest audiences ever for a football match. About 30 million people watched the game on television all over Europe. It was a warm evening, which generated the kind of atmosphere that could only be experienced under the floodlights of the old Wembley Stadium, in the shadow of the twin towers, in a late-English spring.

3

UPTON PARK GOLD

For many Hammers supporters, that magical time in the mid-1960s was the start of West Ham's international record. However, as we have seen, the club had long been familiar with the international game. During the 1950s and 1960s, matches with European opposition from beyond England's shores were meat and drink to the young Hammers, and most of those who played in West Ham's golden era were products of that experience.

Syd King, West Ham's first manager, and his sidekick and eventual successor, Charlie Paynter (manager 1932–1950), introduced teams from mainland Europe, as well as even more exotic climbs, into the Hammers' playing schedule. However, the best part of half a century before this, the best of East London football was carrying their sporting crusade to the continent.

The Parkers

On the eastern borders of London and Essex, Upton Park Football Club was the first big footballing noise in the district. The club had developed during the initial decades of the Football Association and was the first to make an impact in the London Docklands area.

The Parkers established themselves as the top London club when the side won the first London FA (Senior) Cup in 1882–83. They retained the trophy the following season and went on to achieve several impressive results in the FA Cup. As such, they represent the earliest glow of football success in the district, which was to be dominated firstly by Thames Ironworks Football Club and then the team the Ironworks gave rise to, West Ham United.

Upton Park FC were to make an international impact when the club was selected to represent Great Britain in the Paris Olympics of 1900. As all Olympic athletes needed to have amateur status (although professional fencers competed in Paris, at least one, Albert Robert Ayat of France, was awarded 3,000 Fr for his winning efforts), British League clubs would not have been allowed to compete in Paris, being professional outfits. Hence, with the failure of any of the remaining staunch 'Corinthian' clubs to step into the breach, Upton Park FC agreed to travel to Paris.

This said, there is no clear surviving reasoning for the Scarlet and Blacks having been the team of choice. While all participants had to be amateurs and other teams might have turned the opportunity down, it seems the Parkers were in Paris for the Games primarily because they were up for it, and perhaps secondly thanks to being a well-connected side.

They defeated the French representatives, Club Français de Paris (a side reinforced with selections by a Union des Sociétés Françaises des Sports Athlétiques XI—USFSA) 0–4 in what has come to be taken as the final of tournament, although the official record indicates that Upton Park FC played just the one game.

The football tournament of the Games of the II Olympiad was played in the French capital from 20 May to 28 October. Originally, all four football matches had been scheduled to involve a French team:

16 September 1900	France v. Switzerland
23 September 1900	France v. Belgium
30 September 1900	France v. Germany
7 October 1900	France v. England

Quite how this would provide a result is at least questionable. It has been assumed that football (soccer) might have been what was later termed a 'demonstration sport', much like baseball was in the 1936 Games, but there was no such category or designation in 1900. It may have been thought that the visiting teams would sort themselves out once they were in Paris—priority having been given to setting the home team's programme. There seems to have been plenty of time between the scheduled games for this to have been accommodated, but it is recognised that Paris was a particularly chaotic Games largely overshadowed and confused by (and, for many, with) the World Exhibition that was also taking place in the city during 1900.

However, because Switzerland and Germany failed to provide teams, the game between France and England was shifted to 20 September. These two Olympic tournament games were part of the official Olympic programme, although no medals were awarded for the event. That practice, as we might recognise it today, was not instigated until 1904 in St Louis. Most of the winners in 1900 were given cups or trophies, but valuable paintings and works of art were also handed out.

It has been argued that the matches played in Paris on 20 and 23 September in 1900 were contested only to hide the embarrassment of the Olympic organisers' failure to present a football tournament, and as such should be considered friendlies. However, the International Olympic Committee does credit Britain, France, and Belgium with gold, silver, and bronze medals respectively.

Although the founder of the modern Olympic movement, Pierre de Coubertin, personally tried to persuade football players and officials to take part in an Olympic football tournament, there is little evidence that it was discussed within the appropriate authorities in most nations in Europe, and no national sides came forward. Consequently, national champions were approached, but none were willing to make the trip to Paris, including the French champions of 1899 and 1900, Le Havre. The runners-up of 1900, Club Français Paris were, as such, selected by the USFSA to represent France, although they bolstered their side with non-French players. An added bonus of this choice would be that Club Français would attract local spectators, while travelling expenses would be kept to a minimum. This French side did not don club colours; they were kitted out with white jerseys emblazoned with the five Olympic rings.

The Belgium national champions of 1899–1900, Royal Racing Club de Bruxelles, had—along with other national champions—declined to participate in the Games. The Belgian football association turned to Frank König (a well-known striker and popular all-round sportsman) to put a league-select side together. When this did not work out, the *Fédération Universitaire* was approached. However, this organisation failed to find enough students to make up a squad.

Seemingly in desperation, advertisements were taken out in newspapers asking for players to come forward. A 'student' side was assembled, which included the Dutchman 'Henk' van Heuckelum and an Englishman, Eric Thornton. However, on departure for the games, the Belgian team remained a player short. Thus, at the last minute, Eugène Neefs was drafted into the team. For all this, all of the squad played for Belgian clubs—the likes of the Brussels' sides Léopold Club, Royal Racing Club, Skill FC, as well as FC Liégeois, SC Louvain, and Spa FC.

1900 Olympic Games				
Club Français Paris (FRA) Ref: Maignard (FRA)	Vélodrome Municipal de Vincennes, Paris, att: 500	Final 20/09/1900	W 0–4	Nicholas 2, Turner, Zealey
Upton Park FC (GBR): John Jones, Claude Buckingham, Billy Gosling, Alf Chalk, Tom Burridge, Bill Quash, Arthur Turner, F.G. Spackman, J. Nicholas, Jim Edward Zealey Haslom (c)				
Club Français Paris: (FRA): Lucien Huteau, Louis Bach, Pierre Allemane, Virgile Gaillard, Alfred Bloch, Maurice Macaire, Maurice Eugène Fraysse, René Garnier, Marcel Lambert, René Grandjean, Fernand Canelle				

Club Français Paris (FRA)			
Name	Dates	Club	Biography
Lucien Huteau	1878–unknown	Club Français	
Louis Bach	14 April 1883–16 September 1914	Club Français	

Pierre Allemane	19 January 1882–24 May 1956	Club Français	Defender. Born in Montpellier, before 1900 he played for Passy, Club Français (1900–1902), Racing Club de France (1902–1909), and CASG Paris (1909–1914). He won the national tournament in 1907 with RC Paris and was with them as runners-up in 1902, 1903, and 1908. Played for France seven times from 1905 to 1908.
Virgile Gaillard	28 July 1877–unknown	Club Français	
Alfred Bloch,	1877–unknown	Racing Club de France	Bloch came from a Jewish family – aka Jean Bloch
Maurice Macaire		Club Français	
Maurice Eugène Fraysse	August 1879–unknown date of death unknown	Racing club de France	Captain and leading figure within the USFSA
René Garnier	1878 – 1936	Club Français	Aka Georges Garnier
Marcel Lambert		Club Français	
René Grandjean	1872, date of death unknown	Club Français	
Fernand Canelle	2 January 1882 – 11 September 1951	Havre Athletic Club	He was born in Paris and started his career in 1896, at the age of 14, with Club Français. He was with the French Champions in 1899, 1900 and 1919. He won also six French Cups (1897, 1898, 1899, 1900, 1901, and 1903). In 1922 he retired at the age of 40.

Upton Park FC (GBR)		
Name	Dates	Biography
John H. Jones		
Claude Buckingham		
William Sullivan Gosling	19 July 1869–2 October 1952	
Alfred Ernest Chalk	27 November 1874–25 June 1954	

Tom Peter Eustace Burridge	30 April 1881–16 September 1965	Centre-half. His name is sometimes spelled 'Barridge' and his initials given as J. E. by some sources, but he is listed as T. E. Burridge by the IOC.
William Francis Patterson Quash	27 December 1868–17 May 1938	
Arthur Turner		Outside-right with Crouch End Vampires who joined Upton Park FC solely for the period of the Olympics.
F.G. Spackman		
J. Nicholas		
James Edward Zealey	7 March 1868–1934	
A. Haslom		Captain

The opening game of the tournament saw Upton Park FC demolish the USFSA XI. They were 0–2 up at half-time and had doubled this tally by the final whistle.

The game had a sensational start when, after just three minutes, Spackman passed to Nicholas, who beat the Club Français custodian, Huteau, to put the English 0–1 up. In response, the home team committed themselves to a ferocious assault, but found Jones in no mood to capitulate. However, about halfway into the first half, Garnier, in the frantic rush to pull level and attempting to kick the ball out of goalkeeper Jones's hands, fell heavily against the post. He went off for some time. He returned after application of the magic sponge, but as far as could be told, he had made himself pretty much ineffective. For all this, the French continued to push forward with determination, but they still could not manage to find a way past Jones, who stopped everything that came his way.

With half-time looming, Nicholas got his second after a mix-up between Huteau and Bach.

In the second half, Club Français appeared to have decided to throw caution to the wind. Committing to a full forward thrust, a shot by Grandjean had Jones beaten, only for the post to keep the home side out. However the ball rebounded to Canelle, who seemed certain to score, yet somehow Jones managed to push the ball out.

Although seemingly tiring, as the match entered its last quarter the French remained committed to attack—but they were slow to retreat when out of possession. When Turner strolled the ball home after running round Huteau, the game seemed over; Upton Park's 0–4 lead looked unassailable. A long lob from the boot of Jim Zealy just before full time was the predictable icing on the inevitable cake; the French goalkeeper pounded the ground and cursed his defence.

The scoreline was healthy enough, but the Scarlet and Blacks had not had an easy ride. For three-quarters of the game, Club Français had looked capable of putting the East Enders on the back foot. Only the outstanding performance of Jones had shut the Frenchmen out. Buckingham and Gosling at times looked flat-footed in the face of the nippy French attack, and had Garnier stayed out of his argument with the upright his presence might have been telling. The comparative slothfulness of the Parkers' defence had been more than compensated by the clinical finishing of the Upton Park FC forwards; all four goals had been examples of quality finishing.

The conditions had been hot. Indeed, that September would be the warmest Paris would experience for over a hundred years—but against what might have been expected, the game had been a fast and furious event. It seems the fitness of the Upton Park FC players had been the difference between the two sides, as the French had faded noticeably as the second half wore on, effectively playing with a man down.

1900 Olympic Games				
Club Français Paris (FRA) v Université de Bruxelles Student XI (BEL) Ref: Jack Wood (ENG)	Vélodrome Municipal de Vincennes, Paris, att: 1,500	Third-place play-off 23/9/1900	6–2	Gaston Peltier, René Garnier [other French scorers unknown] *Spaunoghe, van Heuckelum*

Club Français Paris: (France): Lucien Huteau, Louis Bach, Pierre Allemane, Virgile Gaillard, Alfred Bloch, Maurice Macaire R. Duparc, René Garnier, Gaston Peltier, Marcel Lambert, Fernand Canelle

Université de Bruxelles Student XI (Belgium) : Marcel Leboutte, René Kelecom, Ernest Moreau de Melen, Alphonse Renier, Gustave Pelgrims, Eugène Neefs, Eric Thornton, Hendrik van Heuckelum, Émile Hilaire Spaunoghe, Albert Delbecque, Lucien Jean Londot

Club Français Paris (FRA)			
Name	Dates	Club	Biography
R. Duparc	1880–unknown	Racing Levallois 92	
René Garnier	1878–1936	Club Français	Captain, a.k.a. 'Georges'
Gaston Peltier	1876–unknown	Racing Levallois 92	

The match between the Belgians and the French, being something of a local derby, was more eventful than the opening game. It seems this contest started at a terrific pace; the home side went ahead in the first minute via Peltier, who had come into the French side to replace Grandjean. However, the plucky visitors scored by way of Spaunoghe and van Heuckelum to put the visitors in front. When Garnier scored in the thirteenth minute, the French overran the hapless 'student' side.

Université de Bruxelles (BEL)			
Name	Dates	Club	Biography
Marcel Leboutte		Spa FC	
René Kelecom		FC Liégeois	
Ernest Moreau de Melen	1879–1968	FC Liégeois	
Alphonse Renier		Racing Club de Bruxelles	
Gustave Pelgrims		Léopold Club de Bruxelles	Captain—a.k.a. 'Georges'
Eugène Neefs		Sporting Club de Louvain	a.k.a. 'Edmond'
Eric Thornton	5 July 1882–5 December 1945	Léopold Club de Bruxelles	British-born national resident in Brussels
Hendrik van Heuckelum	6 May 1879–28 April 1929	Université de Bruxelles	Born in The Hague, nicknamed 'Henk'—a Dutch national resident in Brussels. He played before 1900 at HBS Den Haag in the Netherlands, and in Belgium for Léopold Club de Bruxelles.
Émile Hilaire Spaunoghe		Skill F.C	
Albert Delbecque		Université de Bruxelles	
Lucien Jean Londot		FC Liégeois	

Camille Van Hoorden was a 'reserve' for the Belgians in this match—not that there were any substitutes at the time. His background seems to denote that he was one of their better players, so one can only assume he was carrying an injury. He was born in Watermael-Boitsfort, 1879, and won twenty-four caps for Belgian between 1904 and 1912. He captained his country eleven times and would take part in the Belgium *v*. France game of 1904—the first official match played by the two national teams.

Van Hoorden was with Sporting Club de Bruxelles in 1900, but he later played for Union FC d'Ixelles before moving on to Royal Racing Club de Bruxelles. He played 204 matches in his career, scoring sixteen goals

Van Hoorden won a Belgium Championship medal with Royal Racing in 1908 and was one of the victorious Royal Racing team that claimed the Belgian Cup in 1912. His coaching-management career (1916–1919 and 1919–1922) was with Standard de Liège, where he won the Belgian Second Division in 1921.

Place	Nation	Team	Win	Loss	Goals for	Goals against
1	Great Britain	Upton Park FC	1	0	4	0

2	France	Club Français Paris (USFSA XI)	1	1	6	6
3	Belgium	Université de Bruxelles	0	2	2	6

At first glance, it is hard to see how Upton Park FC came out on top, but the goal difference is strong indicator. However, there is also the consideration that they beat the better of the other two sides.

Great Britain did not enter a team for the next Games in 1904, but the nation that invented football would win gold in 1908 and 1912. For any number of reasons, many of them political, this feat has sadly never been replicated.

Both football games at the Paris Olympics were played at the Vélodrome de Vincennes (officially called Vélodrome Jacques Anquetil—La Cipale), which was the main stadium for the 1900 Games. The stadium is actually situated in Vincennes, near Paris, and was originally built in 1894 as a velodrome, but it played host to cycling, cricket, rugby union, football, and gymnastics. The track-and-field events were staged at the Racing Club de France.

The Vélodrome de Vincennes, which continues to be used for cycling, football, and rugby matches today, was the cycling venue for the 1924 Games, as well as the finish line of the Tour de France between 1968 and 1974 (Belgian Eddy Merckx won all of his five Tour victories at the venue). The stadium has featured in two feature films, La Rafle and Sarah's Key (both 2010), playing the role of the Vélodrome d'hiver in these films about the infamous round-up of Parisian Jews in July 1942.

The Phantom Games?

For everything I have just discussed, there may well have been another venue and even another team involved.

As a boy, my great-uncle showed me a faded sheet of paper that was related to a 'covered' eight-a-side football tournament held apparently as part of the World Exhibition in Paris. This document was in poor condition, but my uncle told me that his father had brought this back from France having worked in Paris from the early summer to the late autumn of 1900. He had even seen the Upton Park FC game at Vélodrome de Vincennes.

The scant leaflet was, of course, written in French, but even as a small lad, I could tell that the game it was supporting was an international team against, from the names of the players, a British side. The only name I recall, however, was what I assumed to be the British goalkeeper, 'Peck'.

As a child, a day out in the school summer holidays sometimes meant a picnic in West Ham Park—my family lived, and still lives, about a twenty-minute walk from there. The erstwhile home of Upton Park FC is a sizable green lung in what is now London's far East End. My brother and I, sometimes with my cousins and our friends, would sit and listen to my grandmother telling us about her days as a child in the

Park—a real escape from the industrial wasteland she lived in as a girl just a couple of miles away. Sometimes, she would talk of the mythical hideout of the legendary highwayman, Dick Turpin, and, at other points, she would tell us of the exploits of the 'Scarlet and Black' at the Olympic Games—particularly beating 'Frenchie' on his own soil. Her father, Jimmy Stone, had been quickly killed (like so many other East End boys) by a German shell soon after arriving in France during the First World War. Oddly, she seemed to hold the French responsible.

I heard a number of versions of the Parkers' accomplishment throughout my boyhood from her, my grandfather, and my great-uncle. All were much more elaborate and so more interesting, and therefore probably much more exaggerated and embroidered than what written history there is. Then, as now, I often wondered if the 'covered' game had anything to do with that triumph. Unfortunately, no-one could answer that question, and I have never found an answer other than the uninspiring 'probably not'. Nonetheless, it is what sparked my interest in Upton Park FC. However, if it was the case that there was more to the Olympic tournament of 1900 than what went on at the Vélodrome de Vincennes, it would explain much. Perhaps there was an 'Olympic' side put together, and maybe part of the Olympic tournament was played out as eight-a-side games, in a 'covered' arena; the World Exhibition would certainly have had some vast venues at its disposal. Maybe Upton Park FC did encounter and beat Université de Bruxelles at the Games of the VIII Olympiad. Perhaps Club Français and Université de Bruxelles also defeated that same, likely hastily put-together side. If so, the final table would have made more sense.

Place	Nation	Team	Win	Loss	Points
1	Great Britain	Upton Park	3	0	6
2	France	Club Français Paris (USFSA XI)	2	1	4
3	Belgium	Université de Bruxelles	1	2	2
3	IOC	Olympic team	0	3	0

In the end, football is a game of the imagination, played out in the hope of balance and romance—two largely incompatible bedfellows. Is that enough to make the dream tournament by conjoining my child's mind and my adult memory acceptable? What is certain is that the groundbreaking club carried their country's name to successfully fulfil the Olympic dream.

The Parkers also played a huge part in creating the world game as we know it today, which is another story. From their East London home in West Ham Park (perhaps twenty minutes sturdy walk to the London Stadium, the centre point of the 2012 Olympics), they produced some of the first England internationals.

Long before clubs like Millwall, Woolwich Arsenal, and West Ham United evolved out of works teams on the river banks of East London, competent and organised football teams had emerged in the Dockland areas. Football was well-established in Britain long before the dawn of the twentieth century. What Sir Geoff Hurst called 'a game of tomorrows' has been shaped by the past, and it is this that gives birth every day to the present.

Upton Park FC faded into history after 1911, but the Upton Park Trophy, an annual play-off between the league champions of Guernsey and Jersey, exists to this day. First contested in 1907, the trophy was donated to the Guernsey FA by Upton Park FC to celebrate their tenth annual Easter tour of the islands in 1906.

When West Ham visited those sunny isles, I like to think the games might have been watched over by the spirits of the Scarlet and Black, and that they might be amused or perhaps a little proud of their legacy.

By the way, Upton Park had a goalkeeper by the name of Peck playing for them in 1900.

Guernsey	The Track	17/05/1981	W 0–2	Goddard, Lampard

West Ham United: Phil Parkes (Bobby Ferguson), George Cowie, Frank Lampard Sr, Banton, Paul Brush, Alan Devonshire, Jimmy Neighbour (Nicky Morgan), Paul Goddard, David Cross, Stuart Pearson, Geoff Pike

Vale Recreation Guernsey	Corbet Field	24/05/1982	L 1–0	

West Ham United: Phil Parkes. George Cowie (Adrian Keith), Everald La Ronde, Neil Orr, Frank Lampard Sr, Pat Holland, Jimmy Neighbour, Dale Banton, David Cross, Nicky Morgan, Geoff Pike (Glen Burvill)

Vale Recreation Guernsey	Cycling Grounds	21/05/1983	W 5–3	Brush, Devonshire, Goddard, Pike, Swindlehurst

West Ham United: Phil Parkes, Ray Stewart (Glen Burvill), Frank Lampard Sr, Neil Orr, Gallagher, Alan Devonshire, Paul Allen, Paul Goddard, Dave Swindlehurst, Paul Brush (Bobby Barnes) Geoff Pike

4

FORWARD TO EUROPE!

The first European tour West Ham undertook was in May 1921 during the managerial reign of Syd King. Over the next decade or so, the Hammers' reputation as learners and teachers grew to such an extent that continental teams began to visit Upton Park to hone their knowledge and skills in the game. In November 1935, for example, FC Austria, winners of the Austrian Cup, practised at the Boleyn Ground at the start of their tour of England and Scotland.

This was the second time the Irons had met an Austrian club. The first was on their 1923 tour of Austria-Hungary.

Club tour Austria-Hungary 1923				
Hakoah Vienna (Austria-Hungary)	Wein	19/05/1923	D 1–1	Watson
West Ham United: Tommy Hampson, Billy Henderson, George Horler, George Carter, George Kay, Syd Bishop, Dick Richards, Bill Brown, Vic Watson, Bert Fletcher and Jimmy Ruffell. Manager: Syd King.				

In 1935, FC Austria included six internationals in their ranks. In particular, their goalkeeper Viktor Havlicek was keen to take tips from his Hammers counterpart, Herman Conway. A full game was organised between the clubs early in December of that year; this was the start of a relationship with Austrian clubs that has endured right up to recent years.

FC Austria (AUT)	Upton Park	02/12/1935	W 2–1	Barrett o.g.
West Ham United: Herman Conway, Alf Chalkley, Albert Walker, Ted Fenton, Jim Barrett, Joe Cockroft, John Morton, Lawrence Conwell, Dave Mangnall, Len Goulden, Jimmy Ruffell				

S.C. Wacker (AUT)	Upton Park	19/10/1954	W 3–1	Southren 2, Sexton
West Ham United: George Taylor, John Bond, Harry Kinsell, Andy Malcolm, Ken Brown Frank O'Farrell, Tommy Southern, Albert Foan, Dave Sexton, John Dick, Jimmy Andrews				

Sportklub Simmering (AUT)	Upton Park, att: 7,000	10/02/1955	W 8–2	Dare 4, Bennett, Hooper, Musgrove, o.g.

West Ham United: George Taylor, Geoff Hallas, Harry Kinsell, Malcolm Allison, Frank O'Farrell, Harry Hooper, Bobby Moore, Billy Dare, Les Bennett. Malcolm Musgrove

SK Rapid Vienna (AUT)	Upton Park	15/11/1955	D 1–1	Dare

West Ham United: Ernie Gregory, John Bond, Noel Cantwell Dave Sexton, Malcolm Allison, Frank O'Farrell, Harry Hooper, Jimmy Andrews, Billy Dare, John Dick, Ken Tucker

FC Austria Vienna (AUT)	Upton Park	05/10/1959	W 2–0	Woosnam, Musgrove

West Ham United: Noel Dwyer, John Bond, Noel Cantwell, Harry Obeney, Ken Brown, Bobby Moore, Mike Grice, Phil Woosnam, Vic Keeble, John Dick, Malcolm Musgrove

First Vienna (AUT)	Upton Park	30/10/1962	W 4–1	Hurst 2, Sealey, Musgrove

West Ham United: Lawrie Leslie, Joe Kirkup, Jack Burkett, Eddie Bovington, Ken Brown, Martin Peters, Peter Brabrook, Phil Woosnam (Ronnie Boyce) Alan Sealey, Geoff Hurst, Malcolm Musgrove

Pre-season European tour 1964–65				
FK Austria (AUT)	Prater Stadium, Vienna, att: 13,000	07/08/1964	W 0–3	Sissons, Moore, Byrne

West Ham United: Standen, Bond, Jack Burkett, Eddie Bovington, Ken Brown, Bobby Moore, Peter Brabrook, Ronnie Boyce, Johnny Byrne, Geoff Hurst, Johnny Sissons (Tony Scott). **Manager: Ron Greenwood.**

Graz AK (AUT)	Graz, att: 6,000	10/08/1964	W 0–1	Byrne

West Ham United: Standen, Kirkup, Jack Burkett, Martin Peters, Ken Brown, Bobby Moore, Alan Sealey, Ronnie Boyce, Johnny Byrne, Geoff Hurst (Peter Brabrook), Johnny Sissons (Tony Scott). **Manager: Ron Greenwood.**

SVL Flavia Solva (AUT)	Roman Stadium	15/07/09	D 1–1	Collison (pen)

West Ham United: Marek Štěch (Péter Kurucz), Julian Faubert (James Collins), Hérita Ilunga (Danny Gabbidon), Jordan Spence, Bondz N'Gala, Georg Grasser (Kieron Dyer), Oliver Lee, Jack Collison (Josh Payne), Savio Nsereko (Junior Stanislas), Anthony Edgar, Zavron Hines

FK Austria Vienna (AUT) Ref: Harald Lechner	Generali Arena, Vienna, att: 7,150	07/07/2012	L 3–1	Baldock

> West Ham United: Stephen Henderson (Jussi Jääskeläinen), Jordan Spence, James Tomkins (George McCartney), Winstone Reid (Mark Noble), Dan Potts, Matthew Taylor (Gary O'Neil), Mo Diamé (Kevin Nolan), Ravel Morrison, Sebastian Lletget, Carlton Cole (Nicky Maynard), Sam Baldock (Ricardo Vaz Tê)

When he hung up his boots, Havlicek, who was capped three times for Austria, went on to become a coach in Germany and the Netherlands. He coached the national Belgian team from 1958 to 1960 under manager Constant Vanden Stock (1958–68). Stock, a former Belgian international himself, became the president of the mighty RSC Anderlecht, the club West Ham would meet in in the 1975–76 European Cup Winners' Cup final. His son, Roger Vanden Stock, is the club's current president. Anderlecht's stadium was named after Constant.

After his role with Belgium, Viktor Havlicek spent a year with the famed Royal Antwerp FC. His brother, Eduard 'Edy' Havlicek, was a coach with the top German side Borussia Dortmund for two years from 1948.

Golden Era

Those early games were the seeds that eventually bore the fruit of West Ham's golden era of the 1960s.

September 1964 brought West Ham's first round, first leg, European Cup Winners' Cup match with the part-timers of La Gantoise, the first Belgian team to compete in the competition. Up to that point, the Hammers had never lost to a side from that part of the world.

Royal Standard Club Liegeois (BEL)	Upton Park	12/05/1951	W 3–2	Barrett, Moroney, Woodgate

> West Ham United: George Taylor, Ernie Devlin, Steve Forde, Tom Moroney, Malcolm Allison, Frank O'Farrell, Harry Hooper, Jim Barrett (Jr), Bill Robinson, Gerry Gazzard, Terry Woodgate

International *Voetbaltornoo* Ghent 1958				
Racing Club de Gent (BEL)	Stadion Jules Otten	Group match 01/05/1958	W 0–1	Keeble

> West Ham United: Ernie Gregory, John Bond, Noel Cantwell, Andy Malcolm, Ken Brown, Andy Nelson, Mike Grice, Mick Newman, Vic Keeble, Malcolm Musgrove. Manager: Ted Fenton.

Club tour of Belgium, Germany, and the Netherlands 1959				
Charleroi (BEL)	Charleroi	30/04/1959	D 0–0	

> West Ham United: Noel Dwyer, Joe Kirkup, John Bond, Andy Malcolm, Ken Brown, Bill Lansdowne, Mike Grice, John Smith, Vic Keeble, John Dick, Malcolm Musgrove. Manager: Ted Fenton.

West Ham manager Ron Greenwood had been based in Ghent with the RAF during the Second World War, and so quite enjoyed the idea of going back. He and his team made their way by coach down to Dover and took the ferry to Ostend. Then it was back on the coach to Ghent. Not everyone in the side was used to going abroad, and two of them turned up without passports. Defender Eddie Presland, an East Ham lad, was due to play in this game, but as he was getting changed Greenwood had to tell him that he had not been registered. This oversight almost certainly changed Presland's future, because chances to break into the side were to be few and far between.

In their first venture into European competition, West Ham learned a few lessons from La Gantoise, who were a rugged side seemingly committed to defence over both legs. They stuck rigidly to their 4-2-4 shape, defending in depth and tackling hard. The Irons countered with a formation that amounted to 1-4-1-4; Brown came back as a centre-half while Bobby Moore acted as general caretaker and Martin Peters played at left-back—his speed and instinct for an opening plagued the Belgian side.

The Hammers created five good chances in the first half, while La Gantoise did not manage one. In the fifty-second minute, Alan Sealey took a corner on the right, Armand Seghers (the forty-year-old home goalkeeper) hesitated, and Boyce got his head to the ball to put it floating over Seghers' head and into the net.

La Gantoise emerged from their shell a little in the second half, but the Buffalos of Ghent had neither the skill nor the method to break down their visitors. Long before the final whistle, the 600 East Londoners in the crowd of 18,000 were looking forward to the second leg at the Boleyn Ground.

When the Belgians came to Upton Park, Alan Dickie played in goal. This was one of his rare first-team outings as Jim Standen had been injured. 'Spider' (as Dickie was known to his teammates) found out about his inclusion late in the day:

> I didn't think I was in the team … I got held up in Blackwall Tunnel—it was murder in those days. We were told to get to the ground by 6.30 p.m. at the latest. I didn't get there till 7.10 p.m., to be told that I would be playing. The kick-off was only twenty minutes away, so I had no time for butterflies.

West Ham's passing was erratic at vital points while their finishing was also inaccurate and, at times, unbelievably poor. The boys from Ghent were a bit more aggressive than they had been in Belgium, but they maintained their determination to defend.

West Ham always appeared destined to move on to the next round, even if they made hard work of it. Johnny 'Budgie' Byrne told me:

> If any side set up just to defend in numbers, they are going to make it hard to score. They were managed by the German, Max Schirschin, who had played for Schalke before the war, and he set them up well. He fought on the Russian front so he was used to making a fight of it. He coached Rouen previously, I think he went on to Fortuna in Holland

and Metz in France; he'd been a prisoner of war in France. He definitely made it hard for us. It was funny, at first I didn't know how to say 'Gantoise' properly but Ron put me right, he had lived in Ghent at some point. But I kept getting it wrong, on purpose like; 'Ganonize', 'Jamonose' and that, and he kept putting me right, saying again and again, 'Gant-was, Gant-was'. I'd say: 'Yea, Gan-waaz', or 'Janways'. Everyone was pissing themselves and he never saw it!

The Hammers should have scored four in the first twenty minutes. The Belgians never fought any less than bravely within the limitations of their system and ability. Even when Denayer, his left thigh strapped, limped out to the wing, forcing Ghellynck and Lambert to drop back, they kept on running and tackling with strength.

However, a moment of outrageous confusion by the Hammers' defence gifted the visitors a goal. Martin Peters intercepted a through ball and turned to make a back pass to Dickie. It looked a formality but, suddenly, things went horribly wrong. The home side custodian advanced along the line of the right post, but the pass from Peters trundled two yards to his right and into the opposite corner of the net.

This rare moment of jubilation for the visitors was followed by more intensive defending on their part.

The Irons might have won by six, but their only goal came eleven minutes after the Belgian opener. Sissons sped along the left wing; his long, diagonal centre was swept into the net first time by Byrne. This was one success, but it had to be set against an endless catalogue of near-things. Sissons hit the side netting twice and was also denied by a post. Hurst forced Armand Seghers to make the save of the night—maybe his life.

In the end, West Ham's opponents deserved a fond farewell. The crowd of 24,000 (who paid record receipts) gave the plucky but outclassed Belgians a huge, spontaneous roar of sympathy as the game concluded. Of course, this might have been ironic, as jeers and slow handclaps had been coming from spectators throughout the match in response to the defensive tactics deployed by the Belgians, who were seemingly intent on keeping the scoreline respectable. Nevertheless, West Ham marched into the last sixteen.

European Cup Winners' Cup 1964–65				
Association Royal Athletic La Gantoise Ref: Birger Nilsen (NOR)	Jules Often, Ghent , att: 5,173	First round, 1st leg 23/09/1964	W 0–1	Ronnie Boyce 51'
Association Royal Athletic La Gantoise: Armand Seghers (c), Antoine Devreese, Richard De Nayer; Norbert Delmulle, Roger Debaets, Lucien Ghellynck; Robert Mahieu, Urbain Seghers, Eric Lambert, Albert Mayama, James Storme. Trainer: Max Schirschin.				
West Ham United: Jim Standen; John Bond, Martin Peters; Eddie Bovington, Ken Brown, Bobby Moore (c), Peter Brabrook, Ronnie Boyce, Johnny Byrne, Geoff Hurst, Johnny Sissons. Manager: Ron Greenwood.				

Association Royal Athletic La Gantoise Ref: Rolf Erling Olsen (NOR)	Upton Park, att: 24,101	First round, 2nd leg 7/10/64	1-1 (1-1)	Peters 33' o.g. Byrne 43'

West Ham United: Alan Dickie, John Bond, Martin Peters; Eddie Bovington, Ken Brown, Bobby Moore (c), Peter Brabrook, Ronnie Boyce, Johnny Byrne, Geoff Hurst, Johnny Sissons. Manager: Ron Greenwood.

Association Royal Athletic La Gantoise: Armand Seghers (c), Noel Van de Velde, Richard De Nayer, Antoine Devreese, Robert Mahieu, Lucien Ghellynck, Albert Mayama, Urbain Seghers, Eric Lambert, Cyprien Bula, James Storme. Trainer: Max Schirschin.

While West Ham had made quite a meal of things, the holders (Sporting Lisbon) bowed out to the English Second Division side Cardiff City. The Welsh Cup winners were carrying on the Welsh giant-killing tradition in the competition started by the Bangor City side that had seen off Napoli in 1962.

Železná Sparta ('Iron Sparta')

The next day, Slavia Sofia of Bulgaria put out Cork Celtic. Galatasaray went through on the toss of a coin, and the Finns of FC Haka ousted Skeid of Oslo. Any one of these sides would have suited West Ham in the next round but they drew Spartak Sokolovo, later to be known as Sparta Prague.

Greenwood and his team knew that they were about to face a hard, disciplined side—one that was leading the Czech League at the time. After going through the Spartak players, West Ham found them to be an awesome crew. John Bond told me about his manager's preparation for the game:

> Ron could have scared the shit out of you going on about former Spartak players like Kvašňák, Tichý, and the outside-left Mašek, he was still with Prague of course, like players of that sort kind of sprung out of the ground for the club. How they got to the 1962 World Cup final. But we took it all with a pinch of salt. They were just human, like us. Don't get me wrong, I knew I'd have my hands full with Mašek, he was an international player and a good one, but we thought they'd have their mind on playing defensively.

Greenwood knew something of the Sparta manager's growing reputation. Václav Ježek would take the Czechoslovakia national team to Yugoslavia for the 1976 European Championships and come home victors having beaten the formidable West Germans in a penalty shoot-out. At forty-one years of age, he was a new, young manager in his first post, but he would lead Sparta Prague to league titles in 1965 and 1967.

Any possible trepidation on the part of West Ham players would not have been allayed by the news that the first leg would be played at Upton Park. But the East Londoner's record against Czech clubs was not good, although things had started well historically.

Club tour of Austria-Hungary 1923				
Slavia Prague (Austria-Hungary)	Prague	16/05/1923	W 1–3	Watson 2, Ruffell
West Ham United: West Ham United: Ted Hufton, Tommy Hodgeson, Jack Hebden, George Carter, George Kay, Syd Bishop, Dick Richards, Bill Brown, Vic Watson, Bert Fletcher and Jimmy Ruffell. Manager: Syd King.				

Sportovni Klub Kladno (Czechoslovakia)	Upton Park	20/04/1938	W 3–2	Archie Macaulay 2, o.g.
West Ham United: Herman Conway, Charlie Bicknell, Steve Forde, Reg Attwell, Charlie Turner, Ted Fenton, Tom Green, Archie Macaulay, Stan Foxall, Len Goulden, John Morton				

The Irons had also matched Sparta in 1957. That said, West Ham had got very little out of more recent encounters with Czech teams generally.

Sparta Prague, (Czechoslovakia)	Upton Park	21/03/1957	D 3–3	Lewis, Dare, Allison (pen)
West Ham United: Ernie Gregory, John Bond, Noel Cantwell, Andy Malcolm, Malcolm Allison, John Smith, Mike Grice, Billy Dare, Eddie Lewis, John Dick, Terry McDonald				

Club tour of of Czechoslovakia 1957				
Sparta Prague-Duklan Prague FC Combined XI (Czechoslovakia)	Prague	22/05/1957	W 1–2	Smith, Dick
West Ham United: Ernie Gregory, George Wright, Noel Cantwell, Malcolm Pyke, Ken Brown, Malcolm Allison, Billy Dare, John Smith, Eddie Lewis, John Dick, Malcolm Musgrove. Manager: Ted Fenton.				
Brno (Czechoslovakia)	Brno	25/05/1957	L 2–0	
West Ham United: Ernie Gregory, George Wright, Noel Cantwell, Malcolm Pyke, Ken Brown, Malcolm Allison, Billy Dare, John Smith, Eddie Lewis, John Dick, Malcolm Musgrove. Manager: Ted Fenton.				
Ostrava (Czechoslovakia)	Ostrava	25/05/1957	D 1–1	Dare
West Ham United: Ernie Gregory, George Wright, Noel Cantwell, Bill Lansdowne, Ken Brown, Malcolm Allison, Mike Grice, John Smith, Billy Dare, Bill Neville, Malcolm Musgrove. Manager: Ted Fenton.				
Bresov (Czechoslovakia)	Bresov	20/05/1957	L 2–1	Musgrove
West Ham United: Bob Wyllie, George Wright, Noel Cantwell, Bill Lansdowne, Ken Brown, Malcolm Allison, Mike Grice, Eddie Lewis, Billy Dare, John Dick, Malcolm Musgrove. Manager: Ted Fenton.				

Bratislava Red Star (Czechoslovakia)	Vienna, Austria	02/08/1959	L 3–2	Brett, Musgrove
West Ham United: Dwyer, Bond (Kirkup), Cantwell, Andy Malcolm (Bobby Moore), Ken Brown, John Smith, Mike Grice, Phil Woosnam, Vic Keeble, Tony Brett, Malcolm Musgrove				

In 1959, the Irons had faced Dukla Prague at Upton Park. They had been Czech champions in 1953, 1956, and 1958 (and would be again in 1961–64, 1966, 1977, 1979, and 1982). Dukla would achieve the Czech league-and-cup double in 1961 and 1966 (in the future the Cup would be there's also in 1965, 1969, 1981, 1983, 1985, and 1990). However, they were held to a 1–1 draw at the Boleyn Ground.

UDA Dukla Prague (Czechoslovakia)	Upton Park, att: 10,300	09/11/1959	D 1–1	Cantwell (pen)
West Ham United: Noel Dwyer, John Bond, Noel Cantwell, Andy Malcolm, Ken Brown, Bobby Moore, Mike Grice, Phil Woosnam, Harry Obeney, John Dick, Malcolm Musgrove				

The American Challenge Cup 1963				
Dukla Prague (Czechoslovakia)	Soldiers Field, Chicago, att: 11,000	Cup final, 1st leg 07/08/1963	L 0–1	
West Ham United: Jim Standen, Joe Kirkup, Jack Burkett, Martin Peters, Ken Brown, Bobby Moore, Peter Brabook, Ronnie Boyce, Johnny Byrne, Geoff Hurst (Alan Sealy), Tony Scott. Manager: Ron Greenwood.				
Dukla Prague (Czechoslovakia)	Randalls Island Stadium, New York, att: 15,000	Cup final, 2nd leg 11/08/1963	D 1–1	Scott
West Ham United: Jim Standen, Joe Kirkup, Jack Burkett, Martin Peters, Ken Brown, Bobby Moore, Peter Brabook, Ronnie Boyce, Johnny Byrne, Geoff Hurst, Tony Scott. Manager: Ron Greenwood.				

John Bond expanded on his thoughts prior to the game with Sparta Prague:

> I was brought back for the game after a calf injury, taking over from Joe Kirkup. I was eager to keep my place and thought, 'Well, if I can keep them from getting by me that'll be alright.' But more than that, I got the bonus of putting a goal by them!

West Ham were not seen as a very attack-minded side at the time, and the cushion of a couple of goals, which were traditionally expected to take to the away leg of a tie, was not a foregone conclusion.

It was thought that Martin Peters and Ronnie Boyce would hold the key in midfield. Ron Greenwood's plan was to let Spartak, being the away team, do their defensive stuff before trying to outmanoeuvre them. The idea was that this would give West Ham control of the game, allowing Hurst, Johnny Byrne, and Sissons to concentrate on goal-getting—simple!

As is so often the case, it did not work out like that. For nearly an hour the Irons flung themselves at Spartak's solidly drilled defence, who never had less than seven men back, and at times this went up to nine. It did not make for exciting football, but it was effective. The burly, uncompromising Gura closely marked Byrne while the equally daunting Steiningel held on to Hurst. The towering Kos swept up behind them.

The Hammers main hope seemed to lie with young Sissons. The left-winger did well against Dyba early on, but the visitors' outside-right was a hard-running defender. By half-time he, alongside Voja and Mráz (who had focused on Boyce and Martin Peters in midfield), had cut off Byrne's supply lines. With Bobby Moore out for this game, the side looked to Martin Peters for inspiration, but it was not happening.

John Lyall, who was at that time managing the West Ham youth team, recalled:

> Our plans weren't working. It seemed like one of those nights when everything you try won't work; you'd have bet on the game being a goalless stalemate. Continental teams could do that well, kill the heart of a game. It was done in a way you didn't really come across in English football then. I think it went against players' instincts in the English game, which of course made it all the more frustrating.

The Hammers were left to fight it out, but in a way that suited them.

Out on the right, Spartak conceded one of a string of free kicks. Alan Sealey curled the ball into the goalmouth where it was beaten out by a defender and landed at the feet of John Bond. From about 25 yards out, the Hammers' defender lashed out. Bond remembered it as, 'a rocket that banged straight into the roof of the net… I hit with my "wrong" left foot'. I laughed as he related this memory. He had a beautiful, antiquated Essex accent hardly heard now, but it made his words lyrical in a straightforward way that brought me right into the moment he was looking back on.

Bond loved to score (who does not?), and with just over half an hour of the leg remaining, the West Ham board and manager Ron Greenwood must have thanked their lucky stars that the veteran full-back had refused to sign for QPR some time earlier. He had not scored for three-and-a-half years, but he could pick his moments. Bond was something of a penalty and dead-ball expert and, although a defender, scored his share of goals—the first against Spartak was his thirty-fourth for the club—and played a number of games as centre-forward in the late 1950s.

One goal was not going to be enough to take to Prague, but the Czech defence now allowed Byrne to buzz and he began to spray passes around in the spaces opening up. With under ten minutes left, he sent a beauty to Ronnie Boyce. Sealey picked up Boyce's volley on the left-hand edge of the Czech penalty-area and struck it firmly—the ball hit the far post. As it came back out, one of the Spartak defenders inadvertently chipped the ball back to Sealey. This time he relaxed, looked up at his target, chose his spot, and fired. Kramerius, their goalkeeper, had no chance. Sealey was ecstatic; he had not scored a goal since early April.

Throwing off their cloak of defence—just previously they had booted the ball out of the ground four times in succession in attempts to waste time—Spartak charged full-bloodedly at the West Ham rearguard. Even in the last minute they were still looking for a reply; Mráz swept a shot across the unprotected goal, but the Hammers held on. The game had attracted nearly 28,000 and the gate receipts were £10,600—a record for the Boleyn Ground at that time.

West Ham grabbed the imagination of the media. Everyone felt that something was happening down in the East End, the magic that comes with putting the Docklands' battling spirit together with football intelligence and an effort to produce something akin to art.

On that cold night of 25 November 1964, east of the Tower and north of the river the night was filled with a celebratory cacophony from the docks that could be heard by children in their beds from Tilbury to Chelsea, from Poplar to Houndsditch. Tugboat toots and the mighty horn blasts of cargo ships sang to signal the alliance of London pride and Essex grit—the stuff that made West Ham a place, not just a football team. They had prevailed, and the fearful ramparts of Iron Sparta, living up to their nickname, had been breached.

Having missed the first leg, Bobby Moore could not make the second leg either, so Boyce switched to play as sweeper in Czechoslovakia. Alan Sealey kept his place, but he and the rest of the side were given a lot to deal with; volatile opponents and a hostile crowd made their task a daunting one.

Sparta—skilful, tough and, apparently encouraged by the Bulgarian referee Hlavni Dinov, rough—rolled wave after wave of attack at the line of claret-and-blue defenders before them. The shield held magnificently; the Czechs must have felt they were hammering a punch bag. No matter how hard they hit, nor from what direction, the ball always came back at them. This was English defending at its best—not the torturous teasing and mucking about so well-crafted in much of the European game. West Ham offered a stoic belligerence fuelled by the will that had its foundation in straightforward cockney defiance.

If he had his say, Byrne was not content to settle for that. In the thirteenth minute, his intuition as a striker came to the fore. He scuttled on to a long clearance from Bond, wrestled free from the desperate arms of Tichý, and squared the ball for Sissons to score with supreme coolness from 20 yards. The goal was a perfect illustration of the counter-attack from a defensive position at which West Ham had become adept.

The band of 120 Irons loyalists broke into exultant tones. The sound of the 'Bubbles' anthem floated once more in Europe across the ground, which was perched high on a hill above the friendly, sun-bathed city. This must have been a very strange experience for the natives.

A cross between a dirge and a ditty, this song of long-lived wanting was used as a celebratory and consolatory resource. Depending on when it is sung, in victory or defeat, to me it is evocative of a statement like, 'we are never beaten', 'down but not out'. It seems to be about fate, destiny, and the need to accept the 'slings and arrows of outrageous fortune'.

As I write this, West Ham have just been knocked out of the FA Cup in an Upton Park replay—the last ever cup tie to take place at the Boleyn Ground. The tie is our story: cheated out of victory at Old Trafford just as we are so often thwarted, but when the Hammers rise again we will be singing 'Bubbles'.

The goal by Sissons was not the end of this Czech saga. Spartak were helped outrageously by the match officials. The referee's partiality reached its peak in the thirty-sixth minute; Bond was pushed and his hand touched the ball as he fell. The outcome was a penalty.

Standen watched Mráz carefully as the forward placed the ball deliberately on the spot. The West Ham goalkeeper went down into a crouch, still studying his would-be executioner. As the ball was hit, Standen flung himself far to his left. Mráz stared, fists clenched at the end of half-raised arms as the Hammers goalkeeper hurled himself towards the Czech missile. The crowd groaned as Standen intercepted for justice. As Martin Peters told me: 'Football has a way of being fair over time, but fairness is helped by a good goalkeeper and Jim was among the best of his time I'd say'.

Spartak scored in the sixty-eight and eighty-eighth minutes. Both goals followed mistakes unworthy of West Ham, but in many ways were typical of the kind of goals the side always and forever seem bound to concede. Mašek grabbed the first while Boyce stood motionless—Standen pushed a Táborský long shot on to the bar before cruel fate intervened and he lost his footing. The second came at a point when the penalty area was populated by eighteen players; Mráz was permitted to flick a header by Kraus into the net. However, these were the only moments in the game when Boyce was still. He pulled back to sweep up loose ends in defence, playing the role as if he were born to it. It is adaptability and planning such as this that made West Ham the European power that they were becoming at the time.

Sissons and Byrne were superb, holding the ball up front to allow things to develop around them.

Although West Ham lost the game 2–1, they went through 2–3 on aggregate. The desperate undertones of the encounter were spelled out in the cuts and bruises sustained. Alan Sealey came off worse than most. He was taken to hospital immediately after the game and had seven stitches in an ugly gash on his left shin.

European Cup Winners' Cup 1964–65				
Sparta Prague (Czechoslovakia) Ref: Jose Maria Ortiz de Mendibil (SPA)	Upton Park, att: 27,590	Second round, 1st leg 25/11/1964	W 2–0	Bond 57', Sealey 82'
West Ham United: Jim Standen; John Bond, John Jack Burkett; Eddie Bovington, Ken Brown (c), Martin Peters; Alan Sealey, Ronnie Boyce, Johnny Byrne, Geoff Hurst, Johnny Sissons. Manager: Ron Greenwood.				
Sparta Prague: Antonín Kramerius; Jiří Gura, Vladimír Táborský; Karel Steiningel, Josef Vojta, Vladimír Kos, Pavel Dyba, Ivan Mráz, Andrej Kvašňák, Tadeáš Kraus (c), Václav Mašek. Trainer: Václav Ježek				

Sparta Prague (Czechoslovakia) Ref: Konstantin Dinov (BUL)	Letnd, Prague, att: 20,462	Second round, 2nd leg 09/12/1964	L 2–1 (W 2–3)	*Mašek 68', Mráz 88'* Sissons 14'
Sparta Prague: Antonín Kramerius; Jiři Gura, Vladimír Táborský; Jiři Tichý, Vladimír Kos, Josef Vojta; Pavel Dyba, Ivan Mráz, Andrej Kvašňák, Václav Mašek, Tadeáš Kraus (c). Trainer: Václav Ježek				
West Ham United: Jim Standen; John Bond, John Jack Burkett; Eddie Bovington, Ken Brown (c), Martin Peters; Alan Sealey, Ronnie Boyce, Johnny Byrne, Geoff Hurst, Johnny Sissons. Manager: Ron Greenwood.				

Subsequently, West Ham played just one more game against a Czechoslovakian side before the country split into the Czech Republic and Slovakia:

Slovan Bratislava (Czechoslovakia)	Upton Park, att: 22,900	02/02/1970	D 1–1	Best
West Ham United: Peter Grotier, Billy Bonds, Bobby Howe, Martin Peters, Alan Stephenson, Bobby Moore, Trevor Brooking, Jimmy Lindsay, Peter Eustace (Clyde Best), Geoff Hurst				

SK Sigma Olomouc (CZE)	Bad Raskersberg, Austria	17/07/2007	L 1–0	
West Ham United: Richard Wright (Jimmy Walker), Jon Spector (Anton Ferdinand), James Collins (Calum Davenport), Matthew Upson (Danny Gabbidon), George McCartney (Christian Dailly), Julian Faubert (Jack Collison), Scott Parker (Mark Noble), Lee Bowyer (Heyden Mullins), Winstone Reid (Luís Boa Morte), Dean Ashton (Craig Bellamy), Carlton Cole (Bobby Zamora)				

West Ham had been told that Spanish officials would be in charge of the second leg, as had been the case at Upton Park. Afterwards, Greenwood said: 'We certainly did not expect Iron Curtain officials. We shall have to take it up with UEFA.'

The overall result was a wonderful achievement for the East London side. They had played well, with a balance of control and innovation. West Ham had outplayed and out-thought class opposition with style and courage as a team—each individual committed to the whole.

5

RAPPAN

Ron Greenwood told me:

> You have to see what the rest of the world is doing. I've always believed football is a developing game—it constantly changes and the possibilities are endless. That's part of its fascination. But if you don't see new and different things, how others do things differently, it's hard to be inventive and you get into a rut; everyone likes best to do what they know—what's hard is to learn what you don't know and then do it better than what you learnt. There's not a great deal of point in anything if you are just going to repeat yourself over and over. Apart from getting found out eventually, people will know what to expect and counter what it is you do, it's unrewarding.

After their exploits against Sparta Prague, The 1964–65 Hammers had a three-month break before their next European game. Alan Sealey's injury put him out for the best part of a month.

The third round of the Hammers' European odyssey pitted them against Lausanne of Switzerland. The Swiss were managed by the legendary Karl Rappan, who had massive experience of the game having spent some forty years at the top level. He had been coach of the Swiss national side and named the 'Master of Swiss soccer'. His 'bolt' system was unique, based on a highly mobile game and theoretically requiring ten men to do the work of thirteen.

This was a man of football. Born in Vienna, Rappan grew up in an era when Austria grew to be a power of the world game. In 1924, he joined the famous Wacker Vienna. His other clubs were FK Austria Vienna and SK Rapid Vienna, where he was part of the 1929–30 team that won the Austrian League.

In 1927, Rappan was capped twice for Austria, scoring a goal in his nation's 6–0 humbling of Hungary. His managerial career started in 1932 with his first post at the Swiss club Servette. He moved on to Grasshoppers, but from 1935 to 1948, he guided FC Zürich to five league titles and seven cup wins. In 1948, he was back at Servette as coach, there to add another league title and cup victory to his list of triumphs.

From 1960 to 1963, Rappan coached the Swiss national side before joining Lausanne—a side he took to the league title in 1965.

Rappan had been the Swiss head coach, while doing other jobs, in stints from 1937–38, 1942–49, and 1953–54. In all, he took control of the side for seventy-seven games, more than any Swiss team coach, and won twenty-nine, another record. Under Rappan, Switzerland qualified for the 1938, 1954, and 1962 World Cups.

As such, Greenwood left his men with no doubt that a team managed and coached by Rappan would not be a pushover; Lausanne were a side to be respected, if not feared.

The Hammers had met Lausanne for the first time more than three decades earlier. Encounters with Swiss sides had provided West Ham with a deal of success over the years.

Club tour of Germany, Switzerland, and France 1924				
Berne (SUI)	Berne	20/05/1924	W 0–1	Yews
West Ham United: Tommy Hampson, Bill Henderson, John Young, Syd Bishop, George Kay, Albert Cadwell, Tom Yews, Vic Watson, Jimmy Collins, Billy Moore, Jimmy Ruffell. Manager: Syd King.				

Continental Motor Tour 1931				
Lucerne (SUI)	Lucerne	20/05/1931	W 0–2	Harris 2
West Ham United: Bob Dixon, Stan Earl, Reg Wade, Fred Norris, Wally St Pier, Albert Cadwell, Tom Yews, Walter Pollard, Jim Barrett, Wilf James, Jim Harris. Manager: Syd King.				
Zürich (SUI)	Zürich	23/05/1931	W 2–5	Barrett 3, Harris 2
West Ham United: Bob Dixon, Stan Earl, Reg Wade, Fred Norris, Wally St Pier, Albert Cadwell, Tom Yews, Walter Pollard, Jim Barrett, Wilf James, Jim Harris. Manager: Syd King.				
Bale (SUI)	Lucerne	25/05/1931	W 3–4	Fereday, Yews, James, Pollard
West Ham United: Bob Dixon, Stan Earl, Reg Wade, Fred Norris, Wally St Pier, Albert Cadwell, Dave Fereday, Walter Pollard (Jim Barrett), A. Robinson (Tom Yews), Wilf James, Jim Harris. Manager: Syd King.				

Club tour of Switzerland 1934				
Berne (SUI)	Berne	10/05/1934	D 2–2	Tippett, Barrett
Berne: Berne: Treuburg, Hannis, Steck, Gerhold, Hoper, Kohler, Bossi, Townley, Billeter, Bosch, Vaccani. Manager: Charlie Paynter.				
West Ham United: George Watson, Alf Chalkley, Albert Walker, Ted Anderson, Jim Barrett, Joe Cockroft, Jim Wood, John Morton, Tom Tippett, Len Goulden, Jimmy Ruffell. Manager: Charlie Paynter.				
Kreuzlingen (SUI)	Kreuzlingen	13/05/1934	W 2–9	Wood 2, Barrett 2, Ruffell 2, Musgrave 2, Fenton
West Ham United: George Watson, Arthur Tonner, Albert Walker, Wally St Pier, Jim Barrett, Joe Cockroft, Jim Wood, Joe Musgrave, Ted Fenton, Len Goulden, Jimmy Ruffell. Manager: Charlie Paynter.				

Swiss International Team (SUI)	Sportplatz Hardturm Stadium, Zürich	16/05/1934	L 3–1	Musgrave
West Ham United: George Watson, Alf Chalkley, Albert Walker, Wally St Pier, Jim Barrett, Joe Cockroft, Jim Wood, John Morton, Joe Musgrave, Len Goulden, Jimmy Ruffell. Manager: Charlie Paynter.				
St Gallen (SUI)	St Gallen	19/05/1934	L 1–0	
West Ham United: George Watson, Alf Chalkley, Albert Walker, Wally St Pier, Jim Barrett, Joe Cockroft, Jim Wood, John Morton, Joe Musgrave, Len Goulden, Jimmy Ruffell. Manager: Charlie Paynter.				
Lausanne (SUI)	Lucerne Stadium	22/05/1934	W 2–9	Musgrave 6, Ruffell, Wood, Goulden
West Ham United: George Watson, Alf Chalkley, Albert Walker, Wally St Pier, Jim Barrett, Joe Cockroft, Jim Wood, John Morton, Joe Musgrave, Len Goulden, Jimmy Ruffell. Manager: Charlie Paynter.				

In two years, Lausanne went from being no match for West Ham to bettering the East London side on an otherwise successful tour for the Irons.

Club tour of Switzerland 1936				
Swiss National Team (SUI)	Zürich	13/05/1936	W 0–1	Barrett
West Ham United: Herman Conway, Charlie Bicknell, Albert Walker, Ted Fenton, Jim Barrett, Joe Cockroft, John Morton, Lawrence Conwell, Peter Simpson, Len Goulden, Jimmy Ruffell. Manager: Charlie Paynter.				
FC Kreuzlingen (SUI)	Kreuzlingen	16/05/1936	W 0–2	Foreman, Simpson
West Ham United: Herman Conway, Charlie Bicknell, Albert Walker, Ted Fenton, Jim Barrett, Joe Cockroft, John Foreman, Stan Foxall, Peter Simpson, Len Goulden, John Morton. Manager: Charlie Paynter.				
Arau (SUI)	Arau	21/05/1936	W 2–4	Foxall 2, Goulden, Ruffell
West Ham United: Herman Conway, Charlie Bicknell, Albert Walker, Ted Fenton, Jim Barrett, Joe Cockroft, John Foreman, Jim Collins, Stan Foxall, Len Goulden, Jimmy Ruffell. Manager: Charlie Paynter.				
Lausanne (SUI)	Lausanne	24/05/1936	L 1–0	
West Ham United: Herman Conway, Charlie Bicknell, Albert Walker, Ted Fenton, Jim Barrett, Joe Cockroft, John Foreman, Jim Collins, Stan Foxall, Len Goulden, Jimmy Ruffell. Manager: Charlie Paynter.				

By 1946, the tables had turned yet again as the Hammers proceeded past Lausanne to complete their tour of Switzerland unbeaten.

Club tour of Switzerland 1946				
FC Luzern (SUI)	Lucerne	09/05/1946	W 0–5	Macaulay 3, Small 2
West Ham United: Harry Medhurst, Charlie Bicknell, Ron Cater, Norman Corbett, Dick Walker, Reg Attwell, Terry Woodgate, Almeric Hall, Sam Small, Archie Macaulay, Jackie Wood. Manager: Charlie Paynter.				

FC Grenchen (SUI)	Grenchen	11/05/1946	W 2–3	Fenton 2, Macualay

West Ham United: George Taylor, Charlie Bicknell, Dick Walker, Norman Corbett, Charlie Walker, Reg Attwell, Terry Woodgate, Dick Dunn, Ted Fenton, Archie Macaulay, Jackie Wood. **Manager: Charlie Paynter.**

Lausanne (SUI)	Lausanne	12/05/1946	W 1–7	Wood 3, Hall 2, Macualay, Woodgate

West Ham United: Harry Medhurst, Charlie Bicknell, Ron Cater, Norman Corbett, Dick Walker, Ron Attwell, Terry Woodgate, Almeric Hall, Sam Small, Archie Macaulay, Jackie Wood. **Manager: Charlie Paynter.**

Young Fellows (Combined Zürich Team) (SUI)	Zürich	15/05/1946	D 2–2	Macaulay, Small

West Ham United: Harry Medhurst, Charlie Bicknell, Ron Cater, Norman Corbett, Dick Walker, Reg Attwell, Terry Woodgate, Almeric Hall, Sam Small, Archie Macaulay, Jackie Wood. **Manager: Charlie Paynter.**

Zug (SUI)	Zug	18/05/1946	W 1–5	Attwell, Woodgate 2, Wood, [unknown]

West Ham United: Harry Medhurst, Charlie Bicknell, Ron Cater, Norman Corbett, Dick Walker, Reg Attwell, Terry Woodgate, Almeric Hall, Sam Small, Archie Macaulay, Jackie Wood. **Manager: Charlie Paynter.**

Schaffhausen (SUI)	Schaffhausen	19/05/1946	W 1–9	Corbett, Macaulay 4, Small 2, Hall 2,

West Ham United: Harry Medhurst, Charlie Bicknell, Ron Cater, Norman Corbett, Dick Walker, Ron Attwell, Terry Woodgate, Almeric Hall, Sam Small, Archie Macaulay, Jackie Wood. **Manager: Charlie Paynter.**

Cantonal FC (SUI)	Neuchatel	22/05/1946	W 0–2	Macaulay, Wood

West Ham United: Harry Medhurst, Charlie Bicknell, Ron Cater, Norman Corbett, Dick Walker, Reg Attwell, Terry Woodgate, Almeric Hall, Sam Small, Archie Macaulay, Jackie Wood. **Manager: Charlie Paynter.**

Servette (SUI)	Upton Park, att: 20,000	06/04/1954	W 5–1	Dick, Arnott 3, Barrett

West Ham United: Peter Chiswick, George Wright, Harry Kinsell, Derek Parker, Malcolm Allison, Doug Bing, Harry Hooper, Jim Barrett Jr, John Arnott, John Dick, Jimmy Andrews

In the 1960s, Lausanne were a different prospect. Unlike Spartak and a world away from the men of Ghent, the club were a very flexible outfit—their ranks bursting with Swiss internationals. In fact, Lausanne was more or less the Swiss national side that was itself was coming fresh from a World Cup Qualifying victory in Belfast. This was part of their eventual group-winning performance that emulated their feat in the same competition in 1962 and would take them to England for the final stages in 1966.

At the time of the tie, Rappan's men were top of the Swiss League and would, by the end of the season, be champions. Lausanne had won the Swiss Cup 2–0 against FC la Chaux-de-Fonds in front of 51,000 in the Wankdorf Stadium (care is required when pronouncing, otherwise some might think one is making a statement as opposed to citing a location). They were five-time Swiss champions and their manager had predicted they would win both their league and the Cup Winners' Cup. They were experienced European warriors, having campaigned in the Cup Winners' Cup and Fairs Cup—a kind of forerunner to the Europa League. During the 1964–65 tournament and prior to their encounter with the Hammers, they had accounted for Honvéd, the crack Hungarian side, 2–1 on aggregate, as well as Slavia Sofia 5–3 overall.

Flying out of London on the Sunday before the first-leg tie, the East Londoners had to prepare for the quarter-final match on Tuesday. They came to the Olympic Stadium, in the shadow of the Alps, with the intention of playing defensively in order to set up the second leg on level terms.

Despite recent snow, the pitch was in good condition. Brian Dear was playing his first senior game outside Britain having been drafted into the side following an injury to Eddie Bovington. It was Dear who put the Hammers in front, snapping up a chance in the thirty-first minute when Künzi failed to hold a Boyce free kick. Earlier, Armbruster had hit the bar. The Hammers' second came from Johnny Byrne—a brilliant solo effort eight minutes after the interval. However, a defensive error allowed the Swiss to halve that lead ten minutes from time, but things still looked good for the return leg in London.

The Swiss had had their chances in a tense first twenty minutes as West Ham struggled to find their form. Armbruster thumped the ball against the bar from 18 yards and had another long-range effort headed away by Kirkup. Then, Standen failed to hold a shot from Hertig, but Martin Peters was there to clear things up.

The flying Dutchman, Kerkhoffs, flashed a rising shot inches wide. He was potentially the most dangerous of the Lausanne forwards, but fluffed a couple of good chances. Had West Ham allowed the Swiss to score at that point, they might well have gone on to take a commanding lead. As it was, the Hammers settled down to some solid defensive stuff and took a firm grip on the game. Bobby Moore and Boyce, often playing behind their own full-backs, quietly and efficiently broke up many a Swiss move in its infancy. Brown, shadowing Kerkhoffs faithfully for much of the match, rarely put a foot wrong, and Kirkup and Martin Peters made sure that the Lausanne wingers were given minimal opportunity to break through.

Early on, Dear cheekily flicked the ball into the net but was offside. Then, around the half-hour mark, West Ham made one of their few upfield sorties and Lausanne conceded an indirect free kick. Ticker drove the ball over the wall at Künzi—the goalkeeper managed only to set up Dear who stuck it home. If Künzi had allowed the ball to pass untouched into the net, a goal could not have been given with the kick having been indirect. To that extent, West Ham had even the fates on their side. To their credit, following that goal, Lausanne made even greater efforts to break through, but the Hammers stood firm until half-time.

On the restart, the Irons looked much more composed, and in the fifty-third minute their endeavour was rewarded. A clearance from a delayed free kick by Bobby Moore bounced to Dear, who touched it to Byrne in midfield. He swept smartly round one defender after another in his 50-yard run before racing into the penalty area. He held off a final tackle to send in a well-placed shot—Künzi touched the ball but could not prevent the second goal.

Ron Greenwood called it 'a brilliant goal', every bit as good as anything seen in Brazil or Italy. 'Budgie' Byrne's own analysis gave nothing away: 'I just kept going and then hit it … you just follow the ball really.'

From then on, West Ham sensibly concentrated on defence as Lausanne's attempts to close the margin became more and more frantic. Eventually, West Ham let them through when Martin Peters misplaced a clearance in his own packed 18-yard box, Hosp promptly slamming the ball into the net.

With the spectators urging them on to even greater efforts, the home side forced three quick corners. However, when the final whistle sounded, they had failed to bridge the gap thanks to the heading of Joe Kirkup, Bobby Moore's cool brain, and the resilient brilliance of Ken Brown. He was to tell me: 'As a defender, you have to think not only of how you are going to stop the man or the ball, like they did way back, but how what you do will set up an attack. You have to be a bit creative.'

West Ham had done well, but the game had turned into something of an intellectual battle for possession. The 500 travelling Hammers fans sent chants of 'East Lon-don!' echoing across the Alps as the 25,000 Lausanne supporters applauded both teams off the pitch. Afterwards, Greenwood commented:

> I'm delighted. We did everything we came out here to do. We gave away a silly goal but the team played magnificently after the first twenty minutes. We were too defensive at that stage when we should have been going for more goals. We got a bit cocky and let Lausanne come back at us when we did not look in danger.

Many years later, he let me know that he considered this result to have been crucial to the advancement of his team:

> We had to be able to do more than one thing, more than just attack or just defend. Against Lausanne, we had to do that; show determination, resilience and, at the same time, invention. That's not as easy as it might sound.

Greenwood had now seen the Swiss three times, once away from home. His assessment had it that they had played better than he would have thought. He said that Brian Dear, 'took his goal well, showed no signs of nerves and did what we asked of him.'

Johnny Sissons got a nasty knock in Switzerland and finished the game limping, but West Ham were already looking forward to the next round. The Germans, TSV 1860 Munich, had a 4–0 first-leg advantage over Legia Warsaw, while Torino had beaten the Finns, FC Haka, 5–0.

The second-leg match against Lausanne was played with much more abandon. Plenty of shots and near-misses made for an exciting night appreciated by the 32,000 who yet again broke the club record for gate receipts at Upton Park. The Hammers' non-stop offense met by Lausanne fighting to get back into the tie made for a good old-fashioned game of football and fine entertainment.

From the kick-off, both sides took risks. West Ham had a fantastic opening burst that saw Hurst twice rattle the woodwork. Then, Künzi saved splendidly from a Dear effort and was fortunate to deny Byrne. The Hammers were blitzing their opponents, obliging the big Lausanne defenders to kick and volley shots clear. At one point, the Swiss gave away three corners in thirty seconds but, with under ten minutes to half-time, they threw a counterpunch. For the first time in the leg, the West Ham defence was caught napping when Dürr took the ball to the right corner flag and crossed it quickly into the goalmouth for Kerkhoffs to head home.

The game did not really need lifting, but the goal elevated it to new heights. Within five minutes, West Ham had scored twice. They were given the first by Tacchella, who swept Sealey's centre passed his own goalkeeper. Sealey also played a part in the second goal when he launched a rocket at Künzi, who desperately managed to palm it away. The ball seemed to go over the byline, but Dear planted it high in the net from an extremely acute angle.

That should have settled the issue, but the Swiss side were unwilling to give in. Four minutes after the interval, they forced the industrious Kirkup into a mistake and there was Hertig, cutting in from the left. He hit the ball with his right foot into the far corner of the rigging. For the next ten minutes, West Ham came under intense pressure. An effort from Kerkhoffs was saved by Standen's legs before the Irons applied extra pace, trying to outrun the slow-it-down Swiss. This began to change the pattern of the game. On the hour, the Hammers forced a corner. Sealey sent a curler into the goalmouth and Peters, the outstanding player on a night of many heroes, calmly headed it home.

Although they now seemed to be fighting a lost cause, the Swiss soldiered on gallantly. Hosp smashed a shot against Standen's bar and Eschmann scored the game's most spectacular goal with an overhead kick that left the West Ham goalkeeper rooted to the ground in disbelief ten minutes from time, to well-earned and rapturous applause from the Hammers fans.

That said, West Ham were in no mood to give way now. With barely a minute to go, Dear thumped the ball into the proverbial onion-bag to clinch victory.

Winning this tie had been no mean achievement. West Ham gained the plaudit of having been the only side to beat Lausanne at home that season. Boyce, playing at right-half, had been immaculate in his prising open the Lausanne defence. Hurst was a tower of strength, while Byrne linked defence and attack with more than a little style. Bobby Moore was his usual impeccable self, and Martin Peters appeared to be the perfect full-back. They all looked international class with the World Cup just over a year away.

European Cup Winners' Cup 1964–65				
Lausanne Sports (SUI) Ref: Paul Schiller (AUT)	Stade Olympique de la Pontaise, Lausanne, att: 18,546	Quarter final, 1st leg 16/03/1965	W 1–2	*Hosp 80'* Dear 33', Byrne 55'
Lausanne Sports: René Künzi, André Grobéty (c) Kurt Hunziker, Heinz Schneiter, Ely Tacchella, Richard Dürr, Norbert Eschmann, Pierre Kerkhoffs, Kurt Armbruster, Robert Hosp, Charly Hertig. Trainer: Karl Rappan				
West Ham United: Jim Standen, Joe Kirkup, Martin Peters; Ronnie Boyce, Ken Brown, Bobby Moore (c), Alan Sealey, Geoff Hurst, Johnny Byrne, Brian Dear, Johnny Sissons. Manager: Ron Greenwood.				
Lausanne Sports Ref: Pieter Paulus Roomer (NED)	Upton Park, att: 31,780	Quarter-final, 2nd leg 23/03/64	W 4–3	Dear 45', 89', Tacchella 41' o.g., Peters 60' *Kerkhoffs 37', Hertig 49', Eschmann 80'*
West Ham United: Jim Standen, Joe Kirkup, Martin Peters; Ronnie Boyce, Ken Brown, Bobby Moore (c), Alan Sealey, Geoff Hurst, Johnny Byrne, Brian Dear, Johnny Sissons. Manager: Ron Greenwood.				
Lausanne Sports: Rene Künzi, Andre Grobéty (c), Kurt Hunziker; Heinz Schneiter, Ely Tacchella, Richard Durr: Norbert Eschmann, Pieter Johannes, Elisabeth Kerkhoffs, Kurt Armbruster, Robert Hosp, Charly Hertig. Trainer: Karl Rappan.				

It was to be two years before West Ham once more encountered Rappan's men. Again, the Hammers found them worthy opponents. The sides have not met since, but the Irons have continued to pit themselves against Swiss opposition without any real success for close to thirty years.

Pre-season tour of Germany 1966				
Lausanne Sports (SUI)	Stade Olympique de la Pontaise	10/08/1966	D 2–2	Byrne 2
West Ham United: Colin Mackleworth, Denis Burnett, Jack Burkett, Ronnie Boyce, Ken Brown, Bobby Moore, Harry Redknapp, Jimmy Bloomfield, Johnny Byrne, Geoff Hurst, Martin Peters. Manager: Ron Greenwood.				

End of season tour 1967				
Grasshoppers Zürich (SUI)	Sportplatz Hardturm, att: 2,000	08/06/1967	W 0–1	Redknapp
West Ham United: Bobby Ferguson, Billy Bonds, Bill Kitchener, Martin Peters, Eddie Bovington, Bobby Moore, Harry Redknapp, Ronnie Boyce, Trevor Brooking, Geoff Hurst, Peter Bennett. Manager: Ron Greenwood.				
Lugano (SUI)	Stadio Cornaredo, att: 5,000	10/06/1967	W 1–4	Sissons, Dear, Hurst, Brabrook
West Ham United: Bobby Ferguson, Billy Bonds, John Charles, Martin Peters, Paul Heffer, Bobby Moore, Peter Brabrook, Ronnie Boyce, Brian Dear, Geoff Hurst, Johnny Sissons. Manager: Ron Greenwood.				

Servette (SUI)	Stade de Geneve, att: 4,500	28/07/1987	L 3–1	Cottee

West Ham United: Tom McAlister, Ray Stewart, George Parris, Gary Strodder, Alvin Martin, Liam Brady, Mark Ward, Frank McAvennie, Alan Dickens, Tony Cottee, Stewart Robson

Uhren Cup Switzerland July 2011				
BSC Young Boys (SUI)	Bruhl Stadium	11/07/2011	L 2–1	Nouble

West Ham United: Ruud Boffin, Julian Faubert (Jordan Spence), Jordon Brown, Hérita Ilunga, Abdoulaye Faye (James Tomkins), Freddie Sears, Joey O'Brien (Oliver Lee), John Moncur, Christian Montano, Luís Boa Morte (Robert Hall), Frank Nouble (Frédéric Piquionne). Manager: Sam Allardyce.

FC Basel (SUI)	Bruhl Stadium	13/07/2011	L 2–1	Stanislas (pen)

West Ham United: Marek Štěch, Jordan Spence (Julian Faubert), Winstone Reid (Abdoulaye Faye) (Carlton Cole), James Tomkins, Hérita Ilunga (Jordon Brown), Freddie Sears (Christian Montano), Joey O'Brien (Oliver Lee), Kevin Nolan (Luís Boa Morte), Junior Stanislas, Robert Hall, Frédéric Piquionne. Manager: Sam Allardyce.

6

ZARAGOZA

In the semi-final draw, West Ham were first out of the hat to face the team they most wanted to avoid: the Spanish side, Real Zaragoza, whose ground was 200 miles from the nearest airport in Barcelona. They were, by far, the best team the Hammers had come up against in the competition.

The team West Ham would face in the last four of the 1964–65 European Cup Winners' Cup was practically the Spanish national side. No-one thought that it was going to be anything less than a difficult tie. The other worry was that West Ham's league form did not bode well for the encounter—ten defeats in thirteen games from a run starting in December that was not to finish until the end of March. West Ham's very first European tour took the club to Spain. In May 1921, the Hammers played six games against Athletic Bilbao (*Los Leones*: 'the lions') in four cities, two in Bilbao.

Club tour of Spain May 1921				
Athletic Club Bilbao	Madrid	08/05/1921	W 0–4	James, Young, Puddefoot 2
West Ham United: Tommy Hampson, Bill Cope, Jack Hebden, Jack Tresaden, George Kay, Dan Woodards, John Calladine, Les Robinson, Syd Puddefoot, Billy James, John Young. Manager: Syd King,				
Athletic Club Bilbao	Vigo	11/05/1921	W 0–4	Watson 2, Tresaden, James
West Ham United: Tommy Hampson, Bill Cope, Jack Hebden, Percy Allen, George Kay, Jack Tresaden, Jim Simmons, Les Robinson, Vic Watson, Billy James, Herbert Cowell. Manager: Syd King.				
Athletic Club Bilbao	Bilbao	13/05/1921	W 0–2	Puddefoot 2
West Ham United: Ted Hufton, Bill Cope, Jack Hebden, Jack Tresaden, George Kay, Syd Bishop, Jim Cumming, Les Robinson, Syd Puddefoot, Billy James, John Young. Manager: Syd King.				
Athletic Club Bilbao	Corruna		W 0–1	Robinson
West Ham United: Ted Hufton, Bill Cope, Alf Lee, Jack Tresaden, George Kay, Syd Bishop, Jim Simmons, Les Robinson, Syd Puddefoot, Billy James, John Young. Manager: Syd King.				
Athletic Club Bilbao	Bilbao	15/05/1921		Robinson 3, James 2, Puddefoot

West Ham United: Ted Hufton, Bill Cope, Jack Hebden, Percy Allen, George Kay, Jack Tresaden, George Carter Les Robinson, Syd Puddefoot, Billy James, Young. Manager: Syd King.				
Athletic Club Bilbao	Bilbao	16/05/1921		Puddefoot 2, James, Robinson
West Ham United: Ted Hufton, Bill Cope, Jack Hebden, Percy Allen, George Kay, Jack Tresaden, George Carter, Les Robinson, Syd Puddefoot, Billy James, John Young. Manager: Syd King.				

Another tour was arranged five years later. However, by the time West Ham welcomed Zaragoza to the Boleyn Ground in 1965, it had been the best part of forty years since the Hammers had played a first-team game against Spanish opposition.

Club tour of Madrid, Corunna, and Vigo May–June 1926				
Spanish International	Madrid	23/05/1926	W 1–2	Watson, Campbell
Spain: Martineuz (Madrid); Pasarin (Vigo); Pallana (Bilbao); Pena (Bilbao); Zahal (Barcelona); Gamborena (Irun); Alcauer (Bilbao); Polo (Vigo); Errazquin (Irun); Samiter (Barcelona); Piera (Barcelona).				
West Ham United: Ted Hufton, Tom Hodgson, JimBarratt, George Carter, George Kay, Jim Collins, Tom Yews, Vic Watson, John Campbell, Billy Moore, Jimmy Ruffell. Manager: Syd King.				
Royal Madrid (ESP)	Madrid	25/05/1926	L 3–2	Campbell, Ruffell
West Ham United: Ted Hufton, Tom Hodgson, Jim Barrett, George Carter, George Kay, Jim Collins, Tom Yews, Vic Watson, John Campbell, Billy Moore, Jimmy Ruffell. Manager: Syd King.				
Corunna (ESP)	Corunna	28/03/1926	W 0–3	Yews, Campbell, Ruffell
West Ham United: Ted Hufton, Tom Hodgson, Jim Barrett, George Carter, Jack Hebden, George Collins, Tom Yews, Billy Ruffell, George Campbell, Billy Moore, Jimmy Ruffell. Manager: Syd King.				
Corunna (ESP)	Corunna	30/05/1926	W 1–2	Yews, Campbell
West Ham United: Ted Hufton Tom Hodgson, Jim Barrett, George Carter, George Kay, George Collins, Tom Yews, Vic Watson, Billy Ruffell, Billy Moore, Jimmy Ruffell. Manager: Syd King.				
Vigo (ESP)	Santiago	03/06/1926	W 1–2	Barrett, Yews
West Ham United: Ted Hufton, Tom Hodgson, Jim Barrett, George Carter, Jack Hebden, George Collins, Tom Yews, Vic Watson, George Campbell, Billy Moore, Billy Ruffell. Manager: Syd King.				
Vigo (ESP)	Santiago	06/06/1926	L 3–2	Barrett, Watson
West Ham United: Ted Hufton, Tom Hodgson, Jim Barrett, George Carter, Jack Hebden, George Collins, Tom Yews, Vic Watson, Billy Ruffell, Peter Cowper, Jimmy Ruffell. Manager: Syd King.				

The first leg of the Cup Winners' Cup tie was at the Boleyn Ground. Geoff Hurst and Ronnie Boyce had been to see Zaragoza play in the previous round against Cardiff in Wales a month earlier. They sang the praises of *los cinquo magnificos*. Ronnie Boyce recalled: 'Zaragoza's "Magnificent Five" forward line, was made up of five internationals ... They looked like a well-tuned machine.' This quintet included the triumvirate of Marcelino, Villa, and Lapetra—the latter had replaced the great Ghento as Spain's outside-left. They had helped Zaragoza find European glory with victory in the Fairs Cup the previous season.

The side had beaten Barcelona and Atletico Madrid in the process of claiming the Copa del Generalísimo, which had qualified them to take part in the Cup Winners' Cup. As if all that was not enough, Zaragoza could score goals. Their victory over Valletta FC of Malta in the preliminary round of the tournament had proved this—they won 8–1 over the two legs. Ron Greenwood was destined to be vindicated when he predicted that they would be tough and uncompromising in defence, and quicksilver, lethal destroyers in attack.

The big Wednesday night came and, within just the first couple of minutes, Marcelino went close. However, with only nine minutes gone, a packed crowd saw local boy Brian Dear get his eighth goal in as many games. The move had begun with Hurst sending a pass bouncing out to Sissons on the left. The wing-man cleverly drew Cortizo out of position, before crossing towards the far post where Dear was waiting to head it home.

Less than a quarter-of-an-hour later, Byrne got a cracker. Bobby Moore chipped a free kick upfield, which was collected by the alert Brown who had left the magnificent Marcelino to work on the right wing. Brown crossed to Sissons. For a second or two, the teenager looked like losing control, but he flicked the ball into the middle for Byrne, who took the pass on his chest, let it drop, and volleyed home. The ball smashed into the roof of the net past the prancing Yarza—Byrne had made contact from almost 20 yards out. Throughout the first half, Dear and Sissons flashed wicked-looking shots inches over. Marcelino shot wide and Canário almost scored.

West Ham had the potential to kill the tie in the second period, but it was never going to be a hat-full as Greenwood went for a play-it-safe policy. The Irons came out after the break with a nine-man defence; the crowd hated it. The Hammers had just two men up top and relied on the 'big boot' to find them. They lost momentum, gave the Spaniards' defence a rest, and allowed their fast, highly skilled attack of Canário, Marcelino, Santos, and Lapetra to take advantage. The visitors suddenly looked quite capable of out-smarting Bobby Moore and the rest of the home defence.

After hitting the post from the right in the fifty-third minute, Canário halved West Ham's lead after ten minutes of the second half. The experienced Brazilian wandered out to the left, tapped the ball through Bobby Moore's legs and dribbled into the six-yard box. His shot hit Standen on the arm, which effectively scooped the ball beyond his reach and over his own goal line.

Boyce had a great chance to make it 3–1 but slashed wide. Then, Canário had a better opportunity to lay on the equaliser, but his shot went high into the silent crowd. After that, Zaragoza were happy to play out time, confident that they could win the tie in front of their own supporters. The Spanish defence, which had booted with all the thunder of a Fourth Division side in the first half, grew more confident as West Ham, desperately needing goals, faltered and slid back on the defensive. The giant Francisco Santamaria Mirones inspired some excellent defensive play that West Ham's two lonely strikers and occasional three-pronged attacks could not break in the second half.

That said, as Ronnie Boyce remembered: 'Ken Brown had never played better … He always matched Marcelino in the air and wasn't a bit intimidated by his reputation or skill. It was a beautiful piece of football and a defensive lesson.'

The 35,000 fans, who had together paid £13,000 in gate receipts to cheer the Hammers, rose as one person to applaud the Spaniards at the close. For the West Ham players, there were only boos and hope. The result did give them some kind of chance for the second leg, although by the next morning, most of the national newspapers had already written off their chances of reaching the final. Have the press not always loved West Ham?

Ron Greenwood was disappointed with the result, having managed to score two early goals. He noted that the Spanish had played better as the game went on and were as good as he thought they would be. He saw it as the toughest game his side had played since he became manager. The Zaragoza manager, Argentinean Roque Olsen, was very pleased with the result, but he did not expect an easy game on his team's home turf, commenting that, 'it will not be easy for us at Estadio de La Romareda. West Ham are a very good team. Ron Greenwood is a very good manager and Bobby Moore ... is very good.' A very good set of comments there for the Hammers.

West Ham's league fixtures concluded just five days before the second leg of the semi-final. Brian Dear had scored a total of thirteen goals in ten league and European Cup Winners' Cup games as West Ham finished ninth in the First Division. Johnny Byrne was top scorer, netting twenty-nine, and Martin Peters won the 'Hammer of the Year' award.

Brian Dear recalled the welcome the team got in Spain: 'At the reception on the Tuesday before the game we each got a bottle of sherry and a silver ashtray. Nice, but maybe they wanted us to have a good smoke and drink before the game.' Defender John Charles, who travelled with the team as a reserve, remembered the same gifts: 'I wasn't that keen on sherry, so I swapped it for a crate of beer with one of the blokes working at the reception. I lost the ashtray in a game of cards ... ashes to ashes so to speak!

Greenwood, as usual, did not take any chances. Before the match, his team trained behind closed doors. Ernie Gregory, the fifty-three-year-old reserve-team manager, went in goal and played brilliantly. 'I wonder if they'll give me a month's trial?' he asked. Years later, he told me:

> They tried to watch you all the time in Spain; everything anyone did there seemed to be someone taking notes or a couple of people talking and pointing things out. We shifted things around a bit to try and confuse them sometimes. They were trying to guess the way Greenwood would play, they thought of lot of him there.

International forward Villa, a twenty-six-year-old local boy, was coming back into the Zaragoza team that night. He had not played in London, but had scored three goals in a recent domestic cup game.

Not having Johnny Byrne available, Greenwood decided against playing with a centre-forward but rather to strike down the wings: Sissons was on the left, Alan Sealey on the right, Hurst and Dear went deep. These tactics would leave the centre-half as the spare man rather than a full-back, who would be free to boost the attack. West Ham did not want the tie to end in a draw—that would mean a play-off in Marseille three days later.

Despite the task ahead, the Hammers felt confident. As Bobby Moore pointed out, the Spaniards had to get two goals to win and West Ham had scored first in all of their European games. He was never one for pep talks, but he did tell his teammates they had the ammunition to beat *los Maños*. This was a night of fine team work—an evening on which West Ham, a side often said to lack that little extra 'devilment', fought with courage, determination, and superbly-disciplined defensive skill.

From kick-off to final whistle, *los Blanquillos* launched attack after attack, but the East Ender's defence held. Consequently, much of the Spanish shooting was from long range, and the artillery did not prove the most accurate of barrages. Nothing looked like beating the alert Standen.

It was probably the best game of Moore's career to date. He put on a true captain's display that received support from the rest of the team. Standen, Kirkup, Jack Burkett, Martin Peters, and Brown all gave everything they had. The same could be said of Boyce who, although nominally chosen as a right-winger, played an important role as an extra defender. The burden of attack rested on the shoulders of Hurst, Sissons, Dear, and Sealey. There were times in the first half when Dear and Sissons looked like boys lost in a grown-up world, but it was this pair who in the end clinched a place in the final for West Ham.

When the first twenty minutes had gone by without a goal, optimistic Hammers fans began to think the danger period had passed and their team might be able to relax. However, three minutes later, the Spaniards levelled the aggregate score from a corner curled into the penalty box met by Marcelino. Standen could do no more than push it away and the ball bounced to Lapetra, who eagerly slammed it home.

Lapetra should have scored again before half-time, but at a crucial moment in the second half following a long period of Spanish domination, Peters cleared the ball to Dear, who chested it down and passed to Sissons. The flying flank-man careered into the Spanish penalty-area to calmly steer the ball into the corner of the net with his right foot as Yarza moved towards him. Just a week or so before, West Ham fans had been jeering young Sissons.

After the goal, Standen and Bobby Moore continued to fight a heroic rearguard, snuffing out one attack after another. Marcelino curled a shot inches wide and Ken Brown headed a Canário drive off the line in a hard footballing trial for the visitors. Still, West Ham managed to hold on. They conceded nineteen fouls in the first half alone. Zaragoza were convinced that the Dutch referee, Leo Horn (a man ripe for double entendre), had 'beaten' them—claiming three penalties should have been given in their favour.

European Cup Winners' Cup 1964–65				
Real Zaragoza (ESP) Ref: Robert Lacoste (FRA)	Upton Park, att: 34,864	Semi-final, 1st leg 07/04/1965	W 2–1	Dear 8', Byrne 28' Canário 54'

West Ham United: Jim Standen, Joe Kirkup, John Jack Burkett, Martin Peters, Ken Brown, Bobby Moore (c), Ronnie Boyce, Brian Dear, Johnny Byrne, Geoff Hurst, Johnny Sissons. Manager: Ron Greenwood.

Real Zaragoza: Enrique Yarza (c), Joaquin Cortizo, Severino Reija, Santiago Isasi, Santamaria, José Luis Violeta; Canário, Eleuterio Santos, Marcelino, Eduardo Endériz, Carlos Lapetra. Trainer: Roque Olsen

Real Zaragoza (ESP) Ref: Leopold Sylvain Horn (NED)	Estadio La Romareda, Zaragoza, att: 29,421	Semi-final, 2nd leg 28/04/1965	D 1-1 (W 2–3)	Lapetra 22' Johnny Sissons 54'

Real Zaragoza: Enrique Yarza (c), Joaquin Cortizo, Severino Reija, Eduardo Endériz, Santamaria, Jose Luis Violeta, Canário, Eleuterio Santos, Marcelino, Juan Manuel Villa, Carlos Lapetra. Trainer: Roque Olsen

West Ham United: Jim Standen, Joe Kirkup, John Jack Burkett, Martin Peters, Ken Brown, Bobby Moore (c), Ronnie Boyce, Alan Sealey, Geoff Hurst, Brian Dear, Johnny Sissons. Manager: Ron Greenwood.

Hammers' chairman, Reg Pratt was correct when he said afterwards that the supporters were 'wonderful' and had given the team 'unequalled support'. They had each paid £15 for their flight (plus £1 for an in-flight lunch). Some of them had left East London at 7 a.m. to make the 10 a.m. flight out and would not get back to the 'manor' until the early hours of the next morning.

No British club had ever taken so many supporters into Europe—more than 1,500 had travelled to Belgium, Czechoslovakia, Switzerland, and Spain to spur their team on. Johnny Byrne considered them marvellous:

> The supporters were West Ham's twelfth man. I know every pro says the supporters at whatever club they are playing for are the best, but what does that mean? They shout more or moan less? West Ham fans in the '60s were funny—a bit mad even. They liked to have fun, they could dish out the complaints for sure, but they were super-loyal; once a West Ham supporter, always a West Ham supporter! These days there's not too many examples of that kind of... well, you have to call it devotion ... They knew we weren't the absolute best in the world but they wanted us to be—and that made us try to be, usually, I think, without knowing it.

Olsen was predictable in his post-match analysis. The Zaragoza manager stated that he thought West Ham were lucky, and that his side had had enough chances in the first half to have won the game comfortably.

Greenwood gave his team all the credit after the match, but it was his ideas that did the trick. Bobby Moore told how once West Ham got their goal, he knew that they would hold on. Johnny Sissons reckoned he felt ten feet tall when he saw his shot go in. It had been only the second goal that he had scored with his right foot all season.

Reg Pratt, the West Ham Chairman, summed it all up when he remarked what a wonderful achievement and magnificent effort it was to reach two Wembley finals in just over a year (the venue had been decided well in advance of the tournament).

Zaragoza had been heralded as the 'new Real Madrid'. They had taken two British scalps before meeting West Ham, having beaten Dundee in the first round and accounting for Cardiff in the quarter-finals. The eleven cockney crusaders had avenged all that.

It had been Bobby Moore's match. He had even been brilliant in the air, which was not always his strong point, and had inspired the defence. With the aid of Boyce and Hurst, the West Ham defence had fragmented and eventually destroyed the most formidable forward line in European club football, allowing it only three clear chances.

West Ham were only the second British team to reach the final of a major European tournament. They would meet either Torino or TSV 1860 Munich at Wembley on 19 May 1965. Spurs had won the European Cup Winners' Cup three years earlier, but the Hammers had the chance to become the first British team to win European glory on their own soil. Also, unlike the Tottenham side, throughout the whole tournament, the Irons had been entirely English.

The newspapers were full of West Ham the next day. The Hammers had put the likes of Yashin, Puskás, and Di Stéfano—playing in a tribute match for Stanley Matthews the same night—in the shadows.

The resignation of Malcolm Allison as manager of Plymouth also made the news. This was something of an irony on the day West Ham had made the biggest final in their history in that Allison had been one of the architects of the club's culture, was out of work and seeking fresh employment for his bold ideas. A colourful individualist, he had also been with Cambridge University, Bath City, and Toronto City since leaving Upton Park. His next stop, Maine Road in Manchester, would be the making of him as a legend. As a West Ham fan, it is hard not to wonder what would have happened had he stayed on at the Boleyn Ground—if 'Big Mal' had inherited the Fenton legacy. Following a warm-up against Shamrock Rovers in Dublin on 12 May, it was back to Wembley.

It seems West Ham liked a game with the Irish Hoops. Thereafter, they met them a couple of more times in the 1960s.

Shamrock Rovers (IRL)	Dalymount Park, Dublin	12/05/1965	W 1–3	Hurst 2, Bennett
West Ham United: Jim Standen, Joe Kirkup, Jack Burkett, Eddie Bovington, Ken Brown, Martin Peters, Alan Sealey (Peter Bennett) Ronnie Boyce, Geoff Hurst, Brian Dear, Johnny Sissons				

Shamrock Rovers (IRL)	Dalymount Park, Dublin	17/05/1967	D 5–5	Hurst 2, Sissons 2, Dear
West Ham United: Standen, Billy Bonds, John Charles (Bill Kitchener), Martin Peters, Paul Heffer, Bobby Moore, Harry Redknapp, Ronnie Boyce, Brian Dear, Geoff Hurst, Johnny Sissons				

On the other side of the border, Lisburn had also been a favoured destination.

Distillery (Ireland)	Grosvenor Park	28/03/1955	D 2–2	Sexton, Musgrove
West Ham United: George Taylor, George Wright, Noel Cantwell, Doug Bing, Malcolm Allison, Frank O'Farrell, Harry Hooper, Bobby Moore, Dave Sexton, Malcolm Musgrove					

Distillery (Ireland)	Upton Park	17/10/1955	W 7–5	Dare 4, Hooper (pen), Dick, Moore
West Ham United: George Taylor, George Wright, John Bond, Gordon Johnstone, Malcolm Allison, Dave Sexton, Harry Hooper, Bobby Moore, Billy Dare, John Dick, Ken Tucker					

However, from the last part of the twentieth century, the Republic has been the Irish host for the Hammers; West Ham have never lost a game after crossing of the Irish Sea.

Munster Select (IRL)	Priory Park, Limerick	13/11/1989	W 0–1	Slater
West Ham United: Allen McKnight, George Parris, Tommy McQueen, Tony Gale, Colin Foster, Alan Devonshire, Kevin Keen, Liam Brady, Mark Ward, David Kelly, Eamonn Dolon. Playing subs: Julien Dicks, Martin Allen, Stuart Slater					

Republic of Ireland International XI	Upton Park	Tony Gale Testimonial 08/05/1994	W 4–2	Dicks, Mitchell, Stuart 2
West Ham United: Ludo Mikloško (Gary Kelly), Tim Breacker (Tony Cottee), Kenny Brown, Steve Potts, Tony Gale (Matt Holland), Martin Allen, Ian Bishop (Paul Mitchell), Steve Jones, Trevor Morely (Darren Currie), Stuart Slater, Mike Marsh (Julien Dicks)					

St Patrick's Athletic Festival of Football 2000—Manager: Harry Redknapp				
St Patrick's Athletic FC (IRL)	Richmond Park	23/07/2000	W 0–1	Sinclair
West Ham United: Stephen Bywater (Alex O'Reilly), Dino Jorge (Benada), Hayden Foxe, Rio Ferdinand (Neil Ruddock), Gary Charles (Adam Newton), Joe Cole, Michael Carrick, Frank Lampard Jr, Marc Keller (Nigel Winterburn), Frédéric Kanouté (Danny Invincible), Trevor Sinclair					

Cork City (IRL)	Turners Cross	Cork International Airport Series 07/07/2013	W 2–6	Diarra, Cole, Taylor, McCallum, Noble (pen), Morrison
West Ham United: Jussi Jääskeläinen (Adrián), Guy Demel (James Tomkins), James Collins (Winstone Reid), Titus Bramble (Răzvan Raţ), Dan Potts, Alou Diarra (Mark Noble), Jack Collison, (Ravel Morrison), Kevin Nolan (Danny Whitehead), Carlton Cole (Ricardo Vaz Tê), Matt Jarvis (Matt Taylor), Modibo Maïga (Paul McCallum)					

Back to 1965, and after a warm-up against Shamrock Rovers, West Ham's Cup Winners' Cup final opponents were the West German club TSV 1860 Munich. They had defeated Union Luxembourg 10–0, Porto 4–0, and Torino 5–3 after a play-off in Switzerland.

7

MÜNCHENS GROßE LIEBE
('MUNICH'S GREAT LOVE')

Bobby Moore knew what had given his team the edge in all their matches—the presence of Martin Peters, who had just established himself in the side. 'In Europe you need more skill,' said Bobby Moore, 'and Martin added an extra quality to our game.'

Before the final, Ron Greenwood sent some of the players to Germany. According to Moore, 'they went to see 1860 [Munich] play in a cup game in Germany. I wasn't able to go, but they got a good idea what to expect in the final.' Alan Sealey recalled:

> Eight players: Joe, Jack, Martin, Ronnie, Geoff, Brian, Johnny Sissons, and myself, along with club officials Albert Walker and Eddie Chapman, had gone see the play-off between Torino and Munich, six days after our draw in Spain. Bobby was on England duty and Ron couldn't make it, but Greenwood had seen them beat Chelsea 2–0 in August.
>
> It was obvious that [TSV 1860] Munich were an impressive, well-organised side. They did well against the skilful Italians, who were emerging as one of the best sides in their country and would have proved difficult opponents for any side in the world. Ron told us to watch our immediate opponent in one of the teams; I chose Munich. They had some good players; Hans Rebele, their outside-left, was one of their youngest players at twenty-two [years old]. A nippy winger who had played well in Europe, he'd once been an inside-forward.

West Ham had been meeting with German clubs for the best part of forty years.

Club tour of Germany, Switzerland, and France 1924				
Cologne (DEU)	Cologne	10/05/1924	W 0–2	Ruffel, Moore
West Ham United: Tommy Hampson, Bill Henderson, John Young, Syd Bishop, George Kay, Jack Tresadern, Tom Yews, Vic Watson, John Campbell, Billy Moore, Jimmy Ruffell. Manager: Syd King.				
Mönchengladbach (DEU)	Gladbach	11/05/1924	W 1–6	Campbell 2, Moore 2, Watson, Carter
West Ham United: Tommy Hampson, Bill Henderson, John Young, George Carter, George Kay, Albert Cadwell, Tom Yews, Vic Watson, John Campbell, Billy Moore, Jimmy Ruffell. Manager: Syd King.				

Mannheim (DEU)	Mannheim	14/05/1924	W 1–4	Watson, Williams, Robinson, Yews

West Ham United: Tommy Hampson, Bill Henderson, John Young, Syd Bishop, George Kay, Jack Tresadern, Tom Yews, Les Robinson, Bill Williams, Vic Watson, Jimmy Ruffell. Manager: Syd King.

Frankfurt (DEU)	Frankfurt	17/05/1924	W 0–4	Robinson 4

West Ham United: Ted Hufton, Bill Henderson, John Young, Syd Bishop, George Kay, Albert Cadwell, Tom Yews, Les Robinson, Bill Williams, Vic Watson, Jimmy Ruffell

Freiburg (DEU)	Freiburg	18/05/1924	L 5–2	Watson 2

West Ham United: Tommy Hampson, Bill Henderson, John Young, Jack Tresadern, George Kay, Albert Cadwell, Tom Yews, Les Robinson, Bill Williams, Vic Watson, Jimmy Ruffell. Manager: Syd King.

Club tour of Germany 1928				
Eintracht Frankfurt (DEU)	Frankfurt-on-Main	09/05/1928	W 1–2	Loughlin, Earle

West Ham United: Ted Hufton, Stan Earl, Cyril Norrington, Matt Smailes, Jim Barrett, Albert Cadwell, Tom Yews, Stan Earle, Joe Loughlin, Billy Moore, Jimmy Ruffell. Manager: Syd King.

Karlsruhe (DEU)	Karlsruhe	12/05/1928	L 4-1	Ruffel

West Ham United: Ted Hufton, Tom Hodgson, Stan Earl, Matt Smailes, Bill Cox, Albert Cadwell, John Payne, George Robson, Jim Barrett, Billy Moore, Jimmy Ruffell. Manager: Syd King.

Nuremburg (DEU)	Nuremburg	13/05/1928	W 2–3	Loughlin, Payne, Yews

West Ham United: Ted Hufton, Stan Earl, Cyril Norrington, Bill Cox, Jim Barrett, Albert Cadwell, Tom Yews, Stan Earle, Joe Loughlin, Billy Moore, John Payne. Manager: Syd King.

FC Bayern (DEU)	Munich	17/05/1928	L 3–3	Yews, Moore

West Ham United: Jim Barrett, Tom Hodgson, Stan Earl, Matt Smailes, Bill Cox, Cyril Norrington, Tom Yews, George Robson, Joe Loughlin, Billy Moore, John Payne. Manager: Syd King.

Hertha BSC (DEU)	Berlin	21/05/1928	W 2–4	Barrett 2, Ruffell, Loughlin

West Ham United: Ted Hufton, Tom Hodgson, Cyril Norrington, Jim Collins, Bill Cox Albert Cadwell, Tom Yews, Billy Moore, Joe Loughlin, Jim Barrett, Jimmy Ruffell. Manager: Syd King.

In 1934, with the rise of Nazism in Germany, both sides lined up in the centre of the field and gave the Nazi salute. Sportgs included four internationals in their ranks.

Club tour of Switzerland 1934				
Sportgs Club 1860 (DEU)	Munich, att: 9,000	24/05/1934	W 0–2	Musgrave, Barrett

West Ham United: George Watson, Alf Chalkley, Albert Walker, Wally St Pier, Jim Barret, Joe Cockroft, Jim Wood, John Morton, Joe Musgrave, Len Goulden, Jim Ruffell. Manager: Charlie Paynter.

VfB Stuttgart (FRG)	Upton Park	05/10/1954	W 4–0	Sexton 2, Hooper, Foan
West Ham United: George Taylor, John Bond, Harry Kinsell, Andy Malcolm, Frank O'Farrell, Tommy Southern, Albert Foan, Dave Sexton, John Dick, Jimmy Andrews				

Kaiserslautern (FRG)	Upton Park, att: 23,000	11/04/56	L 2–4	Blackburn 2
West Ham United: Ernie Gregory, John Bond, Noel Cantwell, Derek Parker, Malcolm Allison, Frank O'Farrell, Mike Grice, Albert Foan, Alan Blackburn, John Dick, Billy Dare				

International *Voetbaltornoo* Ghent 1958

Duisburg SV (FRG)	Stadion Jules Otten	Group match 01/05/1958	W 0–1	Keeble
West Ham United: Brian Rhodes, Joe Kirkup, Harry Cripps, Bobby Moore, Malcolm Pyke, John Smith, Harry Obeney, Derek Woodley, Andy Smilie, Vic Keeble, Tony Scott. Manager: Ted Fenton.				

Club tour of Belgium, Germany, and the Netherlands 1959

Rot Weiss (FRG)	Essen	02/05/1959	L 3–3	Cantwell, Keeble
West Ham United: Noel Dwyer, Joe Kirkup, John Bond, Andy Malcolm, Ken Brown, John Smith, Doug Wragg, Noel Cantwell, Vic Keeble, John Dick, Malcolm Musgrove. Manager: Ted Fenton.				
Borussia Dortmund (FRG)	Rote Erde Stadium	07/05/1959	L 3–1	Musgrove
West Ham United: Noel Dwyer, Joe Kirkup, John Bond, Andy Malcolm, Ken Brown, Harry Obeney, Doug Wragg, Noel Cantwell, Vic Keeble, John Dick, Malcolm Musgrove. Manager: Ted Fenton.				
Aachen (FRG)	Aachen	09/05/1959	L 5–2	Dick, Musgrove
West Ham United: Ernie Gregory, Joe Kirkup, John Bond, Andy Malcolm, Ken Brown, Harry Obeney, Doug Wragg, John Hills, Vic Keeble, John Dick, Malcolm Musgrove. Manager: Ted Fenton.				

International Soccer League 1963

Preussen Munster (VfB)	University of Detroit Stadium	16/06/1963	W 2–0	Peters, Hurst
West Ham United: Jim Standen, Joe Kirkup, Jack Burkett, Martin Peters, Ken Brown, Bobby Moore, Alan Sealey, Ronnie Boyce, Johnny Byrne, Geoff Hurst, Peter Brabrook. Manager: Ron Greenwood.				

Pre-season European tour 1964–65

FC Nuremburg (FRG)	Nuremburg, att: 30,000	12/08/1964	L 1–0	
West Ham United: Standen, John Bond, Jack Burkett, Eddie Bovington, Ken Brown, Bobby Moore, Peter Brabrook, Ronnie Boyce, Johnny Byrne, Geoff Hurst (Martin Peters), Johnny Sissons (Alan Sealey). Manager: Ron Greenwood.				

Tickets for the Cup Winners' Cup final had sold out long before the game was to be played. At Upton Park, the allocation shifted at a rate of 4,000 an hour on the day they went on sale, but because of the television audience, it was to be one of the most watched games in history.

Johnny Byrne had been injured in the England *v.* Scotland game, so Brian Dear was brought in. This was a worry—even though Dear had done well in Spain, 'Budgie' was an exceptional player and, alongside Peters and Moore, one of the Irons' most classy and talented performers. Once again Hurst was position to play behind the main attack, which was comprised of Alan Sealey and Sissons. The team looked very different from the FA Cup-winning side of the previous year; the right flank had been transformed. John Bond had made way for Joe Kirkup at right-back, Martin Peters had come into Eddie Bovington's right-half position, and the right-wing place had been transferred from Peter Brabrook to Alan Sealey.

West Ham went into the final with the best record of any British club in Europe. Neither of the teams were keen for a replay at the Stadion Feijenoord in Rotterdam a couple of days later, so the final promised to be a memorable encounter.

From the first kick, West Ham went full throttle at the Germans, who were playing in all white—a change from their usual blue and white. It was a cracking first half with some immaculate football displayed and, although no-one managed to score, it could have been 3–3.

Before fifteen minutes had been played, Sissons had put a shot wide from some 12 feet out. Petar Radenković, the thirty-year-old, black-garbed Yugoslav in the Munich goal (the press called him 'Peter the Great') pulled off a string of magnificent saves, foiling Dear more than once. In Germany, where Radenković had played for five years, he was seen as something of a clown, but he was one of the finest goalkeepers in the Bundesliga; good in the air and when going to ground.

Both Dear and Alan Sealey failed to connect with a cross by Sissons that (if diverted) would almost certainly have put the Hammers ahead. Hennes Kuppers, the fair-haired inside-right, was perhaps Munich's outstanding forward and also had his chance to open the scoring. At twenty-six-years-old, he was one of those perpetual motion performers. Two months before the final, he had partnered outside-right Alfred Heiß at international level against Italy. The pair won their first caps together in December 1962. Heiß was a speedy winger, and his outstanding club form that season had given him West Germany's number seven shirt.

The second forty-five minutes started where the previous period left off. Dear again went close. Sissons hammered a shot against the post. Sealey put the ball in the net a couple of minutes later, but he had instinctively used his hands and no goal was given.

Rudi Brunnenmeier, Munich's all-action skipper and a West German international centre-forward, was a constant threat. He had nearly been transferred to Torino, but the Italian FA had barred new foreign imports until the end of July 1966. Brunnenmeier had a bullet-like shot and blinding pace—his twenty-four Bundesliga goals in 1964–65 were the product of the combination of those abilities. He had been the first TSV 1860 Munich player to be capped that season and had recently scored for his country in a 1–1 draw against Sweden.

Inside-left Peter Grosser was tall, lean, and clever with the ball. At twenty-five years of age, he had missed only one league match all term. These two and Kuppers were denied only by the skill and courage of Standen. At one point, the Hammers goalkeeper hurled himself across goal to deflect a shot from Grosser, and just seconds later saved from the blond Kuppers.

With only about twenty minutes of the match remaining, Ronnie Boyce intercepted a pass just over the halfway line, immediately drawing two men to him. 'Ticker' carried the ball up the right flank beyond the full-back. Sealey went in close and then Boyce placed a perfect pass between two Munich defenders, leaving Sealey with just the left-back to worry about.

Boyce gave it to Sealey at just the right time. He went forward, firing a rocket of a drive from the edge of the box from what looked to be an impossible angle, only for it to whistle beyond Radenković into the high right-angle. Nobody would have got near it.

Sealey somersaulted out of pure delight and followed this with a bit of a dance. He said afterwards:

> It could have gone over the bar as easy as flying in the top corner of the net, but without going over the top, I can say that I could hit a ball. I can't say I had any feelings. It's all over ... a sudden rush of blood, that's all ... but once you've scored one, straight away you want to score another.

Brian Moore, the BBC Radio commentator, described it:

> Hurst, looking for a man, decides to sling one over left-footed, but he finds Bena. He didn't mean to do that, but the ball bounces off Bena fortunately to Grosser, his inside-left, who is tricking West Ham players left, right, and centre now, and then slings a good pass there for... Oh, but the left-half missed it and its Boyce coming through for West Ham. A chance here for Alan Sealey inside the box. Can he get in a shot? It's a goal! A goal for West Ham!
>
> So, West Ham are a goal ahead from Alan Sealey, twenty-four minutes into the second half. A mistake by the German left-half Luttrop gave Alan Sealey his chance and from a narrow angle he fairly belted the ball into the Munich net!

For a while afterwards the goal was screened on television as part of an advertisement for Oxo. It was typical of the type of goals West Ham had been scoring in and out of Europe. Alan Sealey recollected: 'I remember the ball hitting the roof of the net. It was my style of goal, the kind I would score. Quick... Bang!' He also reflected:

When I came to West Ham from Orient, I never dreamed all this could happen to me. I've been to Ghana, Rhodesia, America, Austria and Germany and, of course, the European Cup Winners' Cup travels.

When I went on that first trip to Africa, I played with people like Jackie Dick, Malcolm Musgrove, Ian Crawford, Lawrie Leslie and Brian Rhodes. It seems strange that they had all gone by the Final. A year before, I had sat on the sidelines at Wembley and watched us win the FA Cup. Now it was great to be back, this time playing and scoring.

I know the other lads who missed Wembley last time—Martin Peters, Brian Dear and Joe Kirkup—all felt the same. Martin had, of course, played there for England Schoolboys, but that was not quite the same. It had been a great four years for me.

In the fraction of a second after a crucial goal has been scored, there is a space in time. Therein can be found the roar that emerges in recognition, squeezed into the quietness—not a total silence, but sound retreats, like the tide going out prior to a tsunami. In this tiny period between an occurrence and the realisation of the same, there is a gap made for what is to become, and regard for that which is passing away. This was palpable as the fans (of which I was one—albeit, just before my tenth birthday) watched the ball enter the goal at Wembley, now more than half a century ago.

The relatively appreciable numbers of those who had followed TSV 1860 Munich to Wembley gazed incredulously at the leather sphere as it bounced, happily, inside its cosy net of a nest. The bellow of the Irons supporters gouged out a dome in the dusky skies. The German fans turned their eyes up from the ball to stare, shocked and questioning, at the voices of all the Hammers—the fount of the massive noise. The roar smashed hard into every niche of the famous, old stadium. The Munich supporters intuitively dipped down as one, trying to avoid what seemed like a wall of sound coming their way.

West Ham had caught their opponents on the ropes. Just two minutes later, the knockout blow was delivered. Dear, having got by Munich's defence with a late run, was poleaxed by a desperate German defender and a free kick was awarded.

The Hammers had the kind of thing they were going to do sorted out well in advance. Sealey described the tactics:

> We used to make a nice big hole that Bobby could just knock the ball into, and we would pull people wide. We would just nominate somebody to make the hole. I was the last one that should have gone because I was the worst header of the ball in the world, but I saw the hole and went early.

Hurst ran over the ball, leaving Boyce to send it to Bobby Moore—a commanding figure on the night. The West Ham skipper lifted it, floating the ball in from an attacking left-half position between 15 and 20 yards outside the penalty-area. Sealy recollected:

[Moore] drove it in towards the far post, in my direction. I was supposed to run in and head the ball. That was the intention, but, as I say, heading wasn't the strongest part of my game. Sure [sic] enough, I missed it, the ball whizzed by me and then, luckily, it hit Martin Peters, who had moved into the middle from a characteristically late run.

He didn't quite control it—the ball must have gone out of his vision or something—and it hit him on the leg. That got everyone on the wrong foot and, as the ball bobbled, it ran for me. That lack of control turned out to be a perfect pass. It came beautifully, if unintentionally, into my path about five yards out. I'm lethal from that range [he smiled]. It only needed turning in. I applied the finishing touch.

Again, the radio commentary painted a picture for listeners:

And a free kick to West Ham. Some of the most cunning free kick takers these West Ham boys. I wonder what they've got up their sleeves now?

West Ham, that brilliant goal ahead by Alan Sealey, and now looking for another one. Here comes Hurst, runs over the ball, it goes to Boyce. To Bobby Moore. Bobby Moore clipping it forward... And... Oh ... And... Oh, it's a goal! Another goal for West Ham! Alan Sealey the scorer again! West Ham 2–0 up now and surely that must be the killer goal.

Ron Greenwood remembered the work and faith that went into that goal:

We had repeatedly rehearsed the moves that led to the second goal ... There was a young lad called Trevor Dawkins at the club at the time and we went through it with him. I remember Alan [Sealy] saying that 'it would never work'. I was delighted that he was the match-winner that night at Wembley.

West Ham could have had three more goals in that final period of the game. Sissons hit the post again with a right-foot shot, and Dear, twice, had Radenković deflecting shots wide. Nevertheless, when the final whistle sounded, it was 2–0.

This was the signal for celebration. Delirious fans, tossing claret-and-blue bowlers and scarves high into the night air, had to be dragged away from Alan Sealey and the rest of the team. Bobby Moore led the way up the stairs to receive the trophy from Gustav Wiederkehr, the Swiss President of UEFA. He grinned as he handed the cup over to the West Ham skipper, but as he did so, in a low voice, he said 'Zar Vold cup vill not be so easy for you'. Bobby just smiled his cool smile. Brian Dear carried a captured Munich flag in triumph on his lap of honour, and Ken Brown cuddled a huge claret-and-blue hammer. Ron Greenwood, Johnny 'Budgie' Byrne, Eddie Bovington, Peter Brabrook, Alan Dickie, Tony Scott, and John Bond stood on the touchline and applauded.

It was a classic match—the end of 810 minutes of football in four different countries. Even the referee, István Zsolt, said what 'a good and wonderfully clean game it had been', and that 'West Ham and Munich are two fine teams.'

It was one of the great Wembley Finals, and the high-point in the history of West Ham United.

The game would give rise to many more stories over the years. Alan Dickie shared just one. Like so many players of his generation, 'Spider' is a romantic and generous man:

All the players who played in the Cup Winners' Cup winning team got a gold Omega watch from the directors, inscribed with their name and 'WHUFC CWCW 1965'. I gave it to my son for his twenty-first birthday. He asked me what he should do with it. I told him to give it to his son on his twenty-first.

The Wembley Final had been a satisfying affair. Both teams had played the fast, open football that the nearly 100,000 spectators had wanted to see. Munich tried to match West Ham by playing attacking football, and this had made for an entertaining game that swung back and forth. Both sides had played with flair and determination. One Fleet Street sports journalist wrote: 'There could have been no greater match to put before the greatest night audience in England's football history.'

European Cup Winners' Cup 1964–65				
TSV Munchen 1860 Ref: István Zsolt (HUN)	Wembley, att: 97,974	Final 19/05/1965	W 2–0	Sealey 69', 71'
West Ham United: Jim Standen, Joe Kirkup, Jack Burkett, Martin Peters, Ken Brown, Bobby Moore (c), Alan Sealey, Ronnie Boyce, Geoff Hurst, Brian Dear, Johnny Sissons. Manager: Ron Greenwood.				
TSV Munchen 1860: Petar Radenković, Manfred Wagner, Hans Reich, Wilfried Kohlars, Stefan Bena, Otto Luttrop, Alfred Heiß, Hans Küppers, Rudi Brunnenmeier (c), Peter Grosser, Hans Rebele. Coach: Max Merkel (AUT)				

The Cup Winners' Cup of 1964–65, culminating at Wembley, had been a great success. West Ham had faced all the leading scorers (apart from the former Cardiff and Aston Villa centre-forward Gerry Hitchens), and Brian Dear was among those in third place in the final scoring table for the competition:

Six goals: Václav Mašek, Ivan Mráz (Sparta Prague), and Pierre Kerkhoffs (Lausanne Sports)
Five goals: Alfred Heiß, and Otto Luttrop (TSV Munchen 1860)
Four goals: Brian Dear (West Ham), Carlos Lapetra (Real Zaragoza), Rudolf Brunnenmeier (TSV Munchen 1860), and Gerry Hitchens (AC Torino)

Among the telegrams that poured into Greenwood's office after the final was one from Bill Shankly, whose Liverpool side had lost to Inter Milan in the European Cup semi-final. It read: 'Well done. I feel that British club teams are more than ready for these European clubs.'

Chelsea sent two telegrams: one from Stamford Bridge, and one from Tommy Docherty leading the Chelsea party in Australia. Bill Nicholson, manager of Spurs, wrote: 'Those were the days. Hope they are yours too.' Fulham manager, Vic Buckingham, messaged: 'Well done you East End lot—a real West End show.'

As an East Ender, Alan Sealey was a typical example of what West Ham were built of:

> The ideas that Ron came up with, working with us, were too unbelievable for words. We used to come in every day and there was something different. Being a bunch of young lads, we were just so keen to listen, learn, and develop. Things started to happen from the moment that Ron arrived. This was invaluable, but I think if you look at the team, nine or ten came through the system. They weren't bought, they were local lads.

Just a cursory look at the team would prove Sealey right. Johnny Sissons came from West London, but the majority of the team were local cockney or Essex boys. Alan Sealey elaborated: 'Bobby Moore was a little bit older than us, but of those who played in the final, there were Geoff, Martin, Johnny Sissons, Ronnie Boyce, Jack Burkett, and Brian Dear who had all come through at a similar age.' This meant that the side had the resources of camaraderie and togetherness. People like Ken Brown and Jim Standen, who were a little bit older, stabilised the whole thing, but as Alan said: 'We all came through together and we all did things together.'

West Ham later found out that they had beaten two teams that would be playing in the European Cup the following season. Not only did Lausanne win the Swiss title, but Sparta Prague also topped the Czech League by seven points form Dukla.

Ron Greenwood was in his element facing foreign sides, starting from the point when he was put in charge of the England Under-23s while at Arsenal. Although he relished these encounters with continental clubs, he would describe the experience as 'interesting' because it was 'testing'. He saw it as his team's proving ground and a kind of football laboratory.

Greenwood loved to travel abroad and watch teams play. He built up a footballing encyclopaedia within his own mind. As John Bond put it:

> When Greenwood came to West Ham and got the club into Europe he had the chance to put into practice all the things that he'd got in his head. A lot of players had trouble understanding some of it though, but if you stuck with it, persisted, it made sense. Although he wasn't a people person—that was his biggest weakness—he was quite school teacher-like, not [that] everyone warmed to that. He got over that eventually, I think, when he managed England.

Alan Sealey said of Greenwood's idea of play:

It was brilliant because it agreed with us; it suited our players, it was to do with movement. If you're playing from the back, then there's got to be a lot of movement up front to let the ball get there. It's got to be built up. We had the players to do this. We revelled in it. We loved it!

Greenwood later remarked that winning the Cup Winners' Cup was not ultimate success—West Ham still had to win the European Cup. For him, only then would West Ham be a great team. After Wembley, he declared this to be the aim of the club.

(I am not too sure we are any nearer that goal half a century later. What happened?)

When the Hammers had come back from playing international opposition in the USA a couple of years earlier, Greenwood had called it a new era for the club—and he had been right. He saw that West Ham's success was founded on a belief by everyone in the club, and it was this that had to be built upon. It had caused a team of great style to be developed in London's East End—a team that passed the ball with players like Martin Peters, Johnny Byrne, Bobby Moore, and Geoff Hurst. Alan Sealey asked himself:

> Why was I part of this creative evening? The great referee in the sky might have just looked down, stretched out his ringer and touched Alan Sealey on the shoulder. But I was an aggressive, very quick forward. Ron took on many of my ideas about what I wanted to do. I tried to be innovative and he cottoned on to this. Sometimes my mind raced ahead of myself, but a lot of the time it paid off, as at Wembley in 1965 in the Cup Winners' Cup final. They were two great goals. Since those goals, a lot of people have said how good it was to see an East Ender do the business. I have always said that it was my pleasure.

However, most people who were at Wembley for those ninety minutes in 1965 simply thought like Johnny Byrne that it was 'Sealey's finest hour and his night.'

The Prime Minister, Harold Wilson, had sent West Ham a congratulatory telegram after the victory over TSV 1860 Munich. The First Secretary of State, George Brown (a West Ham supporter) was a guest of honour at the banquet held on the evening of the final. The match, alongside West Ham's victory in in the 1964 FA Cup final, would be a cross-road for the English game. Nothing would be the same again. West Ham had carried the future into their dreams—the past was now a memory.

Meanwhile, as was typical of him, Bobby Moore (like Greenwood) was looking forward to the European Cup. He was always up for the next hurdle. He said that the Cup Winners' Cup final had been West Ham's best-ever team effort: 'There was a lot of good football and we played really well against a good side.'

He was not wrong. The game had been an example of what working together can achieve. Jack Burkett had been as solid as a rock at left-back playing just behind Bobby Moore. Burkett had sustained a back injury on Boxing Day and fought his way back into the team to face Zaragoza. Greenwood said that, 'when Jack returned, we started looking like a team again.'

Jim Standen had yet another good day. The instinctive save with his legs from the Munich skipper, Brunnen, may well have been critical to the final result.

Boyce had made the first goal. It was a great pass; Alan Sealey recalled how he, 'saw the keeper was slightly out of position and so decided to shoot.' He was later to reflect: 'But it was instinctive, you don't really 'think' at times like that—it's sort of "in" you.'

Johnny Sissons thought he had scored when he hit the post. He was desperate to make up for that miss and worked like a Trojan.

Ken Brown, who thought the whole experience was better than winning the FA Cup, had been a giant in the centre of defence.

Alan Sealey, smiling his gap-toothed smile as he looked back on at the day, commented:

> That Wembley day passed me by so quickly. It came and went. You have your little bit of success and you go home. You don't really take it all in, but it was a marvellous night. It had to be the best night of my career.
>
> My dad, God rest his soul, was there, and that's all you want in life really; to give your parents just something back for what they gave you. If you do that, you have achieved what you want.

The occasion had been made by odd chemistry. Sealey and Greenwood were two very different football people, but they both enjoyed the night of their lives: Alan Sealey, the bustling striker who grew up next door to West Ham's ground; Ron Greenwood, a northerner and very much a coach. It is peculiar how people's lives come together.

About three-quarters of the nearly 100,000 fans who attended Wembley (the biggest crowd ever to watch a Cup Winners' Cup final at that point) were Hammers supporters. They paid an average ticket price of around 15s (75p).

The post-match atmosphere was unique. The queue at Wembley Park station seemed to be more than a mile long at one point, but many West Ham fans remained outside the stadium into the early hours of the next day. It was a night in which few in London's Docklands saw sleep. Ships and tankers paid a foghorn tribute up and down the Thames, accompanying millions of joyful renditions of 'Bubbles'. Ronnie Boyce recalled how, 'when we came back to East London, not a soul was about. This felt odd after the huge reception we'd got bringing the FA Cup home.'

However, hours after the game, most of the local population continued to bask in the reflected glory of their side at home or around the environs of Wembley. Others had stopped off from the game to 'do the right thing' by the club 'up west' and gone AWOL, in some cases for days.

By the Sunday, and the 'homecoming' of the Irons, few might have been little more than exhausted. Only about 5,000 people turned up—about 20,000 fewer than the club's average home gate at the time. It was a real surprise because, as Boyce had remarked, the team's return from the FA Cup Final had been greeted by hundreds of thousands lining the streets. However, the arrangements had been made at the last minute, and many street parties took place in the afternoon.

When Bobby Moore spoke to the supporters, he said that without them, it would not have been possible; Ron Greenwood told them that the side was proud to represent them in the world.

After watching TSV 1860 Munich play against Torino, Alan Sealy had told how he had studied the German defence:

> I watched their backs carefully. Manfred Wagner, on the right, was their longest-serving player. He'd earned a reputation for his versatility. He could play in either full-back position and revert to wing-half if he had a mind. On the left was Rudolf Steiner. He was another one who could move over if he had to. Their centre-half, Hans Reich, was not yet twenty-three and had been with the club as a youngster. He'd played at right-half and right-back. Their style was almost typically English, with two fast wingers, a hard-hitting centre-forward, and a solid defence.

West Ham had returned to the twin towers for the second year running following their victory over Preston North End in the FA Cup Final. Greenwood had been obliged to reshuffle his side because Peter Brabrook and Johnny Byrne were both injured.

The Hammers had been England's last hope in Europe that season—Liverpool having been beaten in the European Cup in Milan. The Lions of Munich had roared into Wembley knowing, like West Ham, that they had to win to stay on the money-spinning European football circuit. They were out of their league race and out of the cup they had won the year before by beating Eintracht Frankfurt 2–0 in the German Cup final. In 1964–65, they had been eliminated by giant-killers Mainz 05 in an early-round replay.

TSV 1860 Munich are the oldest club in Germany. The '1860' in their title refers to the founding of the sports organisation out of which the football club grew. The football section did not come into being until 1899. It was only a few years before the 1965 Final that they had emerged from the shadow of FC Bayern and FC Wacker—Munich's other big clubs during that era.

Honours were few under the regional system, which involved top clubs meeting in end-of-season play-offs. TSV 1860 had reached this stage only once, in 1931, when they lost to Hertha BSC 3–2. It was eleven years before they won their first cup final, beating FC Schalke 04 2–0. Under former Dutch national coach Max Merkel, the forty-five-year-old ex-Austrian international (formally with SK Rapid Vienna), they won their first league championship and entered the Bundesliga when it was formed in 1963. TSV 1860 Munich had not been out of the top six in the 1964–65 season, bettering their seventh place of the previous term.

Eddie Bovington, the teak-tough iron man of the FA Cup-winning side, was fit but did not get a place in the team as Bobby Moore came back safely from England games against West Germany and Sweden. The whole TSV 1860 Munich team had turned out to watch Bobby Moore against the West German national team. England's spring tour of 1965 brought them to Nuremberg where they claimed a slim 0–1 victory in the seventh time the teams had met—England had then beaten the Germans six times with the first match in 1930 having been a 3–3 draw. It was the home side's first-ever defeat in the Frankenstadion. It is likely that few of the players that day, German or English, would have predicted they would be playing in England's last victory on German soil for more than thirty years.

Ron Greenwood was full of praise for all those in his Cup Winners' Cup team, but he was correct when he said, 'this was Bobby Moore's greatest game: technical perfection.'

8

THE VOICE OF PASSION

The voice of passion is better than the voice of reason.
The passionless cannot change history.
'Child of Europe'
Czesław Miłosz

Ron Greenwood was always something of an enigma for West Ham supporters. He continued to be after 1965.

For some reason, he was not as loveable as the likes Shankly or Busby. He lacked the panache of Allison or the no-nonsense appeal of Docherty. He did not carry himself like Joe Mercer or Jock Stein. He lacked the slight mystique of Alf Ramsey. These giants of the game seemed to have a different attitude to football than Greenwood's almost passionless, technical outlook. He did not seem to have any sense of humour or fun.

Maybe his very serious attitude to football had something to do with the fact that, unlike Shankly, Stein, and Busby for example, he had never really done anything else. When one has worked at the coal face down a pit, there tends to follow some idea of proportion. Results might be upsetting, but proportion helped prevent a fall into a deep depression or, as it sometimes seemed in Greenwood's case, a sulk.

He did get better as he got older, but while few players would be willing to gainsay the likes of Malcolm Allison or Tommy Docherty, as time went on Greenwood, by his relative detachment, seemed to practically invite the defiance of his more senior players. This was less noticeable once the affable but tough John Lyall became Ron's sidekick. Lyall was capable of laying it on the line to players in no uncertain terms, as described by Eddie Lewis:

[Lyall] was a lovely bloke, brave and honest, but he could call a spade a spade and then shove it up your arse if he had a mind to. John was granite hard, but no-one was more polite or kind. He made time for people, but no-one scared him, on or off the field. He was the complete other way to Greenwood really. Ron had a reputation for torpedoing people. He held a grudge rather than get it out in the open.

While never a man to harbour rancour, Lyall, the one-time uncompromising defender, hardly left anyone in doubt where they stood with him. This was almost the diametric opposite to Greenwood. While most players respected Greenwood's seemingly boundless knowledge, few detected deep-seated passions. According to Ronnie Boyce:

> Everyone understood that Ron had a huge knowledge of the game and great perception. He was a champion of the way the game should be played. He liked it to be open; he liked it to be attractive, he wanted the game to be honest. Football was, for him, at its best, a battle of wits. He viewed any match on a slightly higher plane than most other managers. He was a real student of the game, always looking to expand his knowledge, but he was also a realistic man.

As John Bond commented, Greenwood was a paradox:

> He was often accused of being a blackboard theorist, and that, to some extent, was true, but there was never a more practical manager than Ron Greenwood. These things did not go together. I mean, you can't be a no-nonsense philosopher can you. With players you got [sic] to be on their side, even with bad news; you got [sic] to get them to see what's best for them. For Ron, the person wasn't central. Sometimes I think, on some level, he thought people just got in the way of football.

Similarly, while Greenwood's rather cold attitude did not always make for good 'people management', this was contradicted by his obvious understanding of how people could get the best out of themselves and learn to contribute to the work of the whole. He seemed to understand humanity well (groups, teams, and mechanistic and instrumental interaction), but this was not matched by his awareness of individual human sensibilities—even though he was an emotional man who often seemed more easily hurt and certainly more thin-skinned than some of the legendary managers of his era. Perhaps these contradictions demonstrate a complex character—humanitarianly intelligent, socially inarticulate, but often naïve about human nature. Bond said:

> Greenwood, quite rightly, got a lot of credit for what happened at West Ham in the mid-1960s. However, you've got to remember that when he arrived at Upton Park, the place had a way of doing things that did not really change when Ron came along, but he built and strengthened the structure. What happened in 1964 and 1965 wasn't the result of just one mind or person, with a number of others just following instructions. Dozens of people were involved, all pulling together, handing on and working on ideas and moves over years, from the late 1950s in fact.
>
> This was the 'Academy': straightforward stuff done with quality, but with an ethical code and a sense of doing things properly, a sort of morality. True, our big ideas and

principals could be literally kicked off the park, but West Ham's football was a gospel and Ron was its prophet. For him, the way you played was much more important than getting results—if you couldn't get results righteously, then the game wasn't worth playing. The players of course wanted to win.

Greenwood's belief was that a commitment to skill, fairness and generosity of spirit (teamwork) were the only means to attain the highest levels in football, or anything else. Considerations like nobility, honesty, integrity and honour were important to him; to this extend he was a throwback to the Corinthian age of the sport.

Ron spelt out what he thought about the game, what he expected of the players, and even if they didn't catch on to everything he said, like 'putting players in vacuums', they appreciated that he had intelligent ideas.

Greenwood was great on different styles of play that were new to the English game. He wanted to take a continental approach to football, a fluid, passing game. When West Ham got into European games they tended to do pretty well. For some reason, they couldn't sustain this kind of poetry over a forty-two-game programme. That was West Ham's big problem.

We were always different from other clubs in London. The club belonged to their own patch. Players and fans identified with each other. You felt when you went to Upton Park that you were actually part of something quite special.

Expressing ideas was important. Ron had players who believed in what he believed in. It's no good if a manager says what he wants and the players don't believe in it. We gelled together. Ron developed his ideas with the players—that is, he didn't just come to transplant a way of doing things, although in the first instance I think that he had a notion of creating a kind of 'Arsenal light'. What was produced was something quite unique, and I think even he was surprised.

West Ham was seen as a side that will never threaten to win the League, that's for more consistent sides. But in the cups it was a different story altogether. Ron, in the end, almost came to accept this belief, that we were better suited for Cup football than the nine-month rigour of a league championship. The suspicion grew in his own mind, almost into a certainty, over the period in which we were winning the FA Cup. We had won the cup with quite a bit of style. In fact, the semi-final was taken beautifully, with panache. This level of Ron's thinking limited us; it smacked of a kind of excuse (more than a reason). It became part of a negative myth that he paid into, the other part of which was that we were an easy team to play against. People used to say that they loved playing against West Ham because we allowed them to play. This rumour or legend started with Greenwood. In the 1950s, West Ham was [sic] always thought of as a hard team, which gave little away.

For all this, Bond understood that Europe was really what Ron had been waiting for:

He was so pleased that the Cup Winners' Cup Final was seen all over the continent and he congratulated Munich for making it such a good game. We were suited to the European game. West Ham players who were injured were sent out to spy on the opposition. They came back and were able to talk to players on players' terms with a player's view of things. We went into games thoroughly prepared. Ron adapted tactics to suit the occasion and the score, whether West Ham played at home or away.

But remember, West Ham had always played European opposition. Tours and friendlies were part of life at Upton Park. We weren't surprised what we come across in Europe; we'd experienced it all before.

The Cup Winners' Cup was a great achievement for Ron Greenwood. The final was a game in which his principles and beliefs fell in line with the way West Ham played. Bond continued:

It was the perfect example of how he wanted the game thought about and performed. I don't know if it ever happened for him again. Maybe that would have been the best time for him to have left the club. It's difficult to build on something that has already reached your ideal. It's got to be all downhill when you've come to the top of the mountain, hasn't it? A Malcolm Allison or a Noel Cantwell coming in at that time would have driven West Ham on to bigger and better things, and a move to somewhere like Arsenal or Chelsea would have given Ron a more comfortable situation in terms of his personality.

As it was, his problems with the post-match celebrations were to be indicative of the next few years. Another former player told me:

It was a real mess up. The team complained about it because all Ron had been concerned about was getting to the stadium and doing well. No arrangements had been made for anything afterwards. At Wembley they had the two teams sat down, but there had been no arrangements made for the wives. So all the families of the players were left standing outside somewhere. Ron was occupied for some time after the match taking drinks and bits of food out to the wives. He did his best, but that was a bit of a lash-up.

Ron was looking forward to the two-leg challenge with European Cup holders Inter Milan at Wembley. This never happened, but the idea was taken on by UEFA and in 1972 the European Super Cup was born.

As West Ham had not won the league in 1965 (they finished ninth), the Hammers' European ambitions were confined to the defence of the trophy they had won the previous season. West Ham faced the Greek side, Olympiakos, in their first game of the 1965–66 Cup Winners' Cup campaign.

The Irons had never met a Greek side in senior football, and nor would they again until the managerial reign of Billy Bonds.

The Makita Tournament 3–4 August 1991				
Panathinaikos (GRE)	Highbury	04/08/1991	D 1–1	Parris

West Ham United: Ludo MiklOško, Kenny Brown, Houghton, Tim Breacker, Colin Foster, George Parris, Ian Bishop, Simon Livett, Clive Allen, Stuart Slater, Iain Dowie. Playing subs: Leroy Rosenior, Dean Martin. Manager: Billy Bonds.

Pre-Season tour of Greece August 2006				
Aris FC (GRE)	Kleanthis Vikelidis Stadium	04/08/2006	D 2–2	Harewood, Zamora

West Ham United: Jimmy Walker, Tyrone Mears (Carlton Cole), James Collins, James Tomkins, Paul Konchesky (Hogan Ephraim), Mark Noble, Heyden Mullins, Matthew Ethrington (Winston Reid), Marlon Harewood, Bobby Zamora, Teddy Sheringham. Manager: Alan Curbishley.

PAOK FC (GRE)	Toumba Stadium	06/08/2006	L 2–1	Dean Ashton

West Ham United: Roy Carroll, Tyrone Mears, James Collins, James Tomkins, Winstone Reid, Hogan Ephraim, Heyden Mullins, Matthew Ethrington, Dean Ashton, Bobby Zamora, Carlton Cole (Teddy Sheringham). Manager: Alan Curbishley.

Olympiakos (GRE)	Upton Park	12/08/2006	D 1–1	Harewood

West Ham United: Roy Carroll, Tyrone Mears, James Collins, Paul Konchesky, Anton Ferdinand, Nigel Reo-Coker, Heyden Mullins, Lee Bowyer, Dean Ashton, Bobby Zamora, Marlon Harewood

Panathinaikos (GRE)	Fussballplatz, Kitzbuhel	23/07/2010	W 0–1	Hitzelsperger

West Ham United: Marek Štěch (Péter Kurucz), James Tomkins (Fry), Manuel da Costa (Jordan Spence), Danny Gabbidon (Radoslav Kovac), Hérita Ilunga (Fabio Daprela), Scott Parker (Kieron Dyer), Thomas Hitzisperger (Alessandro Diamanti), Mark Noble (Christian Montano), Julian Faubert (Freddie Sears), Carlton Cole (Benni McCarthy), Luís Boa Morte (Junior Stanislas)

The first leg of the second round of the Cup Winners' Cup (West Ham, as holders, were given a bye in the first round) was at the Boleyn Ground. The Greeks, who had overcome AC Omonia Nicosia just 2–1 on aggregate in the first round, proved to be quite a handful.

Olympiakos came to Upton Park spitting, kicking, and elbowing. Geoff Hurst got to a pass from Bobby Moore to blast the first past goalkeeper Fronimidis. Hurst got the second with his head. Just over ten minutes after half-time, Johnny Byrne jumped on a mistake by Fronimidis to make it 3–0. Brabrook finished them off when he nodded in the fourth with seventy-two minutes gone.

John Charles was the only new boy to European football in West Ham's line up. He was just twenty-one years old and looked a little incredulous at times, aghast at the visitor's behaviour, but he did well enough to keep his place for the second leg.

Charles was a Canning Town boy, and one of the first black players to break through in London football. Indeed, he was the first black player to turn out for West Ham's first team and, when he was chosen for the Under-18s, the first to be selected to play for England (see Belton 2004, 2006, and 2013). 'Charlo' was a good full-back and always strove to live up to one of the most famous names in football. He captained West Ham's Youth Cup-winning side, won his England honours, and made his league bow in a 0–1 home defeat against Blackburn—all in 1963.

European Cup Winners' Cup 1965–66				
Olympiakos Ref: Karl Marc Keller (SUI)	Upton Park, att: 27,250	Second round, 1st leg 24/11/1965	W 4–0	Hurst 23', 43', Byrne 65', Brabrook 82'
West Ham United: Jim Standen, Joe Kirkup, John Charles, Eddie Bovington, Ken Brown, Bobby Moore, Peter Brabrook, Martin Peters, Johnny Byrne (c), Geoff Hurst, Johnny Sissons. Manager: Ron Greenwood.				
Olympiakos: Giannis Fronimidis, Orestis Pavlidis, Dimitris Stefanakos, Kostas Polychroniou (c), Pavlos Vasiliou, Giorgos Sideris, Nikos Gioutsos, Vasilis Botinos, Giannis Gaitatzis, Mimis Plessas, Christos Zanteroglou. Trainer: Márton Bukovi.				

In Greece, the 45,000 crowd were hurling bangers around the huge Olympiakos soccer bowl well before the match. Indeed, about an hour before kick-off they were lobbing them at the West Ham team as they inspected the pitch. The bombardment continued throughout the game—a thunderflash was burning away in Jim Standen's goal as he took up his place.

It was a European baptism of fire for young John Charles on his first trip abroad as a playing team member. Injuries meant that Martin Peters was moved to centre-forward. Both Standen and Hurst had been suffering with stomach bugs, which was part of the reason why Hurst played something of a defensive role that night.

From the off, it was clear that the Hellenics were going to continue to be a rough and uncompromising side. After twenty minutes, the Greek World Cup skipper, Polychroniou, left Martin Peters with a nasty gash on his shin. The same player converted a penalty for the first goal—Ken Brown having been picked out as the offender by the referee, Mr Bahramov, a Russian who was later to find fame in a World Cup Final with heavy West Ham involvement. The decision was a complete mystery—even Ron Greenwood questioned him, a thing that he hardly ever did.

West Ham were not doing too well. Too many passes out of defence were going astray, but the Hammers had a couple of first-half shots and one, from Martin Peters, was particularly unlucky, going just inches wide. Then again, West Ham's first goal was somewhat fortunate. Stefanakos missed a chip forward by Sissons and Martin Peters scored with an angled shot that was deflected beyond Fronimidis by a defender. Peters said later that he had meant it to go to Johnny Byrne.

The second goal was an Irons' special. Byrne sent Sissons away. The wing-man jinked around a couple of defenders before flighting a perfect cross to the head of

Peters. Not surprisingly, both goals by Martin Peters were greeted by the home crowd with almost perfect silence.

West Ham's 120 or so fans, of course, went mad.

A couple of minutes or so after Peters' second, Eddie Bovington scored a strange own goal, sending a high ball past Jim Standen. At this, the Greek crowd became animated, but the atmosphere was stilled and silent as the teams left the field following the final whistle. A 2–2 scoreline on the night sent the Hammers through 2–6 on aggregate.

European Cup Winners' Cup 1965–66				
Olympiakos Ref: Tofik Bakhramov (USSR)	Karaiskaki, Peiraias, att: 32,826	Second round, 2nd leg 01/12/1965	D 2–2 (W 2–6)	*Bovington 57' o.g., Polihroniou 81'* Peters 28', 53'
Olympiakos: Giannis Fronimidis, Dimitris Stefanakos, Evangelos Milisis, Kostas Polihroniou (c), Paulos Vasileiou, Nikos Gioutsos, Aristidis Papazoglou, Vasilis Botinos, Giannis Gkaitatzis, Dimitris Plessas, Grigoris Aganian. Trainer: Marton Bukovi.				
West Ham United: Jim Standen; Joe Kirkup, John Charles, Eddie Bovington, Ken Brown, Bobby Moore, Peter Brabrook, Martin Peters, Johnny Byrne (c), Geoff Hurst, Johnny Sissons. Manager: Ron Greenwood.				

After the match, Greenwood identified Jim Standen as man of the match, pointing out the magnificence of two saves in the first part of the game.

West Ham now had a rather crowded fixture list in March: two Cup Winners' Cup quarter-final games and the two-leg League Cup final, on top of four matches in Division One—eight games in three weeks.

The Hammers' grip on the Cup Winners' Cup seemed to loosen at Upton Park when they failed to create the big lead they had hoped to take to East Germany for the second leg of the last eight of the Cup Winners' Cup. They left themselves an uphill task against FC Magdeburg (nicknamed, with the famed inventive flare of the East Germans, *Der Club*).

Die Jungs aus Sachsen-Anhalt had accounted for the Swiss side FC Sion (8–3) in the previous round and, in their first game of the tournament, CA Spora Luxembourg (3–0). Unless there was to be a marked improvement in their performance, West Ham would disappear from the competition. For a team now so experienced at this level of football, the Hammers were thrown surprisingly easily out of their stride at Upton Park by Ernst Kuemmel's side. The German club would have a bright future in Europe, but they would be relegated to the second tier of the DDR-Liga that term.

This was the first time West Ham had met a team from East Germany since the partition of Germany in 1949. However, between then and their triumph over TSV 1860 Munich at Wembley, the Hammers had gained some more experience of German football.

End of season tour of America 1965				
TSV 1860 Munich (FRG)	Randalls Island Stadium, New York	20/06/1965	W 2–1	Peters, Sealey

West Ham United: Jim Standen, John Bond, Jack Burkett, Eddie Bovington, Ken Brown, Bobby Moore, Peter Brabrook, Martin Peters, Geoff Hurst, Ronnie Boyce, Johnny Sissons. **Manager:** Ron Greenwood.

Pre-season tour of Germany 1965				
VfB Stuttgart (FRG)	Neckar Stadium, att: 25,000	03/08/1965	L 1–0	

West Ham United: Jim Standen, Joe Kirkup, Jack Burkett, Martin Peters, Eddie Bovington, Bobby Moore, Alan Sealey (Harry Redknapp), Ronnie Boyce, Geoff Hurst, Peter Bennett (Brian Dear), Johnny Sissons. **Manager:** Ron Greenwood.

Eintracht Frankfurt (FRG)	Waldstadion, att: 25,000	07/08/1965	W 1–2	Peters, Sealey

West Ham United: Alan Dickie, Denis Burnett, Jack Burkett, Martin Peters, Ken Brown, Bobby Moore, Harry Redknapp (Alan Sealey), Ronnie Boyce, Geoff Hurst (Peter Bennett), Brian Dear (Eddie Bovington), Johnny Sissons. **Manager:** Ron Greenwood.

TSV 1860 Munich (FRG)	Grünwalderstraße, att: 40,000	09/08/1965	D 1–1	Peters

West Ham United: Jim Standen, Joe Kirkup, Jack Burkett, Martin Peters, Eddie Bovington, Bobby Moore, Alan Sealey, Ronnie Boyce, Geoff Hurst, Peter Bennett, Johnny Sissons. **Manager:** Ron Greenwood.

The Irons always seemed hurried and allowed themselves to be hassled into mistakes by Magdeburg. The long-ball game West Ham played resulted in too much possession being gifted to their opponents. The home side snatched at shots and the ball flew high or wide again and again, even from close range.

At the same time, errors were forced by the close-covering, intelligent marking, and swift interception of the Germans. With Busch sweeping up behind a four-man line of defenders, and Segger and Seguin harassing in midfield. When the Germans were not launching counter-attacks, they were tying down the off-colour Boyce and hard-working Martin Peters for long periods. Johnny Byrne was almost always closely guarded, and Hurst could not find the time he needed for a well-directed shot. Brabrook rarely got through on the right, and Sissons too often was left to strike on his own.

Not surprisingly, West Ham did not get their noses in front until a minute after the interval when Byrne hammered a cross from Peters into the net after Hurst had just failed to meet the ball with his head. Thereafter, the Irons launched raid after raid, but few were carefully built and none was accurately finished. They squandered their chances of building a tie-winning lead by trying to batter their way through the wall their visitors had erected.

European Cup Winners' Cup 1965–66				
1. FC Magdeburg (DDR) Ref: Jean Iricot (FRA)	Upton Park, att: 30,620	Quarter-final, 1st leg 01/03/1966	W 1-0	Byrne 46'
West Ham United: Jim Standen, Dennis Burnett, Jack Burkett, Martin Peters, Ken Brown, Bobby Moore, Peter Brabrook Ronnie Boyce, Johnny Bytne (c), Geoff Hurst, Johnny Sissons. Manager: Ron Greenwood.				
1. FC Magdeburg: Wolfgang Blochwitz, Rainer Wiedemann, Manfred Zapf, Günter Kubisch, Dieter Busch, Günter Fronzeck, Wilfried Klingbiel, Wolfgang Seguin, Rainer Geschke, Rainer Segger, Hermann Stöcker (c). Trainer: Ernst Kummel.				

West Ham were not, however, without hope of squeezing into the semi-finals, provided they could revert to their counter-attacking style in East Germany. This would surely prove far more effective against a fit, fast, and earnest side like Magdeburg, than the old fashioned 'hit hard and run' stuff seen at Upton Park.

In East Germany, the Hammers supporters were obliged to have an armed police escort to enter Magdeburg, which still bore the scars of the Second World War. Officials were concerned that any or all of the five West Ham coaches might harbour West German stowaways. Police, armed with pistols, rummaged through luggage racks and seats looking for defectors, checking and double checking British passports. For almost four hours the fans were stuck on East-West German frontier.

West Ham achieved a noble end by harshly efficient means. They were uncompromising in defence, hard, and well-ordered overall. 1. FC Magdeburg, meanwhile, proved to be a team with greater ability, vision, and bite than they had suggested in the first leg, but they too were a side well-versed in a few of the game's naughtier tactics.

All the pressure was on the Hammers in the first half. Hirshmann hit the base of a West Ham post with a 20-yard free kick in the opening minute; Sparwasser blasted over from two yards; and after fifty-five minutes Standen had to catapult across his goal to turn away Seguin's 25-yard drive.

The goals came in the space of forty-five seconds midway through the second half. It was 1. FC Magdeburg who scored first to silence the happy little band of 200 roving West Ham supporters. In the seventy-seventh minute, Sparwasser (soon to win his first full cap) handled the ball, but Mr Laurax, the otherwise admirable Belgian referee, did not see it. Sparwasser centred and, with West Ham's defence dithering for the only time in the match, Walter was able to score easily.

Less than a minute later, the Irons made their reply. Hurst swung the ball across from the left to the far right, Brabrook pushed it inside, and Sissons beat the agile Blochwitz from five yards. It was a rare Hammers attack. The Londoners' defence took the honours.

Denis Burnett had showed why Greenwood felt able to let Joe Kirkup go to Chelsea. Brown and Eddie Bovington relished every moment of the battle, and Standen could not to be faulted. Ronnie Boyce (though still not the 'Ticker' the crowd knew and loved from the previous season) and Martin Peters were the link between defence and the three-man attack: Brabrook, Sissons, and the gallant Geoff Hurst. Although most of the team had or were to play better that season, West Ham had nonetheless achieved a 1–2 win over the two legs.

European Cup Winners' Cup 1965–66				
1. FC Magdeburg (DDR) Ref: Vital Loruix (BEL)	Ernst Grube, Magdeburg, att: 30,926	Quarter-final, 2nd leg 16/03/66	D 1–1 (W 1–2)	*Walter 76'* Sissons 77'
1. FC Magdeburg: Wolfgang Blochwitz, Rainer Wiedemann, Günter Fronzeck, Manfred Zapf, Günter Kubisch, Günter Hirschmann; Wllfried Klingbiel, Jiirgen Sparwasser, Hans-Joachim Walter, Wolfgang Seguin, Hermann Stöcker (c). Trainer: Ernst Kummel.				
West Ham United: Jim Standen, Dennis Burnett, Jack Burkett, Eddie Bovington, Ken Brown, Bobby Moore (c), Peter Brabrook, Ronnie Boyce, Geoff Hurst, Martin Peters, Johnny Sissons. Manager: Ron Greenwood.				

Before the unification of Germany, West Ham would play one more game with an East German club.

FC Groningen Tournament 8–10 August 1986				
Dinamo Dresden (DDR)	Oosterparkstadion	Semi-final 08/08/1986	W 1–2	Cottee, McAvennie
West Ham United: Phil Parkes, Ray Stewart, George Parris, Tony Gale, Paul Hilton, Alan Devonshire, Mark Ward, Frank McAvennie (Geoff Pike), Alan Dickens, Tony Cottee, Neil Orr. Manager: John Lyall				

On the same evening West Ham defeated 1. FC Magdeburg, Dunfermline gained a one-goal lead over West Ham's Cup Winners' Cup semi-final opponents of the previous season (Real Zaragoza) in the first leg of their Fairs Cup quarter-final in Scotland. Dunfermline had the better of the first half, playing crisp, penetrating football, but the Zaragoza defence stood up to terrific pressure. Santamaria, the Spanish centre-half, was injured in a clash with Dunfermline's outside-right and resumed with his head bandaged. Zaragoza should have taken the lead on the resumption when Villa broke through, but he shot wide. The Scots got their goal near the end through Bert Paton. Zaragoza went on to the final of the Fairs Cup but lost to their compatriots, Barcelona, over the two legs.

West Ham faced the club's second European semi-final, but the potential opponents were big boys of the continental game. The draw in Cannes included Liverpool, Celtic, and Borussia Dortmund of West Germany. Most of the public and the press wanted to draw Dortmund—success would mean that West Ham would defend the trophy in an all-British final in Britain.

West Ham's next twenty-one days were now crammed with two legs of a European semi-final, six First Division matches, and the League Cup Final second leg. This was especially demanding given how punishing their previous schedule had been.

FA Cup Final, Wembley; West Ham United defeated Preston. Ashworth, Preston's inside-right, produces an overhead kick, but Standen saves. The victory opened the way for the Hammers to take part in their first ever major European competition.

8 October 1973. Moore (left), captain of Fulham, leads his team off the field at Craven Cottage when a floodlight failure halted play in their match with West Ham in the third round of the League Cup. It was strange to see the man who led the Hammers in Europe playing in a shirt that was not claret and blue. He would be on the Cottagers' side that lost to West Ham in the 1975 FA Cup final.

Above left: Joe Cockcroft, West Ham 1932–39.

Above right: Len Goulden, West Ham 1932–1939; England 1937–39.

Above left: Dave Mangall, West Ham 1934–36.

Above right: Rudi Brunnenmeir, TSV 1860 Munich 1960–1968; West Germany 1964-65.

Above left: Andrej Kvašňák, Sparta Prague 1959–69; Czechoslovakia 1960-70.

Above right: Max Merkel, manager of TSV 1860 Munich 1961–66. He played both for the German (1939) and Austrian (1952) national sides.

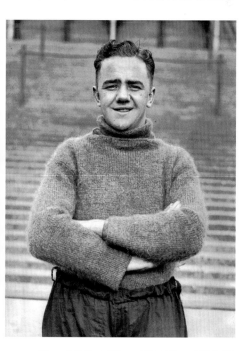

Above left: Jack Weare, West Ham 1936–38.

Above right: Rob Rensenbrink, Anderlecht 1971–80; Netherlands 1968–79.

Charlie Paynter cuts up the pitch, West Ham 1900–1950.

Above left: Dr James Marshall, West Ham 1934–37; Scotland 1932–34.

Above right: Days of iron.

Danny Boffin,
Metz 1997–2001;
Belgium 1989–2002.

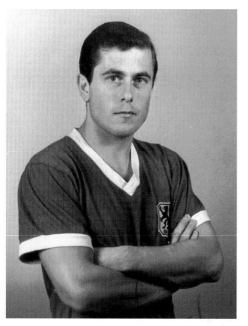

Above left: Alfred Heiß, TSV 1860 Munich 1963–70; West Germany 1962–66.

Above right: Stanley Matthews (England) takes on Nilton Santos (Brazil) at Wembley, 1956. England won 4–2. Legend has it that Tom Mather, manager of Stoke City in 1930, asked Syd King to take the fifteen-year-old Matthews on West Ham's tour of Holland, Denmark, and Sweden in May of that year, so that the lad might get some valuable experience. While there is no record of him playing for the Hammers, it is likely that if he did play, it would have been as a 'ringer' as he was registered with the Potters.

Bernd Nickel
(1 Länderspiel · 0 Tore)

Lothar Emmerich
(5 Länderspiele · 2 Tore)

Clockwise from top left:

Bernd Nickel, Eintracht Frankfurt
1967–83; West Germany 1974.

Sébastien Schemmel, Metz 1999–2001;
West Ham 2001–03.

Lothar Emmerich, Borussia Dortmund
1960–69; West Germany 1966.

Above: West Ham 0 WBA 1 at Upton Park, 14 August 1971. Tony Brown scored the WBA winner— West Brom's Jeff Astle rises above the rest. Left, Frank Lampard Snr, is just behind the Albion's Colin Suggett. Bobby Hove looks on (far left). The Hammers' summer tour of the United States had been a demanding experience, and by the end of the season, it seemed to have taken its toll. A good Hammers' side could do no better than fourteenth place in the old First Division.

Right: Petar Radenković, TSV 1860 Munich 1962–70; Yugoslavia 1956.

Petar Radenkovic
1963-1970: 215 Bundesligaspiele - 0 Tore

Peter Ressel,
Anderlecht
1975–78;
Netherlands 1974.

Above left: Louis Saha, Metz 1997–2000; France 2004–2012.

Above right: Peter Reichel (Eintracht Frankfurt 1970-79; West Germany 1975-76).

West Ham in the '60s: (left to right) Harry Redknapp, Peter Brabrook, Johnny Sissons, Jim Standen, John Charles (England's first black international player), Dave Bickles, Jack Burkett, Ken Brown, and Ronnie Boyce. Martin Peters is looking out of the coach door next to (left) Alan Sealey; Johnny Byrne is at the wheel.

Johnny Byrne scores a penalty.

Left: Frank McAvennie, March 1989. He ran out 153 times in the League for West Ham in his two spells with the club (1985–87 and 1989–92), scoring forty-nine times.

Below: Jim Standen, a perennial figure in the West Ham goal during the Hammers' first European Cup Winners Cup campaigns.

Against Arsenal, Alvin Martin faces up to Alan Smith in the 1980 FA Cup Final. Victory took the Hammers to their second major European final.

Ernie Gregory, a legend in the West Ham goal.

Above: A replay of the semi-final of FA Cup at Stamford Bridge. West Ham's first goal, scored by Alan Taylor, who also scored the Hammers' second and winning goal (left to right: Mick Mills (Ipswich), Alan Taylor, Billy Jennings, and Ipswich goalkeeper Laurie Sivell). The win took the Irons to Wembley to meet Fulham and former skipper Bobby Moore. Winning the final was the passport to the Hammers' second major European adventure.

Left: Paul 'Sarge' Goddard was with West Ham from 1980 to 1986, winning under-21 and full England caps during that time.

Right: John Lyall, arguably West Ham's most successful manager.

Below: Against Leicester at Upton Park, 27 September 1974. From left to right: Malcolm Munro (Leicester, jumping highest), Hammer Billy Jennings, Jon Sammels (Leicester, squeezed out) and Keith Robson (West Ham). The pre-season tour of Norway did not seem to pay dividends during the subsequent league season; a mediocre campaign saw the Hammers finish in thirteenth place on the same thirty-nine points as Wolves, Coventry, and Newcastle. However, winning the FA Cup for a second time was one of the highlights of the club's history.

Left: Kevin Lock, West Ham 1971–78.

Below: Division One game at White Hart Lane, 20 November 1982. Left to right: Alex 'Sandy' Clark (West Ham), Paul Price, and Steve Perryman. Clark would play four games for West Ham against European sides.

Above: Against Manchester City at Upton Park, 29 September 1982. Sandy Clarke scored the first goal of his West Ham career in the 4–1 victory in East London. Tommy Canton and goalkeeper Alex Williams are beaten. Clarke scored ten goals in his thirty-four games for the Irons.

Right: Ron Greenwood, the 'mastermind' behind West Ham's 'golden years'.

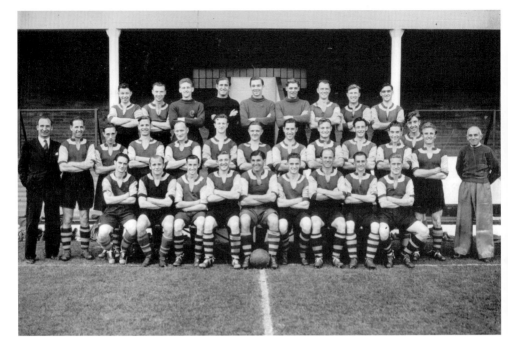

1950–51 Squad (left to right from back row): T. Moroney; unknown; P. Chiswicke; E. Gregory; P. Peters; G. Taylor; S. Forde; J. Yeomanson; F. Kearns; T. Fenlon; Corbett; A. Malcolm; unknown; W. Robinson; unknown; E. Armstrong; F. O'Farrell; G. Gazard; D. McGowan; D. Parker; J. Bond; E. Parsons; D. Wade; E. Devlin; T. Southern; J. Barrett; R. Walker; Betts; T, Woodgate; A. Foan; and R. Cater.

The 1964 FA Cup Final. Preston's goal, which gave them the lead at half-time, headed home by centre-forward Dawson (not in the picture). From left to right: Burkett, Standen, Ashworth, Bovington, and Bond. West Ham scored soon after half-time and won the game in injury time.

Given their selection options, how would they hold it all together? They needed cover badly. Tired cup legs were being sapped by league games, which were still important in terms of the Hammers maintaining their top-flight status. The pace soon began to tell when league form plummeted and the Hammers were left with nothing but disappointment from the League Cup.

It was a battle-scarred West Ham that ran out at Upton Park in the first leg of the European Cup Winners' Cup semi-final. The weariness showed against Dortmund, who were one of the best clubs in Europe at the time. They had hammered Floriana FC (Malta) 1–5 and 8–0, but had been given a fright by CSKA Sofia, the Bulgarian Cup holders. A 3–0 first-leg aggregate lead was almost swallowed up by a 4–2 defeat in Sofia. In the quarter-finals, Dortmund drew 1–1 in Madrid with Atlético and won 1–0 at home. Lothar Emmerich had scored fourteen goals *en route* to the semi-finals.

It was early spring when the Germans came to Upton Park, and nobody seemed to have told Borussia Dortmund that teams playing away in Europe are supposed to defend—they took the game to West Ham at every opportunity.

The night did not begin too promisingly when Moore, the last-but-one-man to take the field, was booed as he came out onto the pitch. He had been replaced by Byrne as captain following a simmering (if undercover) dispute with Greenwood that came to a head that looked like it would send Moore on his way from Upton Park. However, Moore was soon to win the supporters over to his side in the best way he knew—by stamping his authority on the game. He was superlative. This was the Bobby Moore who England would need during the coming summer.

Others also turned it on. Jimmy Bloomfield was at his most cunning, Johnny Byrne darted about incisively, Brown stuck relentlessly to his job, and Peters was at his ubiquitous finest. It was 'Magnificent Martin' who put the Hammers in front just before half-time. Greenwood had brought in the thirty-two-year-old Bloomfield, an old pal from his days at Brentford, and it was the former Bee who gave Peters the ball midway in Dortmund's half. With Byrne running free on the left, it looked as if the movement would continue that way, but Peters suddenly cut inside, drifted past two defenders, and scored with a crisp low drive.

West Ham pushed remorselessly forward in search of the second goal they needed, but it would not come. In the final stages, Dortmund went on the offensive and provided a thunderclap finish to a brilliant and combative game, hitting the Hammers twice in the last four minutes through Lothar Emmerich, West Germany's leading scorer. First Libuda, a wraith-like figure, gave Emmerich the chance to score from 12 yards, and with only two minutes left, Held crossed from the left for the waiting Emmerich to slide the ball smoothly past Standen on the far post. He had knocked in both his goals with his right foot, his left having done all the damage in the competition thus far. His priceless opportunism gave West Ham much to do in the second leg.

Borussia Dortmund were a side of crushing efficiency, wide skill, and indomitable spirit. The match had throbbed with all the best in football. Alf Ramsey, England's team manager, was there to see it all. At the start of the match, Martin Peters may not have been included in Ramsey's first list of forty World Cup potentials. However, his performance must have put him there. Peters proved beyond all doubt that he had the perception and range of skill to tax any opposition.

West Ham had run out of steam in the final stages of the competition. After the game, Ron Greenwood said:

> The way it ended was cruel but a game lasts ninety minutes [always an insight from Ron]. We have not yet given up hope. Dortmund are a good side, but they were not in it. I told my players how good this West German side was to buck them up. But we did not let them be good. I thought Jimmy Bloomfield was the best player on the field and Johnny Byrne has been appointed captain for the rest of the season.

Bobby Moore told the German players that they would, 'have a hard game' in Dortmund. Brave words, but anyone who was at the match could see that West Ham had a steep uphill task in Germany. John Charles stated:

> The team spent the two days before the match with Borussia [Dortmund] talking with Ron Greenwood about the value of an early West Ham goal and the importance of holding the German's early attacks. The away goals meant that we would need to win 2–0 or 3–1. At Dortmund, who were sitting on top of their league, they scored with the first movement of the game—so much for theory!

The Germans cut the West Ham defence in two when Sturm gave Sigi Held a chance to cross the ball to Lothar Emmerich. The tall, dark, round-shouldered winger headed against the bar but banged home the rebound after only twenty-seven seconds. Emmerich had an awkward gait and moderate ability, but he had a feel for scoring goals.

He was not satisfied with the one either. He scored again in the twenty-ninth minute from a bullet of a free kick following a foul by Bobby Moore. West Ham had built their defensive wall with meticulous care, but the lethal left foot, fired from a brisk seven-pace run-up, found the gap that previously did not seem to exist. This brought Emmerich's goal tally to forty-three that winter.

West Ham did what they could and kept going with dogged persistence long after the tie had been won and lost. Byrne managed to get on the scoresheet two minutes before half-time. Brabrook broke free on the right and Byrne headed his centre past Tilkowski into the Dortmund goal. However, with only three minutes left, Cyliax, the Dortmund right-back, was allowed to move forward. His 25-yard shot hit Brown before spinning over Standen's head to cap a 3–1 victory over a well-beaten West Ham.

The night had begun with the band of the Royal Artillery thumping out some English marches. By the end, the 32,500 crowd (several hundred perched on a humped-backed bridge, of all things, at one end of the ground) were happy that their team had mastered the side that had beaten TSV 1860 Munich in the previous year's final.

At least Greenwood's side had the consolation that it took one of the leading teams in Europe to take the cup from them.

European Cup Winners' Cup 1965–66				
Borussia Dortmund (FRG) Ref: Jose Maria Ortiz de Mendibil (ESP)	Upton Park, att: 28,130	Semi-final, 1st leg 05/04/1966	L 1–2	Peters 52' *Emmerich 80', 82'*
West Ham United: Jim Standen, Ken Brown, John Charles, Bobby Moore, Ronnie Boyce, Martin Peters, Peter Brabrook, Jimmy Bloomfield, Johnny Byrne (c), Geoff Hurst, Brian Dear. Manager: Ron Greenwood.				
Borussia Dortmund: Hans Tilkowski, Gerd Cyliax, Theo Redder, Dieter Kurrat, Wolfgang Paul (c), Rudolf Assauer, Reinhard Libuda, Alfred Schmidt, Siegfried Held, Wilhelm Sturm, Lothar Emmerich. Trainer: Willi Multhaup.				
Borussia Dortmund (FRG) Ref: Julio Campanati (ITA)	Rote Erde, Dortmund, att: 33,052	Semi-final, 2nd leg 13/04/1966	L 3–1 (L 5–2)	*Emmerich 1', 28',* *Cyliax 86'* Byrne 43'
Borussia Dortmund: Hans Tilkowski, Gerd Cyliax, Theo Redder, Dieter Kurrat, Wolfgang Paul (c), Rudolf Assauer, Reinhard Libuda, Alfred Schmidt, Siegfried Held, Wilhelm Sturm, Lothar Emmerich. Trainer: Willi Multhaup.				
West Ham United: Jim Standen; Eddie Bovington, John Charles, Martin Peters, Ken Brown, Bobby Moore, Peter Brabrook, Ronnie Boyce, Johnny Byrne (c), Geoff Hurst, Jimmy Bloomfield. Manager: Ron Greenwood.				

In the Cup Winners' Cup final staged at Hampden Park, Glasgow, Borussia Dortmund met Liverpool—a side conditioned to European football. The Merseysiders had done well against strong opposition, beating Juventus, Standard Liège and Honvéd to set up a semi-final meeting with Celtic.

In the first leg at Parkhead, Liverpool, without leading scorer Roger Hunt, struggled to withstand Celtic's attacking momentum, and were fortunate to escape with just a single-goal defeat. At Anfield the roles were reversed, but by half-time Liverpool were still trailing on aggregate to that single, first-leg goal. A venomous free kick from Tommy Smith levelled the scores and then Geoff Strong, who had spent much of the half limping because of an injury, managed to find some extra spring in his legs and rose above the Celtic defence to score. With a minute left, it appeared the Scots had pulled level, but the referee blew for offside.

In the final, the Germans were stronger all round, with a particularly formidable defence. Indeed, they were more sound tactically overall. Siggi Held put them ahead after the interval, only for Roger Hunt to equalise from a controversial centre, which might have upset less resilient teams than the Germans. With just seconds left, Hunt failed with a simple chance and the match went into extra-time. In the 107th minute, under pressure from Held, Liverpool's rotund Scottish goalkeeper, Tommy Lawrence, was forced to punch the ball from the edge of his area. This was a sin for a British goalkeeper in those days—failure to catch the ball was seen as a nasty foreign weakness. Libuda pounced on the clearance and blasted from 40 yards out. The ball took a deflection off the Liverpool centre-half Ron Yeats and whipped past the stranded Lawrence. West Ham had gone out to the winners.

The behind-the-scenes differences with Greenwood centred on pay and the refusal to grant Moore a transfer continued to drag West Ham down. Greenwood had allowed the relationship with Moore to degenerate and fester.

World Cup Winners

While it would be a decade before West Ham returned to major European completion, Bobby Moore made his third Wembley final in two years when he returned to lead England to World Cup victory over West Germany in the spring of 1966.

There have been millions of words written about that game, and I do not intend to add to them here, although I have a fair bit to say about it and the tournament as a whole. However, although it might be too much to say that the Hammers won the World Cup— with Moore as the pivotal, inspirational captain, and Geoff Hurst and Martin Peters playing such a big part in the ultimate victory—it is a claim that, as a West Ham supporter, I argue is worthy of contemplation.

What is undeniable is that England, on that day at Wembley, looked more like West Ham than any other English club team. The trio of Hammers probably knew more about confronting top German players than any three of the rest of Alf Ramsey's side.

Even if West Ham did not actually win the World Cup, English football owed (and still owes) a tremendous debt to the Irons.

9

SCOTLAND

West Ham have played thirty-nine games against Scottish sides and have only lost six times (drawing thirteen). Although every match has been a 'friendly' (or part of a relatively 'friendly' tournament), encounters between English and Scottish football teams confirm my impression that, in the reality of the professional game, there is no such thing as a 'friendly' game. It really is all about winning and losing.

Glasgow Celtic (SCO)	Upton Park	10/04/1924	D 2–2	Gibbins, Moore
West Ham United: Tommy Hampson, Bill Henderson, F. Blake, Syd Bishop, George Kay, Albert Cadwell, Bill Edwards, Vic Watson, Vivian Gibbins, Billy Moore, Jimmy Ruffell				

Glasgow Celtic were the first Scottish team to meet West Ham. The nature, character, and history of football (as in this book) is just a series of games, but it is also far more than that. The story of football can be told in just one game (its 'ins' and its 'outs'), how the fabric of the sport, the passion, and the business intertwines and changes. People, teams, crowds, and individuals not only play their role—they have a part in defining the essence of the activity, the phenomena that combine to give us what we see on the pitch, read on the page, and feel about one's team, side, or club.

You, reading these words, are a representative of the whole, but with a unique take on matters. The journalist, the referee, the agent, the manager, the scout, the player, and the supporter make and remake whatever the experience of football was, is, or might be. Perhaps, we eventually destroy it, or are destroyed by it, even if only in small part, by the decision of a match official, a result, a season, or the transfer of a key player.

The great giants of the game personify this just by the mention of their names, but central in my football taxonomy is Bobby Moore. When we were both young men, we often spoke at local night spots. I last met him in the car park of Roots Hall when he was managing Southend United in the old Division Four—he would preside over arguably Southend's worst ever season of 1984–85. Crowds coming to watch the Shrimpers had dwindled to an all-time low, as home gates averaged fewer than 2,000 for the first and only time in the club's history. An experiment with Rugby League at Roots Hall (Southend Invicta) was also leaking money; eighty-five people paid to watch the game against Huddersfield Barracudas.

I had seen Bobby play many, many hundreds of times. I watched him quell, even blot out and silence Pelé, Best, Law, and Bell—an endless list of brilliance. On sundry occasions, I was present when he would turn a last ditch defence into a winning attack; Bobby Moore was the last line, the first forward.

The derby is a defining factor in football: City *v.* United, Red *v.* Blue, West Ham *v.* Millwall, Lions *v.* Hammers. They happen at every level of the game, but the grandparent of them all is England *v.* Scotland—one of the the oldest battles in sport going right back to the invention of organised football.

Whenever European football brings Scottish and English clubs together, the clash is viewed with relish by everyone who thinks about or follows the game. Pronouns rule: 'we', 'us', and 'them'; music also plays its part: 'Flower of Scotland'; 'Jerusalem'; 'I'm Forever Blowing Bubbles' resonating around Boleyn Ground; and 'The Fields of Athenry' filling every corner of Celtic Park.

Before Celtic came to Upton Park, West Ham's experience of encounters with our Caledonian cousins had been a combination of excitement, skill, passion, and downright aggression and belligerence.

Glasgow Celtic (SCO)	Upton Park, att: 10,000	17/10/1949	W 5–2	Robinson 2, McGory o.g., Woodgate, Bainbridge
West Ham United: Ernie Gregory, Ernie Devlin, Fred Kearns, Derek Parker, Steve Forde, Tommy Moroney, Terry Woodgate, Eric Parsons, Bill Robinson, Gerry Gazzard, Ken Bainbridge				

St Mirren (SCO)	Upton Park	20/04/1953	D 3–3	Dixon 2, Hooper
West Ham United: Ernie Gregory, George Wright, Harry Kinsell, Tom Moroney, Malcolm Allison, Frank O'Farrell, Tommy Southern, Jim Barrett (Jr), Tommy Dixon, Jimmy Andrews, Harry Hooper				

Hearts of Midlothian (SCO)	Upton Park	19/10/1953	W 7–0	Andrews 2, Sexton 2, Gazzard, Parker, Stroud
West Ham United: Ernie Gregory, George Wright, Noel Cantwell, Derek Parker, Malcolm Allison, Doug Bing, Tommy Southern, Roy Stroud, Gerry Gazzard, Dave Sexton, Jimmy Andrews				

St Mirren (SCO)	Upton Park, att.17,000	22/03/1954	W 3–1	Dixon 2, Parker
West Ham United: Peter Chiswick, George Wright, Harry Kinsell, Derek Parker, Malcolm Allison, Dan McGowan, Tommy Southern, Jim Barrett (Jr), Tommy Dixon, Albert Foan, Jimmy Andrews				

International Soccer League 1963				
Kilmarnock (SCO)	Randalls Island Stadium, New York	30/05/1963	D 3–3	Brabrook, Hurst, Peters

West Ham United: Lawrie Leslie, Joe Kirkup, Jack Burkett, Martin Peters, Ken Brown, Dave Bickles, Peter Brabrook, Ronnie Boyce, Alan Sealey, Geoff Hurst, Tony Scott. Manager: Ron Greenwood.

St Johnstone (SCO)	Muirton Park	16/12/1964	W 3–4	Byrne 3, Hurst

West Ham United: Jim Standen, John Bond, Jack Burkett, Eddie Bovington, Ken Brown, Martin Peters, Peter Brabrook, Ronnie Boyce, Johnny Byrne, Geoff Hurst, Johnny Sissons

Kilmarnock (SCO)	Upton Park	17/02/1967	W 2–0	Hurst 2

West Ham United: Alan Dickie, Jack Burkett, Eddie Bovington, Trevor Dawkins, George Andrew, Martin Peters, Alan Sealey, Ronnie Boyce, Peter Bennett, Geoff Hurst, Peter Brabrook

International Cup Soccer USA May 1969				
Kilmarnock (SCO)	Seattle	09/05/1969	L 1–2	Boyce

West Ham United: Bobby Ferguson, Paul Heffer, John Charles (Bobby Howe), Peter Bennett, Alan Stephenson, John Cushley, Ronnie Boyce, Billy Bonds, Trevor Hartley (Harry Redknapp), Trevor Brooking, Johnny Sissons. Manager: Ron Greenwood.

Dundee United (SCO)	Memorial Stadium, Baltimore	17/05/1969	W 6–1	Brooking 2, Boyce, Hurst, Moore, Peters

West Ham United: Bobby Ferguson, Billy Bonds, John Charles, Martin Peters, Alan Stephenson, Bobby Moore, Jimmy Lindsay, Ronnie Boyce, Trevor Brooking, Geoff Hurst, Johnny Sissons. Manager: Ron Greenwood.

Dundee United (SCO)	Dallas	21/05/1969	W 3–1	Hurst 2, Brooking

West Ham United: Bobby Ferguson, Billy Bonds, Bobby Howe, Martin Peters, Alan Stephenson, Bobby Moore, Harry Redknapp, Jimmy Lindsay, Trevor Brooking, Geoff Hurst, Hartley (Ronnie Boyce). Manager: Ron Greenwood.

Dundee United (SCO)	Portland	Exhibition match 25/5/69	W 8–2	Bennett 2, Hurst 2, Peters 2, Howe, Redknapp

West Ham United: Bobby Ferguson, Paul Heffer, John Charles, Martin Peters, Alan Stephenson, Bobby Moore, Harry Redknapp, Ronnie Boyce, Peter Bennett (Trevor Brooking), Geoff Hurst, Bobby Howe. Manager: Ron Greenwood.

Kilmarnock (SCO)	Memorial Stadium, Baltimore	30/05/1969	W 4–1	Bennett, Boyce, Hartley, Lindsay

West Ham United: Bobby Ferguson, Billy Bonds, John Charles, Ronnie Boyce, Alan Stephenson, John Cushley (Trevor Hartley), Harry Redknapp, Jimmy Lindsay (Welch—guest player from Baltimore), Trevor Brooking, Peter Bennett, Bobby Howe. Manager: Ron Greenwood.

For me, the theory that there are no 'chummy' professional football matches was never better exemplified than when Celtic came to Upton Park for Bobby Moore's Testimonial game in 1970. As one newspaper report had it: 'The match was played in a fearfully competitive spirit—perhaps the most fitting tribute to a man who, by common consent is regarded as a model professional.' I believe Trevor Smith of *The Newham Recorder* was spot on when he wrote, 'the fans will argue—and rightly so after this glorious example—that benefit nights can mean something without being bloody minded as the real thing.'

I was a fifteen-year-old on the North Bank at Upton Park the evening the game against Celtic was played. Bobby Moore was in his pomp as a player, not long home from the World Cup in Mexico and captaining (almost certainly) the finest group of players to sally forth from England's shores. Moore had shown himself equal to Pelé and recognised as the best defensive practitioner of the game on the face of the planet.

On his return to his home nation and not long after his testimonial game, Moore was voted into third place in the BBC TV Sports Personality of the Year. He had won the award four years earlier in 1966—fellow Hammer Geoff Hurst had come third. Moore also finished second in the 1970 European Footballer of the Year award behind the great West German striker and top scorer in the World Cup, Gerd Müller. It had been Müller's goal that put England out of the World Cup in the quarter-finals, so avenging the events of 1966.

I had seen Celtic contest the World Club Championship in Uruguay three years prior to their meeting with West Ham for Moore's testimonial (see Belton, 2008), and as such had more than a soft spot for the Glasgow Bhoys. They would forever be 'the Lions of Lisbon'—the first British team to win the European Cup.

Seven members of that wonderful 1967 side (Jim Craig, Tommy Gemmell, Bobby Murdoch, Billy McNeill, Jimmy Johnstone, Willie Wallace, and Bobby Lennox), and eleven of the Celtic side from the European Cup final in May that year turned out for Moore's testimonial.

Visiting East London for the first time in a dozen years, Celtic were among the top two or three clubs in Britain, and one of the leading sides in Europe—maybe the world. Just six months prior to that night in November 1970, the lads from Parkhead had been beaten narrowly in the final of the European Cup, losing 2–1 in extra time to the proud Dutchmen of Feyenoord.

I do not remember it being a cold night relative to the average November of my teens, but it was one of those floodlit evenings at the Boleyn Ground that have not and will not be replicated. There is no way to know what it was like other than to have been there, but the grass always appeared to be greener, and it seemed to smell more strongly than afternoon kick-offs. That, of course, was an impression stoked by expectation, hope, and the passion of stand-up support. However, I am pretty sure the contrast with those claret-and-blue shirts, certainly during my boyhood and adolescent years, had a real psychological impact that translated into the physicality of support.

The floodlit Upton Park had something of a tradition of drawing attractive and high-performing European clubs. Although the Hammers had lost Martin Peters to Spurs, with Moore and Hurst (as recently successful World Cup players) still in the team, West Ham were favourites to be invited to take part in friendly and exhibition games or tournaments.

'Bom-Bom-Bom-Bom—Esso Blue'

Some might recognise this as the strapline of adverts delivered by the cartoon Esso paraffin dealer, 'Joe', during a campaign that continued from the late 1950s into the 1970s. It always comes to mind when I hear or read the word 'Esso'—that and a later campaign, which altered the well-known song 'Smoke Gets in Your Eyes' to put over the message: 'They asked me how I knew, it was Esso Blue. I of course replied, with lower grades one buys, smoke gets in your eyes.' This was meant to enhance the claim that Esso was a non-smoking paraffin. The song was released as a flexi disk and given away free with paraffin in hardware shops. I think we had about eight copies at one point.

(Adverts: the nursery rhymes of children of the 1950s: 'Murray Mints, Murray Mints, too good to hurry mints!')

The above digression is linked to the fact that Moore's testimonial was sponsored and organised by Esso. The operation surrounding the game was innovative in that it was the first and only occasion in the history of the Hammers that a concern separate from the club had taken responsibility for the management and administration of a footballing event.

The petroleum company, expecting a high demand for tickets, increased the price of admission to much higher than that of cup ties or league fixtures. For the game with Celtic, to get into the West Stand cost 30s for a seat that would usually cost between 12s and 18s—a cost hike in modern terms from 60p or 80p to £1.50. I paid 10s (50p) for my place on the North Bank (the Centenary Stand to be). It was the same for the South Bank (renovated in 1993 and then renamed in honour of Bobby Moore), which usually would cost 6s (30p) at a time when a pint of beer cost 15d, and a packet of cigarettes required 25d. A house that might now cost £250,000 could have been bought then for £5,000 , so it is easy to see that football was clearly much cheaper (even at 'Esso prices') than it is today. Not to mention also that the game was about five times more exciting and the players far better—but then I would say that.

For all this, while the night was full of the chanting and singing of East End fans appreciating the quality of football on show, a crowd of less than 25,000 was about as surprising as it was disappointing. The price of the tickets was blamed. At a time when it was not unusual for West Ham to attract a gate of more than 40,000, it was said that had the customary admission charges been asked, many more supporters would have made the effort.

Personally, I doubt it. I was into this type of football—the international game fascinated me. The names of the clubs were poetry to me: 'Rapid Vienna', 'Wacker

Innsbruck', 'Moscow Torpedo', 'Benfica', the 'Eagles of Lisbon' from the 'Estádio da Luz' no less—Estudiantes de la Plata for goodness sake! I loved the romance in the clash of footballing cultures; always something different and attractively cosmopolitan. In truth, full houses were far more likely for boring, 'down-the-road' games with plain as a carrot Tottenham or the other (then 'boring, boring!') north Londoners from the lyrically named Highbury.

I think Esso had done their homework. They were no mugs in terms of market research and pricing up a commodity—even sentiment. The admission fee very likely gleaned the maximum in terms of gate receipts.

Robert Oxby's report of the game in *The Daily Telegraph* urged people to, 'ignore the scoreline, Celtic, playing with the flair that has made them such a force in world football, out-classed the Londoners.'

This is not how I remember it. What I recall is one type of footballing dream encountering another—a complimentary but antagonistic clash reminiscent of something between the clashing of two lines of cavalry; constantly charging and reforming in a game of chess. Desmond Hackett's comments in the *Daily Express* at the time chime more with my recollections of the match: 'This is England *versus* Scotland, a rip-roaring, ear-shattering game that left visiting managers relieved that Celtic were not competing in the Football League.'

What I did find remarkable (and had not really noticed when I watched Celtic previously) was the size of the Celtic players. In the main, they seemed to tower over the Hammers—except for Jimmy Johnstone, that is. Like our own Johnny Aryis, one felt almost as if you might need a magnifying glass to see him.

The account from Welshman Oxby (today a football correspondent for *The Telegraph*) went on—in which he seemingly contradicting himself:

> Until late in the game, Celtic were in total command although a lovely cross by Bobby Moore in the eighteenth minute enabled Hurst to cancel out Celtic's opening goal by Lennox.
>
> Johnstone, flicking in Michael Hughes's short pass, put the Scots ahead again after thirty-four minutes but a mistake by Gemmell allowed the tiny Aryis to lob a surprise equaliser in the sixty-third minute.
>
> Connelly, breaking away, blasted a goal for Celtic within a minute but his withdrawal in favour of Wallace and the introduction of Holland and Bobby Howe for Jimmy Lindsay and Greaves, changed the balance of power and Clyde Best was able to head West Ham level five minutes from time.

While Celtic were in front three times, they were pulled back and thus equalled. Personally, *The [Glasgow] Herald* summed up the game a bit more accurately:

> West Ham are disciples of attacking football, and on the heavy ground they met the European pass masters of attacking football at their peak. The score does justice to the

efforts of both sides in an encounter that turned the green surface to an earthy brown long before the end.

For the early part of the second half Celtic were very much in command with Bobby Murdoch dominating the midfield. But West Ham were determined to give their captain his full reward, and seventeen-year-old Ayris, showing real promise on the right wing, lobbed home an equaliser in sixty-three minutes.

Ayris, at 5 feet 5 inches, was not whopping, but he was from a council flat in Wapping. The gigantic and intensely physical Tommy Gemmel had made his life a misery for most of the match, but I can still see that goal in my mind's eye and the delight and surprise of little Ayris (he was nicknamed 'Rat' by his fellow players, and 'Nipper' by the fans) as the ball entered the net.

With just half a dozen minutes of the match remaining, the visitors were 2–3 up, but Clyde Best's header from a cross by Hurst gave notice to the Celtic players, if they needed it, that West Ham would not be beaten on that night, in that place.

In the dying seconds, Johnstone missed a golden opportunity when, just a few feet from the goal line with no-one between him and the net, he launched the ball over the Hammers' cross-bar.

Writing for the *Daily Mail*, Brian James captured something of the immediate legacy of the match: 'When Celtic sought to dominate their pitch, West Ham drew the line. And thus the prestige friendly rose to become one of the season's minor spectacles.' Trevor Smith of the *Newham Recorder* told of how the 'Hammers, particularly the younger men, refused to lose their nerve against what was reckoned the best team in Britain.'

It had been a fiercely competitive game that demonstrated the combative ethos within professional players that rendered the notion of a 'friendly' football match to be a misnomer. For sure, players might be a bit less cautious and perhaps slightly more inclined to experiment and take chances in a 'friendly', but this just adds to the mix.

The game had been a spectacle of impressive proportions. Indeed, one newspaper had it that Bobby Moore '... had the glory of his testimonial match ... stolen from him by a memorable display from Celtic'. This overlooks that football had been played for its own sake—as an expression of self in relation to others. As in all things, this is when one walks down the road to art. That I am still writing about it today is evidence enough of the game having been well worth the price of the ticket.

Bobby Moore's assist (a cross) for Geoff Hurst's goal was and still remains to me powerfully symbolic of both the England World Cup triumph and West Ham's golden era.

Bobby Moore Testimonial				
Glasgow Celtic (SCO) Ref: J. Finney. Linesmen: J. R. McGowan, R. W. Spires	Upton Park, att: 24,448	16/11/1970	D 3–3	Hurst 19', Ayris 62', Best 84' *Lennox 13', Johnstone 34', Connelly 63'*
West Ham United: Bobby Ferguson, John McDowell, Frank Lampard Sr, Peter Eustace, Tommy Taylor, Bobby Moore, Johnny Ayris, Jimmy Lindsay (Pat Holland 62'), Geoff Hurst, Clyde Best, Jimmy Greaves (Bobby Howe 76'). Manager: Ron Greenwood.				
Glasgow Celtic: Evan Williams, Jim Craig, Tommy Gemmell, Bobby Murdoch, Billy McNeill, Jim Brogan, George Connelly, Jimmy Johnstone, John Michael Hughes (Willie Wallace 73'), David Hay, Bobby Lennox.				

For all this, there was a lot of moaning before and after the game about pricing—enough to motivate Eddie Chapman (then club secretary and the general *factotum* at Upton Park) to seduce the *Newham Recorder* to publish an explanation on behalf of the club. Essentially, this said, 'nuffin' to do wiv me gov'.

Chapman elucidated that Esso had rented the Boleyn Ground for the testimonial, and that the club did not have a clue how much money had been passed on to Moore as that was not the club's business but specifically between West Ham's captain and Esso. Contradictorily, however, West Ham did disclose that following the deduction of commission costs for the gate and programme, the club passed on £19,793 for the gate and £1,633 in programme receipts to Esso—a total £21,426. How much the petroleum company drew off to cover their 'expenses' was, and is, unknown, although Celtic got £5,000 for their troubles.

No-one can really say what Bobby Moore got or did not get. There were estimates quoted, such as one that claimed he was 'guaranteed a reward of at least £12,000', although there is no indication how this sum was arrived at or where the estimate came from. It could, indeed, have been a record amount passed to a Hammer as the attendance was club record for a testimonial game—better than the 21,600 who turned up for Malcolm Allison's (Bobby Moore's footballing guru) testimonial a dozen years earlier.

A cigarette lighter in the shape of the FA Cup was personally presented by Bobby Moore to the players, the referee, and the linesmen. Paradoxically, a poster launched by the World Health Organization around this time was seemingly becoming ubiquitous. It showed a man smoking with the words 'Man Made Killer. Stop Smoking.' This was the first public position against smoking and added impetus to the development of national plans for action against smoking worldwide. One of these testimonial lighters, belonging to linesman J. R. McGowan, coughed up £420 in November 2006 at Graham Budd Auctions.

Bobby Moore's testimonial took place at a time when Esso had fingers, hands, elbows, and feet in a number of promotions connected to football—the 1970 Esso World Cup coin collection being a case in point. This became something of a craze for a time, equivalent to an idea or presentation 'going viral' today.

For some reason, the Esso sponsorship model remained a one-off experiment. Geoff Hurst's testimonial match the next season was kept very much within the ambit of the club.

Esso also oversaw the design and publication of the souvenir programme for the game. They produced two different editions: one on general sale, and another for VIPs. I was not one of the latter, but the programme I bought was far ahead of its time in terms of colour and design. I adored it and hung on to it for decades until my father took it upon himself to sell it on eBay. He did not make much. They were overprinted, and a decent one was readily available for about a dozen quid. It had put me back about three times the cost of the normal shilling or so, but was worth it. It was much bigger, brighter, more dynamic,and packed full of much more content than what was available for the most part at the time; the pathetically dowdy, painfully predictable, anaemically repetitive, flaccid, insipid, totally undistinguished, uninspiring, crappy little A6 leaflets made of paper that crumbled if exposed to even the rumour of damp. Years after the game, programme geeks were still grumbling that the Esso publication was 'too big', to such an extent that they were unable to store it with millions of others they had spent their pocket money on. Life can be a harsh mistress.

The Hammers have had encounters with Scottish clubs since 1970, but East London *v.* East Glasgow perhaps remains the pinnacle of such experiences.

Dunfermline Athletic (SCO)	East End Park	09/08/1971	W 1–3	Geoff Hurst 3 (1 pen)
West Ham United: Bobby Ferguson, John McDowell, Frank Lampard Sr, Billy Bonds, Alan Stephenson, Bobby Moore, Ayris, Clyde Best, Bryan Robson, Geoff Hurst, Tommy Taylor				

The Tennent Caledonian Cup 1979				
Glasgow Rangers (SCO)	Ibrox Park, att: 10,000	Semi-final 03/08/1979	L 3–2	Jennings, Cross
West Ham United: Phil Parkes, Frank Lampard Sr, Paul Brush, Billy Bonds, Alvin Martin, Geoff Pike, Pat Holland (Billy Lansdowne), Dale Banton, David Cross, Trevor Brooking, Billy Jennings. Manager: John Lyall.				

Scottish mini-tour 1978				
Ross County (SCO)	Dingwall	07/08/1979	W 1–8	Cross 2, Holland 2, Brush, Jennings, Banton, Lansdowne
West Ham United: Phil Parkes (Bobby Ferguson), Phil Brignull, Paul Brush, Billy Bonds, Alvin Martin, Geoff Pike (Paul Allen), Pat Holland, Dale Banton, David Cross (George Cowie), Trevor Brooking, Billy Jennings (Billy Lansdowne). Manager: John Lyall.				
Buckie Thistle (SCO)	Victoria Park	09/08/1979	W 1–3	Cross 2, Pike
West Ham United: Phil Parkes (Bobby Ferguson), Phil Brignull, Paul Brush, Billy Bonds, Alvin Martin, Geoff Pike (Billy Lansdowne), Pat Holland, Dale Banton (Paul Allen), David Cross, Trevor Brooking, George Cowie. Manager: John Lyall.				

Scottish mini-tour 1980				
Dundee United (SCO)	Tannerdice Park, att: 5,671	02/08/1980	W 0–1	Cross
West Ham United: Phil Parkes, Ray Stewart, Paul Brush, Billy Bonds, Alvin Martin (Frank Lampard), Alan Devonshire, Pat Holland, Stuart Pearson, David Cross, Trevor Brooking, Jimmy Neighbour. Manager: John Lyall.				
Ayr United (SCO)	Somerset Park, att; 5,671	04/08/1980	D 1–1	Cross
West Ham United: Phil Parkes (Bobby Ferguson), Frank Lampard Sr, Paul Brush, Billy Bonds, Ray Stewart, Alan Devonshire, Paul Allen, Stuart Pearson (Jimmy Neighbour), David Cross, Trevor Brooking (Pat Holland) Stuart Pearson, Geoff Pike. Manager: John Lyall..				

Aberdeen Tournament 1–2 August 1981				
Aberdeen (SCO)	Pittodrie, att: 10,000	01/08/1981	L 3–0	
West Ham United: Phil Parkes, Ray Stewart, Frank Lampard Sr, Billy Bonds, Alvin Martin, Paul Allen, Jimmy Neighbour (Bobby Barnes) , Paul Goddard, David Cross (Stuart Pearson), Trevor Brooking, Geoff Pike. Manager: John Lyall.				

Dundee United (SCO)	Tannadice Park, att: 8,000	01/08/1982	D 3-3	van der Elst, Goddard, Pike
West Ham United: Phil Parkes, Ray Stewart, Frank Lampard Sr, Billy Bonds, Alvin Martin, Alan Devonshire (George Cowie), Jimmy Neighbour (Nicky Morgan), Paul Goddard, François Van Der Elst, Paul Allen, Geoff Pike				

Airdrieonians (SCO)	Broomfield Park	03/08/1982	L 3–0	
West Ham United: Phil Parkes (Tom McAlister), Ray Stewart, Paul Brush, Billy Bonds, Alvin Martin, Alan Devonshire, Jimmy Neighbour (Bobby Barnes), Paul Goddard, Alex Clark, Paul Allen, Geoff Pike				

Dundee United (SCO)	Upton Park	19/02/1983	D 2–2	van der Elst, Donald
West Ham United: Phil Parkes, Ray Stewart, Frank Lampard Sr (Paul Brush), Billy Bonds, Alvin Martin, Alan Devonshire, François Van der Elst, Paul Goddard, Nicky Morgan (Tony Cottee), Warren Donald, Geoff Pike				

Dundee United (SCO)	Tannadice Park	13/08/1983	L 4–0	
West Ham United: Tom McAlister, Frank Lampard Sr, Paul Brush, Billy Bonds, Neil Orr, Paul Allen (Alan Dickens), Steve Whitton, Tony Cottee, Dave Swindlehurst (Bobby Barnes), Trevor Brooking, Geoff Pike (Alvin Martin)				
St Mirren (SCO)	Love Street	Challenge match 2/8/86	L 3–0	

West Ham United: Phil Parkes (Tom McAlister), Ray Stewart, George Parris, Tony Gale (Steve Walford), Alvin Martin, Alan Devonshire (Paul Goddard), Mark Ward, Frank McAvennie, Alan Dickens, Tony Cottee, Neil Orr (Geoff Pike)

Falkirk (SCO)	Brockville Park	23/07/1992	D 1–1	Allen

West Ham United: Ludo Mikloško, Tim Breacker, Julien Dicks, Steve Potts, Alvin Martin, Kevin Keen, Kenny Brown, Ian Bishop, Mitchell Thomas, Mike Small, Clive Allen
Playing subs: Tony Gale, Colin Foster, Trevor Morely

St Johnstone (SCO)	McDiarmid Park	25/07/1992	W 4–1	Small 2, Allen, Potts

West Ham United: Ludo Mikloško, Tim Breacker, Julien Dicks, Tony Gale, Alvin Martin, Steve Potts, Ian Bishop, Kevin Keen, Kenny Brown, Mike Small, Clive Allen

Falkirk (SCO)	Brockville Park	29/07/1993	D 1–1	Dicks (pen)

West Ham United: Ludo Mikloško, Tim Breacker, Julien Dicks, Steve Potts, Tony Gale, Martin Allen, Stewart Robson, Peter Butler, Trevor Morely, Clive Allen, Dale Gordon. Playing subs: Matty Holmes, Darren Currie.

Dunfermline Athletic (SCO)	East End Park	31/07/1993	L 2–1	Trevor Morely

West Ham United: Ludo Mikloško, Tim Breacker, Julien Dicks, Steve Potts, Tony Gale, Danny Williamson, Stewart Robson, Matty Holmes, Trevor Morely, Steve Jones, Dale Gordon. Playing sub: Darren Currie.

Dunfermline Athletic (SCO)	East End Park	02/08/1994	L 1–0	

West Ham United: Ludo Mikloško, Tim Breacker, Kenny Brown, Steve Potts, Alvin Martin, Julien Dicks, Ian Bishop, Matt Holland, Trevor Morely, Martin Allen, Tony Cottee

St Johnstone (SCO)	McDiarmid Park	04/08/1994	D 0–0	

West Ham United: Gary Kelly, Tim Breacker, Kenny Brown, Steve Potts, Alvin Martin, Julien Dicks, Matt Holland, Paul Mitchell, Tony Cottee Darren Currie, Martin Allen

Hearts of Midlothian (SCO)	Victoria Road, Dagenham FC	14/11/1994	W 0–1* (floodlight failure—match abandonded)	Morely (pen)

West .Ham United: Les Sealey, Tim Breacker, Kenny Brown, Alvin Martin, Marc Rieper, Michael Hughes, Danny Williamson, Matty Holmes, Darren Currie, Lee Chapman, Trevor Morely

Clyde (SCO)	Broadwood Stadium	19/07/1997	W 0–2	Hughes, Hartson

West Ham United: Ali Boumnijel, Danny Williamson, Graeme Philson, Steve Potts, Rio Ferdinand, David Terrier, Eyal Berkovic, Steve Lomas, John Hartson, Iain Dowie, Michael Hughes. **Playing subs:** Keith Rowland, Marc Rieper, Frank Lampard Jr, Paul Kitson

Dunfermline Athletic (SCO)	East End Park	23/07/1997	D 2–2	Moncur, Hartson

West Ham United: Ali Boumnijel, Danny Williamson, Grahame Philson, Steve Potts, Rio Ferdinand, David Terrier, Frank Lampard Jr, Eyal Berkovic, Paul Kitson, John Hartson, John Moncur

St Johnstone (SCO)	MacDiarmid Park	25/07/1997	W 0–1	Hartson

West Ham United: Craig Forrest, Stan Lazaridis, Michael Hughes, Steve Lomas, Rio Ferdinand, David Terrier, Frank Lampard Jr, John Moncur, Paul Kitson, Iain Dowie, Danny Williamson

Hibernian (SCO)	Easter Road	23/07/1998	D 1–1	Mean

West Ham United: Shaka Hislop, Trevor Sinclair, Lee Hodges, Ian Pearce, Steve Potts, Chris Coyne, Scott Mean, John Moncur, John Hartson, Eyal Berkovic, Manny Omoyinmi. **Playing subs:** Frank Lampard Jr, Samassi Abou

Motherwell (SCO)	Fir Park	25/07/1998	D 1–1	Hartson

West Ham United: Ludo Mikloško, Trevor Sinclair, Lee Hodges, Steve Potts, Ian Pearce, Chris Coyne, Scott Mean, Frank Lampard Jr, Eyal Berkovic, John Hartson, Manny Omoyinmi. **Playing subs:** Stephen Purches, John Moncur, Ian Wright

Glasgow Celtic (SCO)	Parkhead, att: 10,000	25/07/2000	L 2–1	Di Canio

West Ham United: Stephen Bywater, Dino Jorge (Gary Charles), Nigel Winterburn (Marc Keller), Neil Ruddock (Tyrell Forbes), Igor Štimac, Michael Carrick, Steve Lomas, Frank Lampard Jr, Frédéric Kanouté (Jermaine Defoe), Paolo Di Canio, Trevor Sinclair (Adam Newton)

10

SPIEGLER

In the late 1960s and early 1970s, I (along with other fellow West Ham supporters) was denied the type of international football diet I had been exposed to in the mid-1960s. The preseason (1970–71) prospect of a trip to Leyton for the meeting between the Hammers and Orient, our East London neighbours, was not going to be compensation. The fairly entertaining 1–1 draw (Peter Eustace scoring for the visitors) did have a spark of the kind of international magic that Ron Greenwood spiced his sides with throughout most of his reign. For instance, Ade Coker would join the cause of the Irons the following season, and, of course, Clyde Best had been with the club for a couple of years.

West Ham fielded a substitute, Mordechai Spiegler, the striker and skipper of the Israeli side at the 1970 World Cup. He took the field for the third time during the Hammers build-up to the new season. He had previously turned out for the West Ham team that beat Portsmouth 0–2 and was in the team defeated at Bristol City (1–0).

Spiegler had impressed in the qualifying games Israel played to get to Mexico. This was Israel's first (and so far, only) appearance at the World Cup Finals. They had qualified as an Asian team, but for political (and other reasons) were expelled from the Asian Football Confederation in 1974. As a result, from 1991 the nation competed in the European zone as a member of UEFA, hence why Israeli teams are included in this book.

Israel received a bye for the first round of qualifying games for the 1970 World Cup, but in the second round got what looked like a tough draw grouped with New Zealand and North Korea. The latter nation had impressed in 1966, taking a 3–0 lead over Eusébio's Portugal at Ayresome Park, and although they ultimately lost the match 5–3, they had become the first Asian team to advance beyond the first round in the World Cup Finals.

For political reasons, the North Koreans refused to meet Israel, so the round was decided over two games against New Zealand in Ramat Gan within the Tel Aviv district. On 28 September 1969, Israel won 4–0, and later 2–0 on 1 October 1969.

In the third round Israel met Australia, a side that would make the following 1974 World Cup finals in Germany. In Ramat Gan on 4 December 1969, Israel defeated the Socceroos by the only goal of the game. Ten days later, they held their hosts to a 1–1 draw in Sydney.

At the World Cup Finals in Mexico, Mordechai's men found themselves in another demanding group. In their opening game, the Israelis were defeated 2–0 by Uruguay.

In their second and third matches, they did well to hold the Swedes (1–1) and the losing finalists Italy (0–0) to draws, but they still finished bottom of Group Two. The goal against Sweden had been scored by Spiegler and remains the only Israeli goal at a World Cup Finals. Spiegler, essentially a midfield player, made a major contribution to this relatively successful first venture into the big time of world football. He captained the side in all the qualifying and final group games.

Spiegler had impressed Ron Greenwood; the West Ham manager saw him score four goals against the USA in a warm-up game for the Mexico finals. The USA's manager, Phil Woosnam (West Ham's former skipper and a Welsh international), had recommended Mordechai to Tommy Docherty, who worked with Aston Villa at the time (another of Woosnam's former clubs) and had been interested enough to fly out to Mexico to watch the Israeli. Ultimately, when Greenwood (serving as a FIFA observer during the 1970 tournament) invited Spiegler to London to play alongside Jimmy Greaves, Geoff Hurst, and Bobby Moore in the English First Division, the Israeli opted to do what he could to pit himself against sides like Arsenal and Manchester United.

Described as, 'rangy in build, neat in his work, but perhaps a little short of pace' when first viewed by the English press, Spiegler was born in Sochi (then the USSR) on 19 August 1944. He came to Upton Park on loan from Maccabi Netanya in July 1970 as Israeli footballer of the year—a title he held from 1969 to 1971. He had led his team to the 1970–71 Israeli League title and would do so again in 1977–78 (Maccabi Netanya would also be Champions in 1973–74, 1979–80, and 1982–83). Although he played just three friendly games for West Ham, he made a lasting impression.

Bringing Spiegler to East London the better part of half a century ago was never going to be a straightforward task. He needed permission from his native FA to get a work permit. Alongside this, the English Football League Management Committee would need to rubber-stamp the player's registration.

At the age of twenty-six, Spiegler had amateur status as a player in Israel, and as such was allowed to take part in friendlies, but red tape conspired against Ron Greenwood from bringing the Israeli skipper to the Boleyn Ground on a permanent basis. It was, however, a close-run thing, as evidenced by there being two different West Ham squad photographs for that season; one featured Spiegler standing next to Bobby Moore in the back row, the other did not include the Israeli star. If he had signed for Greenwood, West Ham would have been the first English club to bring an Israeli into their ranks.

Spiegler had feared his way would be blocked. He had told the press that he was worried that the Israeli FA might have misgivings about allowing him to play overseas as it could mean others would follow. He wanted to play for the Hammers so much that he told reporters that he was prepared to get a job outside football and turn out for the East Londoners as an amateur for two years, gain a residential qualification, and go on to play professionally. A trial with Borussia Mönchengladbach in Germany followed, but ultimately he returned to the Sharon plain.

Spiegler's appearance at Brisbane Road was his last before he made his way back to the Middle East and the Diamonds (Maccabi Netanya). Later, he finally appeared in front of West Ham's home fans when he ran out for a European XI in Geoff Hurst's testimonial game. Before the match, Greenwood stated: 'Mordechai likes West Ham and we like him.'

European XI	Upton Park,	Geoff Hurst Testimonial	D 4–4	Hurst, Robson 2, Best McDougall, Marsh
Ref: J. Taylor	att: 29,250	23/11/1971		2, Greaves
West Ham United: Bobby Ferguson, John McDowell (Clive Charles), Bobby Howe, Billy Bonds (Joe Durrell), Taylor, Bobby Moore, Harry Redknapp (Johnny Ayris), Clyde Best, Geoff Hurst, Peter Eustace, Bryan Robson				
European XI Squad: John Jackson (Crystal Palace), Mick Docherty (Burnley), Tommy Gemmell (Celtic), Eusébio (Benfica), Jimmy Greaves (West Ham United), Will Schultz (Hamburg), Dave Mackay (Swindon Town), Jimmy Johnstone (Celtic), Ted McDougall (Bournemouth), Mordechai Spiegler (Maccabi), Uwe Seeler (Hamburg), Rodney Marsh (Queens Park Rangers), António Simões (Benfica). Manager: Tommy Docherty.				

He had been touring Australia with the Israeli national side, but crossed the planet to play the game. Hurst paid about £1,000 in fares to bring him to Upton Park. Such was his distinction in his own country (he would claim thirty-three goals in eighty-three appearances for Israel from 1963 to 1977) that an Israeli television crew was at the Boleyn Ground to record their captain's contribution to the game. Regrettably, Tommy Docherty (at that point the manager of Scotland), who was asked to manage the European XI, waited until the second half to bring Spiegler into play.

Subsequently, the *Daily Mail* had it that the Israeli was interested in playing under Ron Greenwood at Upton Park, even though Nantes (narrowly knocked out of the UEFA Cup by Spurs the month before Hurst's testimonial) had offered Spiegler attractive terms to play in France (a £30,000 signing-on fee was mooted in the press). When asked why he did not take the jump to join West Ham in 1970, Spiegler said: 'Perhaps I should have taken the chance straightaway. My year's ban would now be over and I would be playing for West Ham. Now I still don't know what is best.'

The West Ham manager indicated that Spiegler would be welcomed at Upton Park, but it was not to be. A future in which Spiegler played a part in the future of the Hammers remained a romantic but unfulfilled dream. He returned to Israel's tour of Australia while rumours circulated that Docherty's treatment of him had soured his ambition to play in England. However, it is probably more likely that his decision had more to do with reports about the possibility of the Israeli FA sanctioning him should he decide to play abroad.

However, Spiegler was playing for Paris FC during the 1972–73 term (eleven goals in thirty-nine games) before moving to Paris Saint-Germain in December 1973. In the cause of *les Parisiens*, he scored ten times in thirteen outings.

Spiegler returned to Maccabi Netanya for 1974–75, but he was persuaded to play alongside Pelé and a host of other world footballing stars under the banner of the New York Cosmos. He netted six times in seventeen run-outs for the Cosmos.

In 1975, he once more returned to Israel for his final spell with Netanya. Three years on, having played 342 league games for his club and scored 183 goals, he moved on to Hapoel Haifa, playing twenty matches before breaking into management as a player-manager with Beitar Tel Aviv. He was to pilot a range of clubs including Maccabi Haifa, Hapoel Haifa, his beloved Maccabi Netanya, Hapoel Tel Aviv, Maccabi Jaffa, Tzafririm Holon, before (in 2013) becoming general manager of Maccabi Netanya.

In November 2003, Mordechai was nominated by the Israel FA as the best Israeli player over the previous half-century during their Jubilee Awards. Today, his tally of thirty-three international goals means that he is still the holder of the goalscoring record for an Israeli international player, but he also scored twenty-five times in sixty-two Olympic Qualifying matches. Spiegler skippered the Israeli side at the 1968 Mexico Olympic Games. He was voted the 105th greatest Israeli of all time in 2005 in a poll run by an Israeli news website.

Israel National XI	Upton Park, att: 7,465	Paul Heffer Testimonial 04/04/1973	W 3–2	Lock, Lutton, Robson

West Ham United: Bobby Ferguson, John McDowell, Frank Lampard Sr, Pat Holland (Bertie Lutton), Tommy Taylor, Bobby Moore, Kevin Lock, Clyde Best (Dudley Tyler), Ted MacDougall, Trevor Brooking, Bryan Robson

Israel XI: Wissoker (Michaeli), Gindin, Borba, Primo, Rozen, Oz, Shoum, Talbi, Faigenbaum, Farkash, Brad (Onana)

Israel National XI	Jimmy Bloomfield Stadium, Jaffa, att: 22,000	Invitation Match 03/05/1973	D 2–2	Best, Robson

West Ham United: Bobby Ferguson, John McDowell, Frank Lampard Sr, Billy Bonds, Kevin Lock, Bobby Moore, Clyde Best, Bertie Lutton, Ted MacDougall, Trevor Brooking, Bryan Robson

Israel Select XI	National Stadium, Tel Aviv	Exhibition match 14/5/75	D 2–2	Taylor, Lock

West Ham United: Mervyn Day, John McDowell, Frank Lampard Sr, Pat Holland, Tommy Taylor, Kevin Lock, Alan Taylor, Graham Paddon, Billy Jennings, Trevor Brooking, Keith Robson

Maccabi XI (ISR)	Chadwell Heath	05/08/1982	W 15–0	Matthews 3, Cottee 2, Dickens 2, Donald 2, Schiavi 2, West 2, Campbell, Parris

West Ham United: John Vaughan (Shermer), Glen Burvill (Terry Baker), Everald La Ronde (Paul Goyette), Warren Donald, Chris Ampofo, (Davidson), Keith McPherson, Pat Holland (Andy Skinner), Mark Schiavi (Mark West), Tony Cottee (Gregory Campbell), Alan Dickens (David Matthews), George Parris

11

'FOOTBALL? IT ISN'T ABOUT ANYTHING. IT IS SOMETHING.'
HANS CROON, RSC ANDERLECHT 1975–76

West Ham's 2–0 FA Cup final win over Fulham (the Cottagers included Bobby Moore in their line-up) in 1975 sent West Ham back into major European competition for the first time in a decade.

In the opening round, the Hammers were drawn against Lahden Reipas of Finland. The Irons just about got a 2–2 draw in the frozen north. The home side opened the scoring after the ball ricocheted off Mervyn Day's chest. A gliding Brooking free kick equalised. Tupasela made it 2–1 before Bonds, after a one-two with Pat Holland, made it honours-even.

However, a 3-0 win at home, with goals from Robson, Holland and Billy Jennings sent the Irons comfortably into the second round. To their credit the visitors attacked from the first whistle, but they had no option really, being obliged to score if they were to have any chance of staying in the tournament on the away goals rule. However, the game was killed when Robson picked up a cross from Bonds; his drive hit the post and then the goalkeeper before crossing the goal line.

European Cup Winners' Cup 1975–76				
Reipas Lahti (FIN) Ref: Ulf Eriksson (SWE)	Olympiastadion, Lahti, att: 4,587	First round, 1st leg 17/09/1975	D 2–2	*Lindholm 4', Tupasela 53'* Brooking 29', Bonds 76'
Reipas Lahti: Harri Holli, Pekka Kosonen, Mikko Kautonen, Lauri Riutto, Markku Repo, Harri Toivanen, Timo Kautonen, Ari Tupasela, Pertti Jantunen, Hannu Hämäläinen, Harri Lindholm. Trainer: Keijo Voutilainen				
West Ham United: Mervyn Day, John McDowell, Frank Lampard Sr, Billy Bonds, Tommy Taylor, Kevin Lock, Pat Holland, Graham Paddon, Alan Taylor, Trevor Brooking, Keith Robson (70' Billy Jennings). Manager: John Lyall.				
Reipas Lahti (FIN) Ref: Anthony Briguglio (MLT)	Upton Park, att: 24,131	First round, 2nd leg 01/10/75	W 3–0 (0–0)	Robson 59', Holland 88', Jennings 90'

> West Ham United: Mervyn Day, John McDowell, Frank Lampard Sr, Billy Bonds, Tommy Taylor, Kevin Lock, Alan Taylor (73' Billy Jennings), Graham Paddon, Keith Robson, Trevor Brooking, Pat Holland. Manager: John Lyall.
>
> Reipas Lahti: Harri Holli, Pekka Kosonen, Mikko Kautonen, Lauri Riutto, Markku Repo, Harri Toivanen (73' Seppo Nordman), Timo Kautonen, Ari Tupasela, Pertti Jantunen, Hannu Hämäläinen, Harri Lindholm. Trainer: Keijo Voutilainen.

West Ham were subsequently assigned to play Ararat Erevan (USSR)—a side that had defeated Anorthosis Famagusta 10–1 over the two legs of the first round. Their ground was situated close to the Turkish-Iranian border and the Caucasus Mountains, where Noah's Ark was said to have come to ground following the flood. The stoic Hammers fans that made the journey typically spent a few freezing days in Moscow before taking the 1,500-mile flight south to find themselves sweating in temperatures of around 75 °F.

West Ham had little previous experience of football in the USSR. Looking back on former encounters did not give much cause for optimism.

International *Voetbaltornoo* **Ghent, Belgium 1958**				
Torpedo Moscow (USSR)	Stadion Jules Otten	Final 03/05/1958	D 0–0	
West Ham United: Brian Rhodes, Joe Kirkup, Harry Cripps, Bobby Moore, Malcolm Pyke, John Smith, Harry Obeney, Derek Woodley, Andy Smilie, Vic Keeble, Tony Scott. Manager: Ted Fenton.				

Spartak Moscow (USSR)	Vienna, Austria	30/07/1959	L 5–1	Keeble
West Ham United: Noel Dwyer, John Bond, Noel Cantwell, Andy Malcolm, Ken Brown, John Smith, Mike Grice, Phil Woosnam, Vic Keeble, John Dick, Malcolm Musgrove				

The Irons had to start without Trevor Brooking, who had gone down with stomach problems. Pat Holland took the number-eleven shirt and played a fine game—as did John McDowell in defence. Alan Taylor put the visitors ahead after fifty-six minutes. However, the Soviets pulled level after Day had picked up a high ball. The West Ham goalkeeper was looking where to place the ball when, to his surprise, Nazar Petrosyan headed it out of his grasp and, following a bit of a scramble, the Armenian smacked the ball into the net. Day (with the rest of the team) looked for the foul to be called, but it was not. The German referee gave a goal that had even the locals laughing.

Justice was done at the Boleyn Ground. Continuing an ongoing experiment of playing Brooking in a more attacking role paid off. While he did not have anything to do with the goals, the threat of his presence was clearly effective. A spiralling drive from Graham Paddon's left foot was followed with Robson connecting with a cross from Alan Taylor. Petrosyan was on the mark again before 'Sparrow' (as Taylor was known by the West Ham fans) scored the final goal of the game. For all the visitors demands for offside, this put the game beyond the reach of the Irons' guests.

European Cup Winners' Cup 1975–76				
Ararat Erevan Ref: Hans-Joachim Weyland (FRG)	Razdan, Erevan, att: 70,000	Second round, 1st leg 22/10/1975	D 1–1	*Petrosian 68'* *Taylor 56',*
Ararat Erevan: Alyosha Abramian, Suren Martirosian, Armen Sarkisian, Norik Mesropian, Armen Azarian (70' Sergei Bondarenko), Samuel Petrosian, Sanasar Gevorkian, Arkadi Andreasian, Nazar Petrosian (76' Sergey Poghosyan), Eduard Markarov, Khoren Oganesian. Trainer: Viktor Maslov.				
West Ham United: Mervyn Day, John McDowell, Frank Lampard Sr, Billy Bonds, Tommy Taylor, Keith Coleman, Alan Taylor, Graham Paddon, Bobby Gould, Pat Holland, Keith Robson. Manager: John Lyall.				
Ararat Erevan Ref: Robert Helies (FRA)	Upton Park, att: 30,399	Second round, 2nd leg 05/11/1975	W 3–1 (W 4–2)	Paddon 16', Robson 27', Taylor 59' *Petrosian 48'*
West Ham United: Mervyn Day, John McDowell, Frank Lampard Sr, Billy Bonds, Tommy Taylor, Keith Coleman, Alan Taylor, Graham Paddon, Pat Holland, Trevor Brooking, Keith Robson. Manager: John Lyall.				
Ararat Erevan: Aleksei Abramian, Suren Martirosian, Armen Sarkisian, Norik Mesropian, Armen Azarian, Samuel Petrosian, Sanasar Gevorkian, Arkadi Andreasian, Khoren Oganesian, Eduard Markarov (70' Levon Ishtoian), Nazar Petrosian (70 Sergei Bondarenko). Trainer: Viktor Maslov.				

In the quarter-finals, Lyall's lads were up against FC Den Haag. They were a team of real quality; at that point in the competition they had accounted for Danish side Vejle BK (4–0) and RC Lens (6–3).

The first leg was played in the Netherlands, and by half-time Den Haag were leading 4–0. Two of their goals were highly disputable penalties after both Lock and McGiven were judged to have handled.

The fourth was completely incomprehensible. Rudi Glöckner, the East German referee who had officiated in the 1970 World Cup final, stopped the game after forty minutes when a bottle was thrown in the general direction of Mervyn Day. Lex Schoenmaker, a Den Haag player, went behind the goal to remonstrate with the fans. Glöckner restarted the game with a dropped ball on the centre circle. Graham Paddon stepped up for the Irons, but the referee waved him back, so Schoenmaker just took the ball, made for goal, and scored. Perhaps even more bizarrely than this was when Glöckner brought play to a halt and demanded that Kevin Lock pull his socks up.

John Lyall had been taken ill earlier in the day ('flu), so it was Ron Greenwood who took off Mick McGiven at half-time and sent Keith Coleman out for the second period. The visitors went on to score two second-half goals through Billy Jennings, which would prove decisive.

European Cup Winners' Cup 1975–76				
FC Den Haag (NED) Ref: Rudi Glöckner (DDR)	Zuiderparkstadion, Den Haag, att: 26,000	Quarter final, 1st leg 03/03/1976	L 4–2	*Mansveld 12',* *16' pen, 39' pen,* *Schoenmaker 44'* *Jennings 51', 59'*

FC Den Haag: Ton Thie, Leo de Caluwé, Aad Mansveld, Simon van Vliet, Joop Korevaar, Aad Kila, Dojčin Perazić, Rob Ouwehand, Lex Schoenmaker, Henk van Leeuwen, Leen Swanenburg. Trainer: Vujadin Boškov.
West Ham United: Mervyn Day, Michael McGiven (46 Keith Coleman), Kevin Lock, Tommy Taylor, Frank Lampard Sr, Graham Paddon, Alan Curbishley, Billy Bonds, Billy Jennings, Alan Taylor, Keith Robson. Manager: John Lyall.

There were 30,000 chanting, singing, and shouting fans to greet the Dutch when they came to Upton Park. The visitors wilted visibly. Despite being judged offside on eighteen occasions, the home side won 3–1. After Thie fumbled Brooking's shot, Taylor took maximum advantage. This was followed just three minutes later by the aggregate equaliser, Lampard Sr converting a curling Brooking pass.

West Ham went in front for the first time in the tie when Bonds scored from the spot after Tommy Taylor was brought down. The only goal of the second half came from Schoenmaker to once more bring the sides together, but it was West Ham that went through on the away-goals rule to face Eintracht Frankfurt in the semi-finals.

European Cup Winners' Cup 1975–76				
FC Den Haag (NED)	Upton Park,	Quarter final, 2nd leg	W 3–1 (W 5–5a)	Taylor 29', Lampard 32', Bonds 35' pen *Schoenmaker 59'*
Ref: Karoly Palotai (HUN)	att: 29,829	17/03/1976		
West Ham United: Mervyn Day, Keith Coleman, Tommy Taylor (65 Mick McGiven), Kevin Lock, Frank Lampard Sr, Billy Bonds, Trevor Brooking, Graham Paddon (46 Alan Curbishley), Alan Taylor, Billy Jennings, Keith Robson. Manager: John Lyall.				
FC Den Haag: Ton Thie, Rob Ouwehand, Aad Mansveld, Simon van Vliet, Joop Korevaar, Aad Kila (75 Martin Jol), Roger Albertsen (65 Leen Swanenburg), Dojčin Perazić, Hans Bres, Henk van Leeuwen, Lex Schoenmaker. Trainer: Vujadin Boškov.				

The Germans had claimed their place after beating Austrian side Sturm Graz (3–0) in the quarter-finals, having taken the scalp of Atlético Madrid (3–1) in the second round. Eintracht Frankfurt had opened their European campaign against the Irish side Coleraine, beating them 11–3 on aggregate.

Since their meeting with Borussia Dortmund in 1966, West Ham had played a plethora of games against German sides.

Pre-season tour of Germany 1966				
FC Kaiserslautern (FRG)	Stadion Betzenburg	06/08/1966	W 0–2	Sissons, Byrne
West Ham United: Jim Standen, John Charles, Jack Burkett, Eddie Bovington, Bobby Moore, Martin Peters, Peter Brabrook, Ronnie Boyce, Johnny Byrne, Geoff Hurst, Johnny Sissons. Manager: Ron Greenwood.				
Karlsruher SC (FRG)	Wildparkstadion	13/08/1966	D 2–2	Hurst, Peters

West Ham United: Jim Standen, John Charles, Jack Burkett, Eddie Bovington, Bobby Moore, Martin Peters, Peter Brabrook, Ronnie Boyce, Johnny Byrne, Geoff Hurst, Johnny Sissons

Pre-season tour of Germany 1967

Borussia Dortmund (FRG)	Rote Erde Stadium, att: 22,000	29/07/1967	L 4–1	Peters

West Ham United: Bobby Ferguson, Billy Bonds (Bill Kitchener), John Charles, Martin Peters, John Cushley, Bobby Moore (Bobby Howe), Peter Brabrook (Peter Bennett), Ronnie Boyce, Brian Dear, Geoff Hurst (Trevor Hartley), Johnny Sissons. Manager: Ron Greenwood.

Alemannia Aachen (FRG)	Stadion Tivoli, att: 15,000	02/08/1967	W 2–4	Peters, Bennett, Hurst, Sissons

West Ham United: Bobby Ferguson, Billy Bonds, Bill Kitchener, Martin Peters, John Cushley, Bobby Moore, Harry Redknapp, Ronnie Boyce, Peter Bennett, Geoff Hurst, Johnny Sissons. Manager: Ron Greenwood.

Auswahl Mittelrhein (FRG)	Frechen, att: 3,000	03/08/1967	D 3–3	Peters 2, Kitchener

West Ham United: Bobby Ferguson, Billy Bonds, Bill Kitchener, Martin Peters, John Cushley, Bobby Moore, Harry Redknapp, Bobby Howe, Peter Bennett, Geoff Hurst, Trevor Hartley. Manager: Ron Greenwood.

Borussian Rheine (FRG)	Rheine	05/08/1967	W 2–8	Peters, Hurst 2, Moore, Bennett 2, Boyce, Sissons

West Ham United: Bobby Ferguson, Billy Bonds, John Charles, Martin Peters, John Cushley, Bobby Moore, Harry Redknapp, Ronnie Boyce, Peter Bennett, Geoff Hurst , Johnny Sissons. Manager: Ron Greenwood.

Pre-season tour of Germany 1968

Cloppenburg (FRG)	Cloppenburg, att: 5,000	31/07/1968	W 1–8	Peters, Sissons 2, Dear 2, Brooking 2, Hurst

West Ham United: Bobby Ferguson, Billy Bonds (Paul Heffer), Bobby Howe (John Charles), Martin Peters, Alan Stephenson, Bobby Moore, Harry Redknapp, Ronnie Boyce (Trevor Brooking), Brian Dear, Geoff Hurst, Johnny Sissons. Manager: Ron Greenwood.

Hertha BSC (FRG)	Olympiastadion, Berlin, att: 18,000	03/08/1968	W 0–2	Harry Redknapp, Bobby Moore

West Ham United: Bobby Ferguson, Billy Bonds, Bobby Howe, Martin Peters, Alan Stephenson, Bobby Moore (Trevor Brooking), Harry Redknapp, Ronnie Boyce, Brian Dear, Geoff Hurst, Johnny Sissons. Manager: Ron Greenwood.

Tour of West Germany 27 July–2 August 1969

FC Cologne (FRG)	Hauptkampfbahn Stadion, att: 8,000	29/07/1969	L 4–1	o.g.

West Ham United: Bobby Ferguson (Peter Grotier), Billy Bonds, John Charles (Frank Lampard), Ronnie Boyce, Alan Stephenson, Bobby Moore, Harry Redknapp, Jimmy Lindsay (Bobby Howe), Geoff Hurst, Johnny Sissons, Martin Peters. Manager: Ron Greenwood.				
FC Cologne Karlsruhe (FRG)	Wildparkstadion, att: 9,000	01/08/1969	W 4-0	Bennett 2, Lindsay, Sissons
West Ham United: Peter Grotier, Bobby Howe, Frank Lampard Sr, Martin Peters (Geoff Hurst), Alan Stephenson, Bobby Moore, Harry Redknapp, Jimmy Lindsay, Peter Bennett, Trevor Brooking, Johnny Sissons. Manager: Ron Greenwood.				
Bayern Munich (FRG)	Grunwalder Stadion	02/08/1969	D 0–0	
West Ham United: Bobby Ferguson, Billy Bonds, John Charles, Martin Peters (Bobby Howe), Alan Stephenson, Bobby Moore, Harry Redknapp, Ronnie Boyce, Peter Bennett, Geoff Hurst, Johnny Sissons (Jimmy Lindsay). Manager: Ron Greenwood.				

Summer Tour USA 1971				
Rot Weiss Essen (FRG)	Kezsar Stadium, San Francisco, att: 5,787	09/06/1971	D 1–1	Bonds
West Ham United: Bobby Ferguson, John McDowell, Frank Lampard Sr, Billy Bonds, Tommy Taylor, Kevin Lock, Harry Redknapp, Ronnie Boyce, Geoff Hurst, Bryan Robson, Trevor Brooking. Manager: Ron Greenwood.				
Rot Weiss Essen (FRG)	Seattle High School Memorial Stadium	11/06/1971	2–2	Best, Hurst
West Ham United: Peter Grotier, John McDowell, Frank Lampard Sr, Bobby Howe, Tommy Taylor, Kevin Lock, Harry Redknapp, Ronnie Boyce, Geoff Hurst, Trevor Brooking, Bryan Robson. Manager: Ron Greenwood.				
Rot Weiss Essen (FRG)	Los Angeles Memorial Coliseum	03/06/1971	L 0–1	
West Ham United: Bobby Ferguson, John McDowell, Frank Lampard Sr, Billy Bonds, Tommy Taylor, Pat Holland, Johnny Aryis, Ronnie Boyce, Geoff Hurst, Bryan Robson, Trevor Brooking. Manager: Ron Greenwood.				

TSV 1860 Munich (FRG)	Olympiastadion, Munich, att: 10,000	17/10/1972	L 1-4	Brooking
West Ham United: Peter Grotier (Bobby Ferguson), John McDowell, Frank Lampard Sr, Billy Bonds, Tommy Taylor, Bobby Moore, Dudley Tyler (Johnny Ayris), Clyde Best, Pat Holland (Kevin Lock), Trevor Brooking, Bryan Robson				

The West Germans were the best side West Had had played in the tournament that season. Like many German teams, the Eintracht Frankfurt players could work equally well in defence or attack. They had a very good team, which included Bernd Hölzenbien, Bernd Nickel, and, for my money one of the most skilful German players ever, Jürgen Grabowski, a man with dazzling ball skills. Seeing him play was the thing I most looked forward to when Eintracht came to the Boleyn Ground in the second leg of the semi-final.

West Ham were 1–2 down from the first leg in Germany. That night, the Eintracht goalkeeper, Kunter (the comments of the travelling supporters were easy to imagine), a part-time dentist and their second-choice custodian, had no chance against a Graham Paddon rocket—he struck a ball as hard and cleanly as I have ever seen. This gave West Ham the vital away goal; a beautiful, 30-yard pile-driver of a shot.

It was raining, but when I got to Upton Park it was clear that the game was going to be a sell-out. As I joined the queue to get into the Boleyn Ground, I feared I would not make it. I ultimately got in, but inside the ground was tightest squeeze I could remember since nearly being crushed to death watching Tottenham get a 2–2 draw in 1970. The 42,322-strong crowd was as many as has ever been shoehorned into Upton Park.

This encounter was a *bravura* performance of football. Many supporters of my generation remember it as one of the best games ever played at Upton Park. Even though the pitch was a quagmire that only worsened as the rain pelted down for the duration of the game, the Hammers produced some polished moves. However, in real terms at half-time, with no goals scored the Irons had failed to make headway and were running out of time.

As the rain reached the proportions of a monsoon in the first part of the second half, attacking full-back Frank Lampard Sr found himself on the byline and smacked a cross that was gathered by Trevor Brooking on the near post. The immaculate Brooking looped an adroit header. Use of anything but feet was something of a rarity for the maestro, but the ball travelled across and above Kunter to put the teams level on aggregate. The seething, rain-drenched throng that was the crowd erupted into a single undulating, sloshing creature.

Around the halfway mark of the second half, Brooking slid a fine ball behind the visitor's defensive ranks. Keith Robson had seen this coming and was steaming goalward before Trevor let the ball go. The Geordie flank-man got to it but failed to control the ball. The opportunity for a classic goal passed.

However, Robson made amends when he retrieved the ball and checked back to glance at what was happening in front of him. Kunter's dive was more symbolic than hopeful as the option of a 25-yard curling shot Robson had chosen went straight into the top-corner of the German rigging to send West Ham in front for the first time in the tie.

All the Hammers had to do was hang-on for the twenty-something minutes left. How many times has that thought been had watching West Ham only for what follows to be a dog's dinner of exactly that? Well, that was not the case that evening in the spring of '76.

From a hastily taken throw-in inside the Hammers' half, the ball was touched to Tommy Taylor. The towering, blond centre-half loosed a first-time, 40-yard pass that Brooking collected with no apparent effort whatsoever—it seemed to come to him like a clutch of iron-fillings might to a magnet. He always seemed to play at something just above walking pace, but he was into the German box in but a moment. Trevor dummied a defender on his left foot, turned to face Kunter, and calmly placed a shallow, right-footed drive into the corner of the net to make it 3–0 on the night.

Long after the final whistle, a large proportion of the sodden fans were still chanting and celebrating in the rain that continued to fall. They had seen a display that was more about West Ham's ability than Frankfurt's failings.

The German consolation goal three minutes from time did nothing to foul the impression that we who were at Upton Park that night had seen one of the most complete performances a Hammers team had ever presented. Paddon and Bonds on the left had been faultless. On the right, Brooking had been at his awesome best. The ball moved swiftly on the slick surface, and this suited the home side.

Eddie Gray, one of the most cultured strikers ever to play for Leeds United who played in a style long associated with artistic Scottish frontmen, was known to the Elland Road fans as 'the last waltz'. It epitomised his approach. Brooking evoked the same sort of metaphor, but if anything more so—he often danced the ball into the goal or to the foot of a goalscorer. Kevin Keegan's reputation as an England player owes more than most to Brookings' capacity to do this.

As such, by the art and craft of Brooking and the graft and aggression of Robson, West Ham were on their way to their sixth major cup final.

European Cup Winners' Cup 1975–76				
Eintracht Frankfurt (FRG) Ref: Vladimir Rudnev (USSR)	Waldstadion, Frankfurt/Main, att: 50,000	Semi-final, 1st leg 31/03/1976	L 2–1	Neuberger 29', Kraus 47' Paddon 9'
Eintracht Frankfurt: Peter Kunter, Peter Reichel, Willi Neuberger, Gerd Simons, Klaus Beverungen, Karl-Heinz Korbel, Wolfgang Kraus (70' Roland Weidle), Jürgen Grabowski, Bernd Nickel, Bernd Holzenbein, Rudiger Wenzel. Trainer: Dietrich Weise.				
West Ham United: Mervyn Day, Keith Coleman, Tommy Taylor, Billy Bonds, Frank Lampard Sr, John McDowell, Pat Holland, Graham Paddon, Trevor Brooking, Billy Jennings, Keith Robson. Manager: John Lyall.				
Eintracht Frankfurt (FRG) Ref: Walter Hungerbiihler (SUI)	Upton Park, att: 39,202	Semi-final, second leg 14/4/76	W 3-1 (W 4–3)	Brooking 49', 77', Robson 68' Beverungen 88'
West Ham United: Mervyn Day, Keith Coleman, Tommy Taylor, Billy Bonds, Frank Lampard Sr, John McDowell, Graham Paddon, Trevor Brooking, Pat Holland, Billy Jennings, Keith Robson Manager: John Lyall.				
Eintracht Frankfurt: Peter Kunter, Peter Reichel, Willi Neuberger, Bernd Lorenz, Klaus Beverungen, Roland Weidle, Karl-Heinz Korbel, Jürgen Grabowski, Bernd Nickel, Bernd Holzenbein, Rudiger Wenzel. Trainer: Dietrich Weise.				

Other confrontations with German sides followed in subsequent seasons, including a couple of nostalgic encounters with TSV 1860.

Continental Tour 8–14 August 1984				
Blau-Weiss Lohne (FRG)	Stadion Zeitung	12/08/1984	W 0–4	Cottee 2, Goddard, Whitton
West Ham United: Tom McAlister, Ray Stewart, Steve Walford, Paul Allen, Alvin Martin, Tony Gale, Steve Whitton (Gregory Campbell), Tony Cottee (Bobby Barnes), Paul Goddard, Alan Dickens (Paul Hilton), Geoff Pike. Manager: John Lyall.				
SV Werder Bremen (FRG)	Weser Stadion, att: 9,500	14/08/1984	L 2–1	Whitton
West Ham United: Tom McAlister, Ray Stewart, Steve Walford, Paul Hilton, Alvin Martin, Tony Gale, Steve Whitton, Tony Cottee (Bobby Barnes), Paul Goddard, Alan Dickens, Geoff Pike				

TSV 1860 Munich (DEU)	Stadion an der Grunwalder Strabe	29/07/1995	L 4–3	Martin 2, Rieper
West Ham United: Ludo Mikloško, Tim Breacker, Keith Rowland, Marc Rieper, Alvin Martin, Danny Williamson, Ian Bishop, John Moncur, Stan Lazaridis, Tony Cottee, Marco Boogers. Playing subs: Matthew Rush, Simon Webster, Martin Allen, Matty Holmes				

TSV 1860 Munich (DEU)	Allianz Arena, Munich	40th anniversary match 27/7/05	D 1–1	Harewood
West Ham United: Roy Carroll, Tomáš Řepka, Paul Konchesky (Marcel Licka), Danny Gabbidon (Elliot Ward), Anton Ferdinand, Heyden Mullins (Luke Chadwick), Shaun Newton, Teddy Sherringham (Bobby Zamora), Nigel Reo-Coker (Christian Dailly), Marlon Harewood (Yossi Benayoun), Matthew Ethrington (Gavin Williams)				

Borussia Mönchengladbach (DEU)	Waldstadion, Ruhpolding	17/07/2010	W 0–2	Cole, McCarthy
West Ham United: Péter Kurucz (Marek Štěch), Julian Faubert (Fry), Danny Gabbidon (Manuel da Costa), James Tomkins (Jordan Spence), Hérita Ilunga (Fabio Daprela), Kieron Dyer (Radoslav Kovac), Mark Noble (Christian Montano), Thomas Hitzisperger (Alessandro Diamanti), Luís Boa Morte, Freddie Sears (Junior Stanislas), Carlton Cole (Benni McCarthy)				

Pre-season tour of Germany July 2012				
FC Rot-Weiss Erfurt (DEU)	Steigerwaldstadion, att: 6,750	25/07/2012	W 0–3	Ofosu-Ayeh o.g., Ricardo Vaz Tê 2
West Ham United: Stephen Henderson, Michel Lamey (Callum Driver), Joey O'Brien (Sam Baldock) (Ricardo Vaz Tê), Jordan Spence, Steve Potts, Bilel Mohsni, George Moncur, Robert Hall, Blair Turgott, Nicky Maynard (Matthew Taylor), Colin Kazim-Richards. Manager: Sam Allardyce.				
SG Dynamo Dresden (DEU)	Gluckgas Stadion, Desden	Summer of Champions 27/07/2012	L 3–0	
West Ham United: Jussi Jääskeläinen, Guy Demel, Joey O'Brien (Bilel Mohsni), Winstone Reid, George McCartney, Mark Noble, Gary O'Neil, Kevin Nolan (Nicky Maynard), Ricardo Vaz Tê, Matthew Taylor, Carlton Cole (Modibo Maïga). Manager: Sam Allardyce.				

FC Energie Cottbus (DEU)	Stadion der Freundschaft	29/07/2012	D 2–2	Kazim-Richards, Baldock

West Ham United: Stephen Henderson (Jussi Jääskeläinen), Joey O'Brien (Jordan Spence), Winstone Reid(Lamey), George McCartney, Dan Potts, Mark Noble (Bilel Mohsni), Gary O'Neil (George Moncur), Matthew Taylor (Colin Kazim-Richards), Nicky Maynard (Robert Hall), Modibo Maïga (Sam Baldock), Ricardo Vaz Tê (Blair Turgott). Manager: Sam Allardyce.

Tour of Germany 2013

FSV Mainz 05 (DEU)	Bruchwegstadion	29/07/2013	L 4–1	Cole

West Ham United: Jussi Jääskeläinen, Joey O'Brien (Guy Demel), Winstone Reid, James Tomkins, Dan Potts (Răzvan Raţ), Mark Noble, Jack Collison (Kevin Nolan), Sebastian Lletget (Mo Diamé), Ricardo Vaz Tê (Matthew Taylor), Modibo Maïga (Elliot Lee), Joe Cole (Ravel Morrison). Manager: Sam Allardyce.

Hamburger SV (DEU)	Stadion Flensburg	23/07/2013	W 1–3	Diarra, Tomkins, Morrison (pen)

West Ham United: Stephen Henderson, Guy Demel (Pelly Ruddock), James Collins (Winstone Reid), James Tomkins, Răzvan Raţ, Alou Diarra (Mark Noble), Mo Diamé (Danny Whitehead), Kevin Nolan, Ravel Morrison (Matthew Taylor), Modibo Maïga, Matt Jarvis. Manager: Sam Allardyce.

Eintracht Braunschweig (DEU)	Eintracht-Stadion	27/07/2013	W 0–3	Maïga 2, Diamé

West Ham United: Adrián, Joey O'Brien (Ravel Morrison), James Collins (James Tomkins), Winstone Reid (Pelly Ruddock), Răzvan Raţ (Guy Demel), Mark Noble, Jack Collison (Matt Jarvis), Mo Diamé (Kevin Nolan), Ricardo Vaz Tê (Elliot Lee), Modibo Maïga (Matthew Taylor), Joe Cole. Manager: Sam Allardyce.

Schalke 04 Cup 2014

Schalke 04 (DEU)	Veltins-Arena, Gelsenkirchen,	02/08/2014	D 0–0 (W 6–7 pens)	(Pens: Nolan, Collins, Vaz Tê, Lee, Poyet, O'Brien, Potts, Lletget)

West Ham United: Jussi Jääskeläinen, Joey O'Brien, James Tomkins (Winstone Reid 46'), James Collins, Dan Potts, Kevin Nolan (c), Cheikhou Kouyaté (Mo Diamé 54'), Diego Poyet, Matthias Fanimo (Sebastian Lletget 54'), Carlton Cole, Stewart Downing. Subs: Cresswell, Aaron Jarvis, Mauro Zárate, Ricardo Vaz Tê, Adrián, Josh Cullen, Elliot Lee, Mark Noble, Carl Jenkinson, Amos Nasha, Danny Whitehead, Reece Burke. Manager: Sam Allardyce.

Betway Cup 2015

Werder Bremen (DEU)	Upton Park, att: 9,919	02/08/2015	L 1–2	Sakho 19' *Ujah 20', 31'*

West Ham United: Adrián (Raphael Spiegel 46'), James Tomkins, Cheikhou Kouyaté (Modibo Maïga 63'), Mauro Zárate (Josh Cullen 63'), Carl Jenkinson (James Collins 46'), Diafra Sakho, Mark Noble (Morgan Amalfitano 63'), Angelo Ogbonna (Doneil Henry 63'), Dimitri Payet (Manuel Lanzini 46'), Reece Oxford (Diego Poyet 46'), Lewis Page (Kyle Knoyle 63'). Manager: Slaven Bilic.

Werder Bremen: Wiedwald, Lukimya, Vestergaard, Fritz, Kroos (Frode 63), Richard Garcia, Ujah, Bartels (Manneh 63'), Grillitsch,

I was able to make the 1975–76 final, spending a night in Amsterdam before making the trip to Brussels the following day.

Since the Cup Winners' Cup tie with La Gantoise in 1964, West Ham's experience of Belgium football had not been massive.

Östers Idrottsförening: Triangelturnering I Vaxjo 1972 (Triangular Tournament)				
Standard Liège (BEL)	Vaxjo	01/08/1972	D 1–1	Bonds
West Ham United: Bobby Ferguson, John McDowell, Frank Lampard Sr, Billy Bonds, Tommy Taylor, Bobby Moore, Dudley Tyler, Clyde Best, Coker, Trevor Brooking, Bryan Robson. Manager: Ron Greenwood.				

At the Heysel Stadium in Brussels, West Ham faced RSC Anderlecht of Belgium, a club with an impressive and proud history of European campaigns stretching back to the 1950s. Although the Hammers fans numbered about 10,000 and gave it all they had, the rest of the 58,000-strong crowd were mostly French-speaking Belgians; the stadium was a sea of the white-and-violet of Anderlecht.

The Belgians had probably experienced a slightly less demanding path to the final than West Ham. Romania's Rapid Bucharest had pushed them hard over the first tie— Anderlecht just doing enough 2–1. Borac Banja Luka (then a Yugoslav side) were less of a challenge (4–0), but the Welsh Cup winners, Wrexham, had given Anderlecht a fright at the Racecourse Ground, pushing the Brussels side hard in a 2–1 aggregate score. In the last four, the German side BSG Sachsenring Zwickau were brushed aside, 5–0.

West Ham had not won a game since beating Eintracht Frankfurt three weeks previously. Outside European competition, Lyall's men had not won a game for the best part of four months: sixteen matches without a victory. The Hammers had won only thirteen games during the league season and just two in both the domestic cups; everything had been focused on the Cup Winners' Cup. The club's league position reflected this: West Ham finished eighteenth.

The Hammers had won four, drawn two, and lost two (both away) in Europe. This was a decent-enough record, and the East Enders had scored eighteen goals and conceded eleven in an exciting European campaign.

RSC Anderlecht were a powerful team. Not only did they have the star of the classy Belgium national side up front (François van der Elst), but two of the Dutch 'total football' World Cup side: Arie Haan and the quicksilver Rob Rensenbrink.

Nevertheless, things started well for the Hammers considering that they were playing on their rivals own turf. Pat Holland put his side in front just before the half-hour mark. It was a good time to score, and a second major European trophy seemed almost secure. However, just before half-time (an even better time to score), the rare mistake by Frank Lampard Sr of a misjudged back pass to goalkeeper Mervyn Day gave Anderlecht the opportunity to take the advantage. Ressel swiped at the ball and laid on Rensenbrink to smash home the equaliser. Not only did Lampard all but set up the goal, he injured himself in the process. Lyall replaced him with Alan Taylor, a forward who had not been having a great season.

The substitution meant an entire reorganisation of the side. McDowell moved to full-back and Holland into midfield, thus drawing Paddon further behind the attack. Almost inevitably, soon after Lampard left the field and just a couple of minutes before the break, Rensenbrink put van der Elst through to score.

West Ham drew level with a Keith Robson header, via the post, from a typically artistic 'Brookingesque' concave cross sent in from the byline. However, fourteen minutes from time, the French referee gave an incomprehensible penalty after Holland had deprived Rensenbrink of the ball. At first, I thought that Robert Wurtz was confirming the corner—but no, he was pointing to the penalty spot. Rensenbrink completed the formalities.

West Ham had no option but to throw caution to the wind and hunt for a goal. With Lampard Sr gone, there were great gaping holes at the back. This situation was exploited by the free-running Anderlecht attack, and with just a couple of minutes of the game left, Rensenbrink found van der Elst with a long through-ball. The little winger darted round McDowell and Day before finishing the Irons off. It was a terrible ending. I was so empty.

European Cup Winners' Cup 1975–76				
RSC Anderlecht (BEL) Ref: Robert Charles Paul Wurtz (FRA)	Stade du Heysel, Brussels, att: 51,296	Final 05/05/1976	L 4–2	Rensenbrink 42', 73' (pen), van der Elst 48', 88' Holland 28', Robson 68'
West Ham United: Mervyn Day; Keith Coleman, Billy Bonds (c), Frank Lampard Sr (46' Alan Taylor), John McDowell, Graham Paddon, Trevor Brooking, Pat Holland, Billy Jennings, Keith Robson. Manager: John Lyall.				
RSC Anderlecht: Jan Ruiter, Michel Lomme, Hugo Broos, Gilbert Van Binst (c), Jean Thissen, Jean Dockx, Ludo Coeck (Franky Vercauteren 32'), François Van der Elst, Peter Ressel, Arie Haan, Rob Rensenbrink. Manager: Hans Croon.				

Rensenbrink was the top goalscorer in the European Cup Winners' Cup 1975–76, netting eight times. Bernd Holzenbein of Eintracht Frankfurt finished second with six goals, equal with Borac Banja Luka's Muhamed Ibrahimbegović.

West Ham have met RSC Anderlecht, as well as other Belgian sides, a couple of times since that fateful day. In 1977, Lyall brought van der Elst to Upton Park.

La Gantoise Tournament: Belgium 6-8 August 1982				
RSC Anderlecht (BEL)	Ghent	Semi-final 06/08/1982	W 0–1	Pike
West Ham United: Phil Parkes, Ray Stewart, Frank Lampard Sr, Billy Bonds, Alvin Martin, Alan Devonshire, François Van der Elst, Paul Goddard, Alex Clark, Paul Allen, Geoff Pike. Manager: John Lyall.				

Arminia Bielefeld Tournament 1983				
Thor Waterschei (BEL)	Bielefeld Alm Stadium	Third-place play-off 07/08/1983	D 1–1 (L 4–3 pens)	Goddard
West Ham United: Phil Parkes, Frank Lampard Sr, Paul Brush, Billy Bonds, Alvin Martin, Alan Devonshire, Steve Whitton, Paul Goddard (Tony Cottee), Dave Swindlehurst, Paul Allen, Geoff Pike. Manager: John Lyall.				

FC Groningen Tournament 8-10 August 1986				
KV Mechelen (BEL)	Oosterparkstadion, att: 2,800	Final play-off 10/08/1986	W 1–3	Cottee 2, o.g.
West Ham United: Phil Parkes, Ray Stewart, George Parris, Tony Gale, Paul Hilton, Alan Devonshire, Geoff Pike, Frank McAvennie, Alan Dickens, Tony Cottee, Neil Orr. Manager: John Lyall.				

Out Performance Display Cup 2004				
RSC Anderlecht (BEL)	Upton Park	31/07/2004	D 4-4 (L 4–5 pens)	Cohen, Melville, Sheringham, McAnuff
West Ham United: Stephen Bywater, Tomáš Řepka (Heyden Mullins), Rufus Brevett, Michael Carrick, Andy Melville (Anton Ferdinand), Christian Dailly, Serhiy Rebrov, Nigel Reo-Coker, (Adam Nowland), Marlon Harewood (Youssef Sofiane), Teddy Sheringham (Stuart Pearson), Chris Cohen (Jobi McAnuff). Manager: Alan Pardew.				

12

SCANDINAVIA

Perhaps the majority of games West Ham have played against European opposition have been with Scandinavian clubs. European tours were organised long before the Second World War, like the one to Scandinavia in 1927. Club Director Albert Charles (A. C.) Davis kept a record of the trip, just as he had done in 1924 and 1926.

Born in Shadwell around fifty-two years prior to the 1927 tour, Charles remained a director of the club until he passed away in East Ham in 1950. His brother, George, was also a director of the club. In 1926, Albert lived at 442 Green Street, which would one day become the boyhood home of David Gold, West Ham's current co-owner and chairman.

> Players: Ted Hufton, Jack Hebden, George Horler, Alf Earl, Albert Caldwell, Jim Barrett, Billy Moore, Jimmy Collins, Joe Eccles, Tommy Yews, Vic Watson, Joe Johnson, Jimmy Ruffell, Joe Loughlin, and George Robson
> Directors: William Frederick White, Frank Pratt, George Frederick Davis, Lazzeluer Johnson, James 'Jimmy' William Youngs Cearns, William Cearns, and Albert Davis, Manager Syd King
> Trainer: Charlie Paynter.

In their first game, played on a Friday, West Ham fielded a strong side.

Tour of Scandinavia 1927				
Combined Copenhagen XI (DEN) Ref: Wilhelm Dino Jorgensen	Copenhagen Stadium, att: 20,000	13/05/1927	W 1–5	Johnson, Watson 2, Yews 2
West Ham United: Ted Hufton, Jack Hebden, Stan Earl, Tom Yews, Jimmy Collins, Albert Cadwell, Joe Eccles, George Robson, Vic Watson, Joe Johnson, Jimmy Ruffell. Manager: Syd King.				

The weather had changed and the sun was shining for the 1.30 p.m. kick-off—the game was played at this time to enable the touring Hammers to go to the races at 4 p.m.

Following their first outing of the tour, West Ham met another Combined Copenhagen XI the following day—the Danes calling on not a single player from the first match. The Irons side was unchanged. The hosts were once more comfortably beaten. As in the initial game, the Danes produced just one goal in reply.

Tour of Scandinavia 1927				
Combined Copenhagen XI (DEN)	Copenhagen Stadium	14/ 05/ 1927	1–3	Eccles, Ruffell 2
West Ham United: Ted Hufton, Jack Hebden, Stan Earl, Tom Yews, Jimmy Collins, Albert Cadwell, Joe Eccles, George Robson, Vic Watson, Joe Johnson, Jimmy Ruffell. Manager: Syd King.				

The game was played in the presence of King Christian X. At half-time, he came on the pitch to chat with the players and match officials. He told Jack Hebden: 'You're a hefty fellow. I should not like to meet you on the left-wing'. Jack's reply was not recorded—probably luckily.

The game kicked off at 7 p.m. The Irons were due to meet the strongest Danish side they had faced thus far; it was pretty much the Danish national side (over the three matches, Copenhagen fielded thirty players). For the Hammers, Moore was brought in for Johnson, while Yews was dropped to make way for Barrett. Once more, the Irons were dominant.

Tour of Scandinavia 1927				
Combined Copenhagen XI (DEN)	Copenhagen Stadium, att: 15,000	16/05/1927	W 0–2	Robson, Watson
West Ham United: Ted Hufton, Jack Hebden, Stan Earl, Jim Barrett, Jimmy Collins, Albert Cadwell, Joe Eccles, George Robson, Vic Watson, Billy Moore, Jimmy Ruffell. Manager: Syd King.				

This part of the tour was the start of an enduring relationship between West Ham and Danish football.

West Ham United in the Netherlands, Denmark, and Sweden 1930				
Copenhagen (DEN)	Copenhagen	06/06/1930	D 3–3	Pollard, Wilkins 2
West Ham United: Ted Hufton, Stan Earl, Reg Wade, Jim Collins, Wally St Pier, George Parkin, Tom Yews, Les Wilkins, K. Barter, Walter Pollard, Stan Cribb. Manager: Syd King.				

AIK (SWE)	Upton Park	26/01/1934	W 6–1	Goulden, Morton, Watson 2, Barrett, Foremen

West Ham United: Herman Conway, Alf Chalkley, Albert Walker, Ted Fenton, Jim Barrett, Joe Cockroft, John Foreman, John Morton, Vic Watson, Len Goulden, Jimmy Ruffell

Club tour of of Denmark 21 May–3 June 1948

AGF Aarhus (DEN)	Aarhus	23/05/1948	L 6–1	Walker

West Ham United: Ernie Gregory, Ernie Devlin, Steve Forde, Norman Corbett, Dick Walker, Ron Cater, Eric Parsons, Almeric Hall, Bill Stephens, Don Wade, Ken Bainbridge. Manager: Charlie Paynter.

EFB Esbjerg (DEN)	Esbjerg	26/05/1948	W 1–2	Wade, Bainbridge

West Ham United: George Taylor, Ernie Devlin, Steve Forde, Norman Corbett, Dick Walker, Ron Cater, Eric Parsons, Almeric Hall, Bill Stephens, Don Wade, Ken Bainbridge. Manager: Charlie Paynter.

Randers Freja (DEN)	Randers	28/05/1948	W 0–4	Hall 2, Parsons, Stephens

West Ham United: Ernie Gregory, Jack Yeomanson, Steve Forde, Norman Corbett, Dick Walker, Ron Cater, Eric Parsons, Almeric Hall, Bill Stephens, Don Wade, Ken Bainbridge. Manager: Charlie Paynter.

Aalborg Pokal Turnering (DEN)	Aalborg	30/05/1948	W 2–5	Bainbridge, Wade, Hall 2, Woodgate

West Ham United: Ernie Gregory, Jack Yeomanson, Steve Forde, Norman Corbett, Dick Walker, Ron Cater, Terry Woodgate, Almeric Hall, Bill Stephens, Don Wade, Ken Bainbridge. Manager: Charlie Paynter.

JBU (Jydsk Boldspil-Union-Jutland Football Association) (DEN)	Jutland	01/06/1948	L 3–2	Hall, Wade

West Ham United: Ernie Gregory, Ernie Devlin, Steve Forde, Norman Corbett, Dick Walker, Ron Cater, Eric Parsons, Almeric Hall, Bill Stephens, Don Wade, Ken Bainbridge/ Manager: Charlie Paynter.

Tour of Scandinavia 1976

Combined XI Valerengen-Frigg (NOR)	Oslo	05/08/1976	W 1–3	Brooking, McDowell, Paddon

West Ham United: Bobby Ferguson, John McDowell, Keith Coleman, Pat Holland, Green, Billy Bonds, Billy Jennings, Graham Paddon, Tommy Taylor, Trevor Brooking, Keith Robson. Manager: John Lyall.

Brøndby IF (DEN)	Opvisningskamp	30/07/1997	L 2–1	Pedersen

West Ham United: Ludo Miklośko (Craig Forrest), Steve Potts, Michael Hughes, Marc Rieper, Rio Ferdinand, Tore Pedersen (trialist), Frank Lampard Jnr, Steve Lomas, Iain Dowie, Eyal Berkovic, Danny Williamson. Playing subs: David Terrier, Stan Lazaridis, Keith Rowland.

FC Copenhagen (DEN)	Parken Stadium, att: 8,907	18/07/2011	W 0–1	Sears

West Ham United: Rob Green (Ruud Boffin), Julian Faubert (Jordan Spence), Winstone Reid, James Tomkins, Hérita Ilunga, Jack Collison (Joey O'Brien), Scott Parker (Jordon Brown), Luís Boa Morte (Christian Montano), Mark Noble, Kevin Nolan (Freddie Sears), Frédéric Piquionne (Frank Nouble)

On 18 May 1927, the Irons made for Gothenburg and played their opening game of the Swedish part of the tour two days later.

Tour of Scandinavia 1927				
Gothenburg (SWE)	Gothenburg Stadium, att: 20,000	20/05/1927	W 3–4	Barrett 2, Ruffell, Yews

West Ham United: Ted Hufton, Jack Hebden, Stan Earl, Jimmy Collins, Jim Barrett, Albert Cadwell, Tom Yews, Billy Moore, Joe Loughlin, Joe Johnson, Jimmy Ruffell. Manager: Syd King.

Gothenburg would host games for the 1958 World Cup, and, in the late 1920s, were thought of by many as one of the best outfits in the European game. The previous year, Gothenburg had defeated Aston Villa 5–1 and 3–2, and Derby County 3–1. As such, the West Ham players understood that they faced tough opposition. The crowd were treated to an exciting encounter as the sides struggled for supremacy. As soon as one team scored, the other responded—the match proceeded 1–1, 2–2, and 3–3 before Jim Barrett settled matters a few minutes before the final whistle.

As with the Danish connection, Swedish clubs played a big part in West Ham's future.

Club tour of the Netherlands, Denmark, and Sweden 1930				
Gothenburg Alliance (SWE)	Gothenburg	05/06/1930	L 2–1	Morris

West Ham United: Bob Dixon, Stan Earl, Bill Cox, Jim Collins, Wally St Pier, George Parkin, Jim Wood, Tom Yews, Arthur Morris, Walter Pollard, Stan Cribb. Manager: Syd King.

Stockholm (SWE)	Stockholm	10/06/1930	L 4–0	

West Ham United: Bob Dixon, Bill Cox, Reg Wade, Jim Collins, Wally St Pier, George Parkin, Tommy Yews, Walter Pollard, K. Barter, Les Wilkins, Stan Cribb. Manager: Syd King.

Gothenburg Alliance (SWE)	Gothenburg	11/6/1930	L 1–2	Walter Pollard, Jimmy Ruffell

West Ham United: Ted Hufton, Stan Earl, Reg Wade, Jim Collins, Wally St Pier, Bill Cox, Tom Yews, Les Wilkins, Arthur Morris, Walter Pollard, Jimmy Ruffell. Manager: Syd King.

Helsingborg (SWE)	Helsingborg	13/06/1930	D 2–2	Cox, Morris

West Ham United: Ted Hufton, Stan Earl, Reg Wade, George Parkin, Bill Cox, Wally St Pier, Tom Yews, Walter Pollard, Arthur Morris, Stan Cribb, Jimmy Ruffell. Manager: Syd King.

Club tour of Sweden 1935

AIK (SWE)	Stockholm, att: 17,000	14/05/1935	W 4–5	Marshall, Morton 2, Fenton 2

West Ham United: Herman Conway, Alf Chalkley, Albert Walker, Jim Collins, Jim Barrett, Joe Cockroft, John Morton, Jim Mike Marshall, Ted Fenton, Len Goulden, Jimmy Ruffell. Manager: Charlie Paynter.

Norrkoping (SWE)	Norrkoping	17/05/1935	W 2–3	Marshall, Fenton, Morton

West Ham United: Herman Conway, Alf Chalkley, Albert Walker, Jim Collins, Jim Barrett, Joe Cockroft, John Foreman, Jim Mike Marshall, Ted Fenton, Len Goulden, John Morton. Manager: Charlie Paynter.

Stockholm Combined (SWE)	Stockholm	21/05/1935	W 0–1	Barrett (pen)

West Ham United: Herman Conway, Alf Chalkley, Albert Walker, Ted Fenton, Jim Barrett, Joe Cockroft, John Morton, Jim Mike Marshall, Dave Mangnall, Len Goulden, Jimmy Ruffell. Manager: Charlie Paynter.

Gothenburg (SWE)	Gothenburg	23/05/1935	W 1–4	Marshall, Fenton, Morton, Foreman

West Ham United: Herman Conway, Alf Chalkley, Albert Walker, Jim Collins, Jim Barrett, Joe Cockroft, John Foreman, Jim Mike Marshall, Ted Fenton, Len Goulden, John Morton. Manager: Charlie Paynter.

Malmö FF (SWE)	Upton Park	30/10/1961	W 4–0	Dick 2, Scott, Sealey

West Ham United: Lawrie Leslie, Joe Kirkup, John Bond, Bobby Moore, Ken Brown, Geoff Hurst, Tony Scott, Phil Woosnam, Alan Sealey, John Dick, Ian Crawford

Tour of Sweden 1972

Combined XI Stockholm (SWE)	Stockholms Olympiastadion, att: 4,000	27/07/1972	W 0–2	Coker, Robson

West Ham United: Bobby Ferguson, John McDowell, Frank Lampard Sr, Billy Bonds, Tommy Taylor, Bobby Moore, Dudley Tyler, Clyde Best, Ade Coker, Trevor Brooking, Bryan Robson (Pat Holland). Manager: Ron Greenwood.

Halmstadt Boldklubben (SWE)	Halmstadt	30/07/1972	W 3–5	Tyler 2, Brooking, Best, Coker

West Ham United: Bobby Ferguson, John McDowell, Frank Lampard Sr, Billy Bonds, Tommy Taylor, Bobby Moore, Dudley Tyler, Clyde Best, Ade Coker, Trevor Brooking, Bryan Robson. . Manager: Ron Greenwood.

***Östers Idrottsförening: Triangelturnering I Vaxjo* 1972 (Triangular Tournament)**

Östers IF (SWE)	Vaxjo	03/08/1972	W 0–2	Lampard, Robson

West Ham United: Bobby Ferguson, John McDowell, Frank Lampard Sr, Billy Bonds, Tommy Taylor, Bobby Moore, Dudley Tyler, Clyde Best, Ade Coker, Trevor Brooking, Bryan Robson. Manager: Ron Greenwood.

Tour of Scandinavia 1976				
Sandakerns SK (SWE)	Grubbe Vallen	29/07/1976	W 1–2	McDowell, Taylor
West Ham United: Mervyn Day, Keith Coleman, Frank Lampard Sr (Alan Curbishley), John McDowell, Bill Green (Kevin Lock), Tommy Taylor, Pat Holland, Graham Paddon, Alan Taylor, Trevor Brooking, Bryan Robson. Manager: John Lyall.				

Atvidabergs FF (SWE)	Kopparvallen	22/07/2003	W 2–5	Cole 2, Defoe 2, Sofiane
West Ham United: David James (Stephen Bywater), Anton Ferdinand, Tomáš Řepka, Christian Dailly, Johnny Byrne, Don Hutchison (Daryl McMahon), Robert Lee (David Noble), Joe Cole (Trent McClenahan), Richard Garcia, Frédéric Kanouté (Youssef Sofiane), Jermaine Defoe				

Djurgerdens IF (SWE)	Norrtalje Sport Centrum	24/07/2003	D 0–0	
West Ham United: David James, Anton Ferdinand, Tomáš Řepka, Christian Dailly, Rufus Brevett, Youssef Sofiane (Daryl McMahon), Robert Lee (David Noble), Joe Cole (Trent McClenahan) Richard Garcia (Shaun Byrne), Frédéric Kanouté, Jermaine Defoe				

Pre-season tour of Sweden 13–19 July 2004				
Umea (SWE)	Umea	13/07/2004	W 0–5	Zamora 3, Sofiane, Harewood
West Ham United: Jimmy Walker (Stephen Bywater), Anton Ferdinand, Christian Dailly, Tomáš Řepka, Rufus Brevett (Nigel Reo-Coker), Jobi McAnuff (Marlon Harewood), Michael Carrick (Steve Lomas), Adam Nowland, Chris Cohen, Bobby Zamora, Youssef Sofiane. Manager: Alan Pardew.				
GIF Sundsvall (SWE)	Solleftea	15/07/2004	W 1–3	Zamora 3, Harewood
West Ham United: Stephen Bywater, Heyden Mullins, Rufus Brevett (Chris Cohen), Steve Lomas, Andy Melville, Christian Dailly (Anton Ferdinand), Nigel Reo-Coker, Don Hutchison, Bobby Zamora (Jobi McAnuff), Marlon Harewood, Matthew Ethrington. Manager: Alan Pardew.				
FriskaViljor (SWE)	Ornsloldsvik	19/07/2004	W 1–3	Hutchison, Reo-Coker, Mullins
West Ham United: Jimmy Walker, Tomáš Řepka, Andy Melville, Anton Ferdinand, Chris Cohen, Youssef Sofiane (Jobi McAnuff), Michael Carrick (Matthew Ethrington), Nigel Reo-Coker (Heyden Mullins), Adam Nowland, Marlon Harewood, Don Hutchison. Manager: Alan Pardew.				

Pre-season tour of Sweden 14–19 July 2005				
Falkenbergs FF (SWE)	Falkenbergs	14/07/2005	W 1–3	Harewood 2, Zamora
West Ham United: Stephen Bywater, Danny Gabbidon, Paul Konchesky, Heyden Mullins (Shaun Newton), James Collins, Elliot Ward, Christian Dailly, Gavin Williams, Petr Mikolanda (Teddy Sheringham), Marlon Harewood (Bobby Zamora), Luke Chadwick (Carl Fletcher). Manager: Alan Pardew.				
FC Trollhattan (SWE)	Trollhattan	16/07/2005	W 0–3	Fletcher, Zamora, Sheringham

West Ham United: Stephen Bywater, Tomáš Řepka, Shaun Newton (Elliot Ward), Danny Gabbidon (James Collins), Anton Ferdinand, Luke Chadwick (Gavin Williams), Carl Fletcher, Nigel Reo-Coker, Teddy Sheringham (Christian Dailly), Bobby Zamora (Petr Mikolanda), Matthew Ethrington (Paul Konchesky). Manager: Alan Pardew.				
Vastra Frolunda IF (SWE)	Kungsbacka	19/07/2005	W 0–3	Mikolanda 2, o.g.
West Ham United: Roy Carroll, Tomáš Řepka, Paul Konchesky, Elliot Ward, Malky Mackay, Carl Fletcher, Christian Dailly, Gavin Williams, Luke Chadwick, Marlon Harewood, Teddy Sheringham. Playing subs: Bucek, Shaun Newton, Danny Gabbidon, Heyden Mullins, Ferdinand, James Collins, Petr Mikolanda. Manager: Alan Pardew.				

Pre-season tour of Sweden 20–25 July 2006				
FC Trollhattan (SWE)	Trollhattan	20/07/2006	W 0–2	Collins, Ashton
West Ham United: Stephen Bywater, Tyrone Mears (Tony Stokes), James Collins, Christian Dailly, Clive Clarke, Mark Noble, Heyden Mullins (Carl Fletcher), Lee Bowyer (Hogan Ephraim), Matthew Ethrington (Winstone Reid), Teddy Sheringham (Dean Ashton), Carlton Cole (Bobby Zamora). Manager: Alan Pardew.				
IFK Gothenburg (SWE)	Gothenburg	22/07/2006	L 2–1	Zamora
West Ham United: Walker, Carl Fletcher, James Collins (Tyrone Mears), Paul Konchesky (Tony Stokes), John Pantsil, Anton Ferdinand (Mark Noble), Heyden Mullins (Clive Clarke), Yossi Benayoun (Hogan Ephraim), Winstone Reid, Marlon Harewood (Teddy Sheringham), Bobby Zamora (Dean Ashton). Manager: Alan Pardew.				
Ljungskile (SWE)	Ljungskile	25/07/2006	W 1–3	Ashton, Benayoun, Zamora
West Ham United: Stephen Bywater, Tyrone Mears (Carl Fletcher), John Pantsil, Christian Dailly (James Collins), Clive Clarke (Paul Konchesky), Mark Noble (Hogan Ephraim), Heyden Mullins, (Tony Stokes), Lee Bowyer (Yossi Benayoun), Matthew Ethrington (Reid), Dean Ashton (Bobby Zamora), Carlton Cole (Marlon Harewood). Manager: Alan Pardew.				

West Ham played the final game of their tour against Oslo. With the King of Norway and Crown Prince Olaf in the crowd, the match kicked off at 1 p.m.

Tour of Scandinavia 1927				
Oslo (NOR)	Oslo, att: 20,000	22/05/1927	W 2–6	Watson, Moore, Ruffell 2, Johnson 2
West Ham United: Ted Hufton, Jack Hebden, Stan Earl, George Collins, Jim Barrett, Albert Cadwell, Tom Yews, Billy Moore, Vic Watson, Joe Johnson, Jimmy Ruffell. Manager: Syd King.				

As reflected in the result, the encounter was a bit of a stroll.

Although it took nearly half a century for West Ham to get back to Norway, between the 1970s and 1980s, West Ham sustained a convivial relationship of competition with Norwegian clubs, gaining many fans *en route*.

Stavanger (NOR)	Stavanger Stadion, att: 12,000	Norwegian Liberty Day Match 17/05/73	W 1–3	Robson 2, MacDougall

West Ham United: Bobby Ferguson, Dave Llewelyn (Ronnie Boyce), Frank Lampard Sr, Billy Bonds, Kevin Lock, John McDowell, Clyde Best, Johnny Ayris (Joe Durrell), Ted MacDougall, Trevor Brooking, Bryan Robson

Pre-season tour of Norway 1974

Viking (NOR)	Stavanger Stadion	25/07/1974	L 0–2	

West Ham United: Mervyn Day, Keith Coleman, Frank Lampard Sr, Pat Holland, Tommy Taylor, Mick McGiven, John McDowell (Kevin Lock), Graham Paddon, Bobby Gould (Johnny Ayris), Trevor Brooking, Clyde Best. Manager: Ron Greenwood.

Start (NOR)	Kristiansund	29/07/1974	W 0–5	Best 3, Gould, McDowell

West Ham United: Mervyn Day (Bobby Ferguson), Keith Coleman, Frank Lampard Sr, Billy Bonds, Tommy Taylor, Mick McGiven, John McDowell (Geoff Pike), Graham Paddon, Bobby Gould, Trevor Brooking, Clyde Best. Manager: Ron Greenwood.

Vard FC (NOR)	Haugesund	01/08/1974	W 0–1	McDowell

West Ham United: Mervyn Day, Keith Coleman, Frank Lampard Sr, Billy Bonds, Tommy Taylor, Mick McGiven, John McDowell, Graham Paddon, Bobby Gould, Trevor Brooking, Clyde Best (Johnny Ayris). Manager: Ron Greenwood.

Pre-Season tour of Norway 1975

Start (NOR)	[unknown]	30/07/1975	W 1–2	Jennings, McDowell

West Ham United: Mervyn Day, John McDowell, Frank Lampard Sr, Pat Holland, Tommy Taylor, Kevin Lock, Alan Taylor, Graham Paddon, Billy Jennings, Trevor Brooking, Bobby Gould. Manager: John Lyall.

Lillestrom Sportsklubb (NOR)	Arasen Stadion	31/07/1975	W 1–4	Paddon 2, Holland, Jennings

West Ham United: Mervyn Day, John McDowell, Frank Lampard Sr, Pat Holland, Tommy Taylor, Kevin Lock (Keith Coleman), Alan Taylor, Graham Paddon, Billy Jennings, Trevor Brooking, Bobby Gould. Manager: John Lyall.

Aalesunds FK (NOR)	Kramyra Stadion	05/08/1975	W 1–5	Gould 2, Paddon, Taylor, Taylor

West Ham United: Mervyn Day, John McDowell, Frank Lampard Sr, Pat Holland, Tommy Taylor, Kevin Lock, Alan Taylor, (Paul Brush), Graham Paddon, Billy Jennings (Keith Coleman), Trevor Brooking, Bobby Gould. Manager: John Lyall.

Os Idrettsplass (NOR)	Os	07/08/1975	W 1–2	Jennings 2

West Ham United: Mervyn Day, John McDowell, Frank Lampard Sr, Pat Holland, Tommy Taylor, Kevin Lock, Alan Taylor, Graham Paddon, Billy Jennings, Trevor Brooking, Bobby Gould. Manager: John Lyall.

Tour of Scandinavia 1976				
FK Bodo/Glimt (NOR)	Aspmyra Stadion	02/08/1976	D 1–1	Taylor
West Ham United: Bobby Ferguson, Keith Coleman, Kevin Lock (Mervyn Day), John McDowell, Bill Green, Tommy Taylor, Alan Taylor, Graham Paddon, Billy Jennings, Trevor Brooking, Keith Robson (Pat Holland). Manager: John Lyall.				
SK Brann (NOR)	Brann Stadion	04/08/1976	W 0–1	Robson
West Ham United: Mervyn Day, John McDowell, Keith Coleman, Pat Holland, Green, Billy Bonds, Billy Jennings, Graham Paddon, Tommy Taylor, Trevor Brooking, Keith Robson. Manager: John Lyall.				

Pre-season tour of Norway 1977				
SK Brann (NOR)	Brann Stadion	02/08/1977	W 2–3	Curbishley 2, Radford
West Ham United: Mervyn Day, John McDowell, Frank Lampard Sr, Alan Curbishley, Bill Green, Mick McGiven, Alan Taylor, Bryan Robson, John Radford, Trevor Brooking, Alan Devonshire (Anton Otulakowski). Manager: John Lyall.				
Moss (NOR)	Mellos Stadion	03/08/1977	W 1–4	Brooking, Curbishley, Otulakowski, Taylor
West Ham United: Mervyn Day, John McDowell (Paul Brush), Frank Lampard Sr, Alan Curbishley, Green, Mick McGiven, Alan Taylor, Bryan Robson B, John Radford, Trevor Brooking, Anton Otulakowski. Manager: John Lyall.				
Select XI (NOR)	Korsgard Stadion	05/08/1977	W 0–5	Robson 2, Brooking, Green, Radford
West Ham United: Mervyn Day, Frank Lampard Sr (John McDowell), Paul Brush, Alan Curbishley, Bill Green, Mick McGiven, Alan Taylor, Bryan Robson, John Radford, Trevor Brooking, Anton Otulakowski. Manager: John Lyall.				

Norway U-21	Tampere	05/08/1988	D 1–1 (W 3–4 pens)	Brady (Pens: Stewart, McQueen, Brady, Keen)
West Ham United: Tom McAlister, Ray Stewart, Tommy McQueen, Tony Gale, Alvin Martin, Mark Ward, Alan Dickens, Eamonn Dolon, Stuart Slater, Kevin Keen, Steve Potts				

Tour of Norway 25–30 July 1989				
Kiruna FF (NOR)	Lavangen Stadion	25/07/1989	D 1–1	Dicks
West Ham United: Allen McKnight, Steve Potts, Julien Dicks, Tony Gale, Alvin Martin, Gary Strodder, Mark Ward, Kevin Keen, Frank McAvennie, George Parris, Stuart Slater. Playing subs: Tommy McQueen, David Kelly, Eamonn Dolon. Manager: Lou Macari.				

Kirkenes IF (Norway Division 2 Select)	Sandnes Gressbane	27/07/1989	W 0–2	Ward, Martin
West Ham United: Phil Parkes, George Parris, Julien Dicks, Tony Gale, Alvin Martin, Simon Livett, Mark Ward, Kevin Keen, Frank McAvennie, Eamonn Dolon, Stuart Slater. Playing subs: Steve Potts, Gary Strooder, David Kelly, Eamonn Dolon. Manager: Lou Macari.				
Fauske Sprint (NOR)	Fauske Stadion	28/07/8199	W 0–7	Dolon 2, Ward, Strodder, Keen, McAvennie 2
West Ham United: Allen McKnight, Steve Potts, Tommy McQueen, Kevin Keen, Alvin Martin, Gary Strodder, Mark Ward, Eamonn Dolon. David Kelly, George Parris, Julien Dicks. Playing subs: Tony Gale, Simon Livett, Frank McAvennie, Stuart Slater. Manager: Lou Macari.				
Finnsnes Idrettslag (NOR)	Fauske Stadion	30/07/1989	W 0–8	McAvennie 2, Parris 2, Ward 2, Dicks, Martin
West Ham United: Phil Parkes (Allen McKnight), Steve Potts, Julien Dicks, Tony Gale, Alvin Martin, Gary Strodder, Mark Ward, Kevin Keen, Frank McAvennie, George Parris, Stuart Slater. Manager: Lou Macari.				

In 1927, the Hammers started their train journey back to East London at 6 p.m. The group had reached Copenhagen by 8.30 a.m. and stayed to watch the second game between Copenhagen and Middlesbrough—the Teesiders had been beaten 4–2 the previous Sunday. The match kicked off at 7 p.m., and Middlesbrough ran out 8–2 victors.

13

'FOOTBALL AT ITS BEST IS A GAME OF BEAUTY AND INTELLIGENCE.'
RON GREENWOOD

Victory over Arsenal at Wembley in 1980 sent West Ham on their third Cup Winners' Cup campaign. The Irons were drawn to meet the Spanish *Segunda División* club, Real Madrid Castilla, who were in reality Real Madrid Reserves. Since the victory over Real Zaragoza in the 1964–65 Cup Winners' Cup, West Ham had gained some of experience against Spanish opposition.

Real Madrid (ESP)	Astrodome, Huston, att: 33,351	19/04/1967	W 3–2	Hurst, Sissons

West Ham United: Jim Standen, John Charles (Denis Burnett), Jack Burkett (Bill Kitchener) (Colin Mackleworth), Bobby Moore, Eddie Bovington (Paul Heffer), Ronnie Boyce, Harry Redknapp, Peter Bennett, Geoff Hurst, Johnny Sissons, Peter Brabrook

Ciudad De Zaragoza: III Trofeo Internacional De Futbol				
Real Zaragoza (ESP)	Zaragoza	Third-place play-off 31/05/73	L 2–0	

West Ham United: Bobby Ferguson (Mervyn Day), Clive Charles, (Ronnie Boyce), Frank Lampard Sr, Billy Bonds, Dave Llewelyn, Bertie Lutton, Clyde Best, Dudley Tyler, Ted MacDougall (Ade Coker), Trevor Brooking, Bryan Robson. Manager: Ron Greenwood.

Prince Felipe Tournament 1976				
Racing de Santander (ESP)	Estadio El Sardinero	12/08/1976	W 2–3	Paddon 2, Ferguson

West Ham United: Mervyn Day, John McDowell (Mick McGiven), Keith Coleman, Pat Holland, Bill Green, Kevin Lock, Tommy Taylor, Graham Paddon, Billy Jennings (Bobby Ferguson), Trevor Brooking, Keith Robson. Manager: John Lyall.

IX *Trofeo* International Tournament 11–13 August 1977				
Real Mallorca (ESP)	Estadio Luis Sitjar	11/08/1977	W 0–4	Curbishley, Green, Radford, Taylor
West Ham United: Mervyn Day, John McDowell (Paul Brush), Frank Lampard Sr, Alan Curbishley, Bill Green, Mick McGiven (Kevin Lock), Alan Taylor, Bryan Robson, John Radford, Trevor Brooking, Alan Devonshire. Manager: John Lyall.				
Real Betis (ESP)	Estadio Luis Sitjar	13/08/1977	D 0–0 (L 6–5 pens)	
West Ham United: Mervyn Day, Paul Brush, Frank Lampard Sr, Alan Curbishley, Bill Green, Kevin Lock, Alan Taylor, Bryan Robson, John Radford (Anton Otulakowski), Trevor Brooking, Alan Devonshire. Manager: John Lyall.				

Preparations for the first leg of the tie with Castilla in Spain started out as a welcome distraction from the everyday of the football season. The 'Irons' travel club' advertised air transport for £112, or a coach trip for £80—both included accommodation.

The match was an exasperating one for the Irons. After Cross headed home the opening goal following Devonshire facilitating a curling Brooking centre to the far post, the visitors dominated the first part of the game. Four clear opportunities were squandered.

The Hammers clung to their slim advantage for more than an hour before a juddering dozen minutes did for West Ham. In their previous six games, West Ham had kept a completely clean sheet. In those twelve minutes, the Hammers conceded three.

European Cup Winners' Cup 1980–81				
RM Castilla (ESP) Ref: Alain Delmer (FRA)	Estadio Santiago Bernabeu, Madrid, att: 40,000	First round, 1st leg 17/09/1980	L 1–3	*Paco 64', Balin 72', Cidon 77'* Cross 17'
RM Castilla: Miguel Recio, Juan Antonio Felipe (Chendo 63'), José Antonio Salguero García, José Manuel Espinosa, Casimiro Torres, Ricardo Álvarez, José Sánchez Lorenzo, Miguel Bernal (c), Balín, Francisco Paco Machín, Valentín Cidón (Vicente Blanco 82'). Trainer: Juan José García Santos.				
West Ham United: Phil Parkes, Ray Stewart, Frank Lampard Sr, Billy Bonds, Alvin Martin, Alan Devonshire (Paul Brush 86'), Nicky Morgan (Bobby Barnes 73'), Paul Goddard, David Cross, Trevor Brooking, Geoff Pike. Manager: John Lyall.				

Although both Devonshire and Morgan were booked, the match was not remotely vicious. It seems the frustration infected the travelling West Ham fans; Spanish police ejected around fifty of them from the Santiago Bernabéu Stadium in the face of a sizable fracas. Frank Sait, a West Ham fan and carpenter who was only eighteen years-old, was killed as the ruckus continued outside the stadium after he was run-down by a bus.

The next day, the British newspapers had a field day with headlines like: 'Shame Night', 'Hammers Fans in Police Battle'; 'Hammers Europe Bid Turns Sour—3–1 Defeat as Fans Go on the Rampage'; and 'Havoc'. One prophetic script wrote: 'The ugly face of English football again emerged here in Madrid last night and could cost West Ham further involvement in the European Cup Winners' Cup.' Another hack told the world: 'West Ham's hopes of an all-conquering return to European football look a long way off following the sad events at Madrid's magnificent Bernabéu Stadium.' West Ham captain, Billy Bonds was quoted as saying: 'Deep down I wonder if one day UEFA will say: "That's it, we've had enough," and ban British clubs.'

John Lyall's reaction was given under the headline, '"These Crazy Fans"—Lyall':

> West Ham manager John Lyall, horrified by last night's events in Madrid, said: 'I wonder what the game is coming to. This sort of behaviour just lowers all the standards. All our efforts that went into this game now mean nothing. We took every precaution possible and then this happens. We will carry out an investigation and, if we are satisfied that some of our fans did these dreadful things, they will be punished. The incidents on the terraces certainly didn't help us, because they only incited the home crowd. We had a nightmare fifteen minutes during the second half. We gave away the second goal with a mistake that happens only once in a blue moon. To do it again for the third goal was unbelievable.'

Here, Lyall was referring to two horrendous back passes by Bonds and Pike, each had cost West Ham dearly. Lyall's piece continued:

> Skipper Billy Bonds, who had written an open letter to West Ham fans before they left England begging them to behave, said: 'Whatever we do, still some of them don't listen. The players were aware of what was going on but I can't offer that as an excuse. What can you do with people like this? We want support for West Ham, but not from fans like these.'

Trevor Brooking said: 'We don't know yet if those involved came with the official tour parties or not. That could be a key issue. West Ham supporters without match tickets were able to buy them from the Madrid club before the match.'

The Bernabéu was light years away from the Boleyn Ground. It held 100,000, and most West Ham fans did not even notice anything untoward was going on that night—there were around 40,000 people in the stadium and they looked a bit lost in all the space; perhaps all the room went to the heads of one or two of the Upton Park faithful.

Following the furore, UEFA was obliged to act. On 22 September, they declared that West Ham would be fined £7,750. On top of this, the club was instructed to play their two subsequent European home ties 300 km (187 miles) from London.

The following day, West Ham accepted an offer from Sunderland to play the second leg at Roker Park—although on 26 September, the Hammers appealed against UEFA's ruling. The appeal was upheld; the fine was dropped and West Ham would be allowed to play the second leg of the tie at Upton Park. However, it was stipulated that the match would take place behind 'closed doors', meaning that no spectators would be allowed into the Boleyn Ground for the game. This was clearly a punishment for the fans rather than the players who, after all, had done nothing wrong.

What came to be known as the 'ghost match' entered the mythology of the Hammers. A handful of club officials and administrative staff, players, and journalists made up the official attendance of 262. Surprisingly (or not), this stands as the club's lowest attendance for a competitive first-team game played at Upton Park.

The idea was mooted to broadcast the game live to cinemas locally and perhaps to another stadium, but UEFA refused They reiterated that the interpretation of 'behind closed doors' meant no fans were allowed to watch the game as it happened. Hans Bangerter, general secretary of UEFA, stated: 'I want to strongly warn West Ham against such a plan as it would lead to even more sanctions. West Ham may not obtain any financial benefit from the game.' This made it clear that not only closed-circuit television coverage but also highlights of any sort were disallowed. Bangerter continued: 'We want to get the message across to British fans that they cannot expect to misbehave in Europe and get away with it.'

This response was not unexpected. Shortly after the UEFA appeals board in Zürich, Brian Cearns (as leader of the West Ham delegation) had talked about the potential for some kind of live coverage: 'I think they might well regard this as an attempt to beat the ban.'

That said, Eddie Chapman (by that point in time the club's chief executive) had spent most of his weekend negotiating closed-circuit options and had reached a provisional agreement for coverage. He explained: 'We were trying to recoup some of the money we would lose.' The figure was estimated at the time to be around £40,000. Chapman elaborated: 'They won't allow us to make money from television either, so only three minutes of footage can be shown on the news.' Nevertheless, with West Ham appealing (via Chapman) to the fans to stay away, 'unless you want to get us into more trouble', the BBC and London Broadcasting Company were given the go-ahead to broadcast a live second-half commentary on the radio.

Prior to the game, John Lyall commented: 'It's going to be a strange experience, but I feel we have the right attitude. Since that game in Madrid, we've played three matches and won them all. So we shouldn't be short of confidence.'

At 7.30 p.m. on Wednesday 1 October 1980, the hooligans listened to the second leg on the radio before going out to smash up bus stops—as is presumably the wont of hoolgans. Geoff Pike pulled one back before the twenty-minute mark with a blinding 25-yard scorcher—Pat Holland having beaten a trio of defenders to trundle the ball back to the lad from Lower Clapton to rifle it home.

West Ham drew level over the two legs when David Cross got his head to a floater of a free kick taken by Brooking. Close to half-time, Cross provided the assist for Paul Goddard's first goal of the tournament.

Castilla came out for the second half gunning for the home side. In the fifty-sixth minute, captain Miguel Bernal scored what was arguably the best goal of the game from 30 yards, to bring the score on the night to 3–1, but 4–4 on aggregate. Both sides had one away goal, so the tie required half an hour of extra-time.

It was Nicky Morgan who started the move that led to Cross heading his second goal of the leg. He achieved his hat-trick with a minute left on the clock.

On the night: 5–1, and 6–4 overall—a tale of two cities; so much for the crucial role of the supporters. Perhaps when the Hammers are next punished by UEFA, the club will be ordered to play in front of a full stadium.

European Cup Winners' Cup 1980–81				
RM Castilla (ESP) Ref: Jan N. I. Keizer (NED)	Upton Park, att: 262 (behind closed doors) 01/10/1980	First round, 2nd leg	W 5-1 a.e.t. (W 6–4)	Pike 19', Cross 30',102',119', Goddard 39' *Bernal 56'*
West Ham United: Phil Parkes, Ray Stewart, Frank Lampard Sr, Billy Bonds, Alvin Martin, Alan Devonshire, Pat Holland (Paul Brush 106'), Paul Goddard (Nicky Morgan 91'), David Cross, Trevor Brooking, Geoff Pike. Manager: John Lyall				
RM Castilla: Miguel Recio, Chendo, José Antonio Salguero García, José Manuel Espinosa, Casimiro Torres, José Sánchez Lorenzo, Balín, Ricardo Álvarez, Francisco Paco Machín (Francisco Ramírez 106'), Miguel Bernal (c), Valentín Cidón (Vicente Blanco 46'). Trainer: Juan José García Santos.				

In fact, the 'crowd' on the night was larger than it should have been. UEFA had stipulated that only seventy representatives from each club—including players—should be allowed into Upton Park. However, the ruling had allowed for the attendance of journalists and officials from the FA, Spanish FA, UEFA, stadium staff, and the police.

Although the occasion was somewhat macabre, West Ham had done amazingly well to overcome the deficit they had carried from Spain to East London. Perhaps the visitors were more thrown than the home side by the eerie quiet. West Ham's goalkeeper, Phil Parkes, recalled being able to hear parts of the second-half commentary on a radio someone had brought to the terraces. What was striking was that, following the goal, the usual euphoric celebrations did not happen. After Cross had completed his hat-trick, there was so little noise that he felt obliged to check with the referee that he had in fact scored.

Nevertheless, there was a sense of defiance even in the practically deserted Boleyn Ground. As one newspaper reported: 'Strains of West Ham's famous 'Bubbles' song echoed around the deserted Upton Park last night as the final whistle heralded the club's European Cup Winners' Cup victory over the Spaniards of Castile.' The players, journalists, and club officials thus reminded the world that football is made by its supporters.

The game was played out in a convivial manner without out any suggestion of violent confrontation. No one was booked.

The next day, the press seemed totally intrigued by the game, slapping up headlines that yelled 'Blacked Out', 'Ghosts of Glory', and 'Cross Ghosts In'. One tabloid featured a view of the pitch with a police officer in the foreground. The caption read: 'LONELY! A policeman watches an empty terrace as West Ham and Castilla battle away.'

This said, Cross was called the 'Hammers' goal hero' under the banner: 'David's Extra-Time Double Lifts the Hammers to Silent Night of Euro Glory'. Brian Woolnough wrote in *The Sun*: 'Thousands of fans held their own bubbles party outside Upton Park last night the moment they heard David Cross had completed West Ham's magnificent European comeback.'

While fans were not permitted to watch the match, a restricted number of programmes were printed. They are relatively rare find today.

It would be twenty years before West Ham met another Spanish side; it was perhaps fitting that it was a team the Hammers had faced in their first European tour seventy years previously. The game, at long last, allowed the Spaniards to get some payback.

Julian Dicks benefit match				
Athletico Bilbao (ESP)	Upton Park	11/08/2000	L 1–2	Kitson
West Ham United: Shaka Hislop, Gary Charles (Dino Jorge), Nigel Winterburn, Steve Potts, Igor Štimac (Norman Mapeza), Javier Margas, Trevor Sinclair, Frédéric Kanouté (Jermaine Defoe), Davor Suker (Paul Kitson), Paolo Di Canio (Julien Dicks) (Michael Ferrante), Michael Carrick. Manager: Harry Redknapp.				

Since then, West Ham have pretty consistently pitted themselves against Spanish opposition.

Out Performance Display Cup				
Osasuna (ESP)	Upton Park	06/08/2005	D 1–1 (L 7–8 pens)	Ferdinand
West Ham United: Roy Carroll (Shaka Hislop), Tomáš Řepka, Paul Konchesky (Elliot Ward), Anton Ferdinand (James Collins), Danny Gabbidon, Nigel Reo-Coker (Mark Noble), Christian Dailly (Heyden Mullins), Yossi Benayoun, Matthew Ethrington (Gavin Williams), Marlon Harewood (Bobby Zamora), Teddy Sheringham (Shaun Newton). Manager: Alan Pardew.				

Bobby Moore Cup				
Villarreal (ESP)	Upton Park	09/08/2008	D 1–1	Cole
West Ham United: Rob Green, Lucus Neill, Matthew Upson, Calum Davenport, Ben Thatcher (Lee Bowyer), Valon Behrami, Mark Noble (Zavron Hines), Scott Parker, Matthew Ethrington (Winstone Reid), Carlton Cole (Freddie Sears), Dean Ashton (Julian Faubert). Manager: Kevin Keen.				

SBOBET Cup 2010				
Deportivo de la Coruña (ESP) Ref: K. Friend	Upton Park, att: 14,295	07/08/2010	D 0–0 (W 5–3 pens)	
West Ham United: Rob Green, Danny Gabbidon, James Tomkins, Scott Parker, Carlton Cole, Thomas Hitzisperger, Matthew Upon, Mark Noble, Julien Faubert, Hérita Ilunga, Alessandro Diamanti. Manager: Avram Grant.				

Real Zaragoza (ESP)	Upton Park	20/07/2011	W 2–0	Taylor, Sears
West Ham United: Rob Green, Joey O'Brien (Jordan Spence), J. Lloyd Samuel (Christian Montano), James Tomkins, Winstone Reid, Julian Faubert (Pablo Barerra), Matthew Taylor (Freddie Sears), Mark Noble (Junior Stanislas), Scott Parker (Carlton Cole), Kevin Nolan (Freddie Sears), Frédéric Piquionne (Frank Nouble)				

Ciutat De Barcelona Trophy—Memorial Fernando Lara (POR) 2013				
RCD Espanyol (ESP)	Estadi Cornella El-Prat	05/09/2013	W 0–1	Noble (pen)
West Ham United: Adrián, Guy Demel (Driver), James Tomkins, Pelly Ruddock, Matthew Taylor, Kevin Nolan (George Moncur), Mark Noble (Matthias Fanimo), Ravel Morrison, RicardoVaz Tê, Modibo Maïga (Elliot Lee), Matt Jarvis (Sebastian Lletget). Manager: Sam Allardyce.				

Absolute Sports Travel Cup				
Espanyol (ESP)	R Costings Abbey Stadium, Cambridge	20/07/2014	W 2–4	McCallum, Lee 2, Cullen
West Ham United: Tim Brown (Danny Boness 71'), Kyle Knoyle (Sam Westley 60'), Nathan Mavila (Lewis Page 60'), Emmanuel Onariase (Reece Burke 60'), Jamie Harney (Reece Oxford 60'), Moses Makasi (Josh Cullen 60'), Amos Nasha (Kieran Bywater 60'), Trialist (Sebastian Lletget 60'), Djair Parfitt-Williams (Kieran Sadlier 60'), Jerry Amoo (Jaanai Gordon 35'), (Blair Turgott 60'), (Alex Pike 74'), Paul McCallum (Elliot Lee 60'). Manager: Sam Allardyce.				

Schalke 04 Cup				
Málaga (ESP) Ref: Arne Aarnink	Veltins-Arena, Gelsenkirchen, Germany	03/08/2014	L 2–0	
West Ham United: Adrián, Carl Jenkinson (Amos Nasha 61'), Winstone Reid (Dan Potts 78'), Reece Burke, Aaron Cresswell, Mark Noble, Danny Whitehead, Mo Diamé (Josh Cullen 46), Jarvis, Ricardo Vaz Tê, Mauro Zárate. Subs not used: Jussi Jääskeläinen, Cheikhou Kouyaté, Sebastian Lletget, Stewart Downing, Elliot Lee, Diego Poyet, Matthias Fanimo. Manager: Sam Allardyce.				

Following the phantom victory, West Ham faced the Romanians of Politehnica Timişoara. This was their second European campaign, and they had put
Celtic out in the first round—Celtic had won the first leg in Glasgow 2–1, but
the second leg was notable for the preposterous decisions of its Greek referee,
Nikolaos Lagoyannis.

The game had been a 50,000 sell-out in the University town of Timişoara. Danny McGrain guessed right on the toss, but Lagoyannis allowed the home side to take centre and make choice of ends; Celtic were obliged to play into a strong wind. At the start of the game, loud music was piped through the stadium's sound system and, contrary to UEFA rules, allowed to continue throughout the game.

In the warm sunshine, just a dozen minutes after the 2 p.m. kick-off, Frank McGarvey was the subject of a waist-high tackle. Lagoyannis' response was to have a go at the Celtic man. Five minutes on, Roddie MacDonald challenged the Politechnica goalkeeper after Moise had fumbled the ball. The referee sent MacDonald off, along with Manea, the Poli Timişoara centre-half, who had pushed MacDonald. Neither action had looked much like a foul—certainly nothing that would constitute an offence requiring a dismissal.

The referee booked Peter Latchford (the Celtic custodian) prior to McGarvey shooting wide, missing a good opportunity to put his side in front.

Just after the hour, Alan Sneddon's hard drive brought a brilliant save from Moise. However, with nine minutes of the game left, Păltinişanu unmistakably obstructed Latchford as he went for a high ball. Roy Aitken called the foul as Păltinişanu recovered to fire the ball into the goal. It looked like final nail in the coffin when McGarvey got sent off for arguing with the referee, but after the match, John Clark, the former Celtic player, had a storming row with the match official and as a result received a two-year touchline ban from UEFA. At the after-match reception McGarvey was accused of assaulting Lagoyannis.

The upshot of all this was that Celtic were fined £6,000, while MacDonald was banned for two games (after appeal), and McGarvey for one match.

West Ham's first-leg game against Poli Timişoara was something of a stroll. The second leg of that tie in Romania, a bit like the Celtic game, was something of a humdinger. It was Culloden all over again, only with the Romanians in place of the Scottish.

Poli Timişoara boasted players good enough to make the Romanian national side—the team that had beaten England 2–1 in the World Cup Qualifying game in Bucharest shortly before the first-leg tie. On top of this, they had contributed to the Under-21 team that beat their English counterparts 4–0 the day before.

Celtic's Billy McNeil had handed John Lyall a dossier on the Romanians, which seemed to prove useful when a Billy Bonds' header found the net in London. A Stewart free kick in the twenty-fourth minute put Goddard on target. A couple of minutes later, following Visan pushing Goddard in the area, the typically powerful penalty from Stewart made it 3–0. Later, after Moise fouled Goddard, Stewart missed the chance of putting West Ham four up, but David Cross completed the rout with a goal seven minutes from time.

Surely this demonstrated just how poor the England set-up was. Who was in charge of the England team? The beloved Ron Greenwood, formally of the Boleyn Ground Parish.

Poli Timişoara, nicknamed the *Banat* ('grief') Boys or The Violets, appeared to believe they could rescue the situation on their own turf. They might have done so had Phil Parkes had not been on such excellent form.

Just as in the game with Celtic, the sound system bellowed out loud music throughout the match, seemingly the Romanian version of the Beatles' idiotic ditty, 'Yellow Submarine'.

However, it appeared that although they could not score goals, Poli Timişoara were determined to leave their mark on the West Ham players in a physical sense.

The responsibility for the only goal of the game must, ironically, be laid at the door of Parkes' lack of luck—a drive ricocheted off his arm. Anyway, this turned out to be irrelevant, and Poli Timişoara and their submarine were sunk. Down periscope!

This game was the first in twenty-eight Cup Winners' Cup outings that West Ham had failed to score.

European Cup Winners' Cup 1980–81				
Politehnica Timisoara (ROM) Ref: Heinz Fahnler (AUT)	Upton Park, att: 27,157	Second round, 1st leg 22/10/1980	W 4–0	Bonds 25', Goddard 27', Stewart 30' pen, Cross 83'
West Ham United: Phil Parkes, Ray Stewart, Billy Bonds, Alvin Martin, Frank Lampard; Pat Holland, Jimmy Neighbour, Alan Devonshire; Paul Goddard (Nicky Morgan 88'), David Cross, Geoffrey Pike. Manager: John Lyall.				
Politehnica Timisoara: Aurel Moise, Dumitru Nadu, Gheorghe Serbanoiu, Dan Păltinişanu, Aurel Şunda; Ion Dumitru, Emerich Dembrovschi (Titi Nicolae 69'), Gheorghe Cotec, Viorel Visan, Stelian Anghel, Leonida Nedelcu. Manager: Ion Ionescu				
Politehnica Timisoara (ROM) Ref: Riccardo Lattanzi (ITA)	1 Mat, Timisoara, att: 25,000	Second round, 2nd leg 5/11/80	L 1–0 (W 1–4)	Păltinişanu 54'
Politehnica Timisoara: Aurel Moise, Viorel Visan, Dan Păltinişanu, Gheorghe Serbanoiu, Nicolae Mircea Murar, Titi Nicolae (68' Ioan Palea), Emerich Dembrovschi (36' Aurel Şunda), Ion Dumitru, Stelian Anghel, Leonida Nedelcu, Gheorghe Cotec. Manager: Ion Ionescu.				
West Ham United: Phil Parkes, Ray Stewart (Paul Brush 32'), Frank Lampard Sr, Billy Bonds, Alvin Martin, Paul Allen, Pat Holland, Paul Goddard, Jimmy Neighbour (Trevor Brooking 63'), David Cross, Geoff Pike. Manager: John Lyall.				

Things were going well for West Ham. Good domestic form placed them at the top of the league and they had the quarter-finals of the European Cup Winners' Cup waiting. Then, they lost to Luton—those mighty legends of world football.

The quarter-finals of the Cup Winners' Cup paired West Ham with Dinamo Tbilisi. Prior to the match, John Lyall had declared they were the best side left in the competition. They had beaten Liverpool 4–2 in the European Cup the previous season and were champions of the Soviet Union. At that point in the tournament, they had put the Greeks of Kastoria FC to the sword (0–2) and then thrashed Waterford FC (0–5).

At Upton Park, it was clear from the first quarter-of-an-hour that Dinamo Tbilisi were masterful technicians; very cool on the ball, they kept it simple off the ball. The game was a masterclass of clever, supple, and penetrating football by Tbilisi. The visitors showcased some of the finest counter-attacking football many at the Boleyn Ground that evening had seen. The Hammers seemed to spend a lot of their time pursuing elusive white phantoms, all the while doing what they could to keep the scoreline from reaching embarrassing propotions. The veritable rampage began with a glorious goal.

Following a series of swift, single-touch passes, the central defender, Aleksandr Chivadze, gathered a knockdown 10 yards inside the Tbilisi half and charged forward into the heart of West Ham's territory. From 30 yards, the man who would be capped forty-six times for the USSR delivered a dipping shot that glided over the head of the watching Phil Parkes.

The Georgian had staggeringly good ball control—as good as any creative player I had seen in the British game. I had become accustomed to the plodding British centre-half; the type that would batter, bombard, and wallop balls around the pitch, into the crowd, or out of the stadium—the likes of Jack Charlton. Taking in this physically inconspicuous sweeper, stroking and elegantly manipulating the ball to perform his will, taunting opponents into making mistakes and misjudgements, was an eye-opener.

The whole team were cast in the same mould. Ramaz Shengelia was strong, with an almost telekinetic ability, and an uncanny consciousness of where his playing colleagues were or were likely to be. Vladimir Gutsayev was gifted with what might be called 'goaldar'. Vitali Daraselia had a lively, scurrying manner that allowed him to identify improbable compartments of space on the field. David Kipiani, with rapid, smart feet, was so proficient at unbalancing those who stood in his way. They had magic names, like mythological warlocks.

The match became a stage for teamplay of the highest technical level, exemplifying what exceptional coaching, player ability, and human will can accomplish. Tbilisi were a side made up of focused athletes, confident in their touch, adroit at feints and flicks, clever in terms of developing and generating passing angles.

The Soviets were fast, but at the same time had that uncommon control of the multifaceted dynamics that establish the rhythm of a match. They grasped the concept that their opponents would be more perplexed by a quick alteration of cadence than commitment to maintaining a constant, absolute pace. They were resolved, as one, to manipulate the tempo of games. When expedient or necessary, they could slow the game down to a walk—prior to blasting away at a lick. They confounded, surprised, and quickly overwhelmed the other team, who would find themselves powerless to adjust immediately to the faster game forced upon them.

West Ham could do not very much more than roam around the field trying to understand why they felt so stunned and disabled. All they could do was hope for the luck needed to interrupt the intricate passing shapes Dinamo Tbilisi created almost instinctively. The Hammers found it almost impossible to keep up with the movement of the Soviets across the pitch.

With just over half an hour gone, Chivadze and Vladimir Gutsaev had put the visitors two up. David Cross, whose name was more like a hot bun than a warlock, got his sixth goal of the competition about five minutes from the hour—only for Shengalia to bang in two and make it 1–4 on the night. The crowd of 35,000 East Enders applauded the Georgians off the pitch—the best team that I had ever seen at Upton Park. It was an honour to watch them.

I went to Georgia for the second leg. Timișoara and back had taken thirty-five hours—a mere jaunt compared to Tbilisi. The city was not far from the Iranian border via a snowy, minus 16 °C Moscow. The total trip distance was 4,000 miles, but it was worth it to be in the fantastic, bleakly splendid, 80,000 all-seater Lenin Dinamo Stadium—a completely different experience to the Bernabeu.

West Ham played intelligently, holding on to the ball in the search for breaks as the Soviets came forward, but it was no match for what I had seen at the Boleyn Ground. Stuart Pearson, who was brought on in the sixty-fifth minute, scored the only goal of the game in front of about 2,000 West Ham supporters and 78,000 others. It was a very tasty volley from a right-wing centre by Cross.

The rather soulless victory made West Ham only the third side to win in the Lenin Dinamo Stadium in six years of European competition. Incidentally, Ray Houghton was one of the unused subs for the away leg against Tbilisi. He did not get on the pitch that evening, although later in Ray's career he would enjoy European competition with the mighty red machine known as Liverpool.

European Cup Winners' Cup 1980–81				
Dinamo Tbilisi (USSR) Ref: Antonio Jose da Silva Garrido (POR)	Upton Park, att: 34,95	Quarter-final, 1st leg 04/03/80	L 1–4	Cross 54', *Chivadze 24', Gutsaev 31', Schengeliya 55', 67'*
West Ham United: Phil Parkes, Ray Stewart, Frank Lampard Sr, Billy Bonds, Alvin Martin, Alan Devonshire (Paul Allen 46'), Jimmy Neighbour, Paul Goddard, David Cross, Trevor Brooking, Geoff Pike. Manager: John Lyall.				
Dinamo Tbilisi: Otar Gabeliya, Nodar Khizanishvili, Aleksandr Chivadze, Shota Khinchagashvili, Georgi Tavadze, Vitali Daraselia, Zaur Svanadze, Tengiz Sulakvelidze, Vladimir Gutsaev, David Kipiani, Ramaz Schengeliya. Trainer: Nodari Akhalkatsi.				
Dinamo Tbilisi (USSR) Ref: Walter Eschweiler (FRG)	Tbilisi, att: 80,000	Quarter-final, 2nd leg 18/03/1981	W 0–1 (L 2–4)	Pearson 87'
Dinamo Tbilisi: Otar Gabeliya, Nodar Khizanishvili, Aleksandr Chivadze, Shota Khinchagashvili, Georgi Tavadze, Georgi Chilaia (David Mudzhiri 77'), Zaur Svanadze, Tengiz Sulakvelidze, Vladimir Gutsaev, David Kipiani, Ramaz Schengeliya. Trainer: Nodari Akhalkatsi.				

West Ham United: Phil Parkes, Ray Stewart, Frank Lampard Sr, Billy Bonds, Alvin Martin, Paul Brush, Jimmy Neighbour, Paul Goddard (Stuart Pearson 65'), David Cross, Trevor Brooking, Geoff Pike. Manager: John Lyall.

As the archetypal West Ham fan, I decided to become a temporary supporter of Tbilisi, and went to Düsseldorf with about a dozen other 'resting' Irons fans to see them win the Cup against FC Carl Zeiss Jena. We were well at home. With only 9,000 (officially 4,750) in the stadium, it was like playing Castilla all over again, this time with (to the tune of the Sandpipers' old number 'Guantanamera'):

> *There's only one Sydney Puddefoot*
> *One Syd-ney Puuud-defoot,*
> *There's only one Sydney Puddefoot...*

At half-time, it was 'Bubbles'. We managed to teach about forty ex-pat Tbilisi supporters something like the words: 'Eyesfur-heffas blo-isk bubills, pity bubills isk de aar.'

This came with free coaching in the 'Hokey Cokey': 'U doo da oky cockney han uoo ter awn, han daz vot eats halls abot!'

They took it very seriously. I am sure they saw it as some mad cockney ritual to summon up the spirits of the ancestors or something. A potential gold medal team for the welterweight 'Knees-Up-Muvva-Brown' Olympiad, we thought; cultural exchange and all that.

CONCLUSION

West Ham have been campaigning in European football for not far off a century now. All-in-all, the club has a record to be proud of. The Hammers are, of course, not Manchester United or Liverpool, and I have not the slightest wish that they might be—the abomination known as a 'cockney red' notwithstanding. However, as I am about to send the manuscript of this book to the publisher (toward the conclusion of the 2015-16 season), the Hammers look like they might, once more, have played their way into major continental competition.

At points, some have allowed themselves to contemplate a first sortie into the Champions League. Fanciful? Perhaps, but we've beaten Liverpool three times this season (a Premiership double and knocked them out of the FA Cup at Upton Park) so there were some grounds for optimism.

The last time the Irons won at Anfield, in September 1963, Hurst and Peters had scored in the 1–2 result. 'She Loves You' by the Beatles had just knocked 'Bad to Me' by Billy J. Kramer and the Dakotas from the top of the singles charts. The Dakotas were not (as their moniker might imply) part of that branch of the Sioux nation but a Manchester band, while Billy (seventy-three years old at the time of writing and still performing) was from Bootle. Also that September, Christine Keeler was arrested for perjury in her part in the Profumo affair, and the Sindy fashion doll was first marketed by Pedigree. Vauxhall launched the new Viva—yours straight from the production line for under £500; a new Viva will cost you well over £8,000 today.

Things do change. Time alters everything. But what draws people to the game endures.

Soon, we will no longer gather that the Boleyn Ground, having being exalted to the heady heights of the London Stadium (formerly the Olympic Stadium) in Stratford, but the sentiment, expectation, disappointment and hope will not be touched by that, nor the years that have rolled by since those '60s days at Anfield, Wembley, or any of the many wells of football West Ham visited in those shimmering times. The likes of Mark Noble, a successful Hammer born in the 'manor', are not as thick on the ground as they once were, but the shirt is still claret and blue, the crossed hammers remain, and bubbles continue to fly so high.

Those days, however, do give way to these days. In the tale of days, these are ours. We will make the future history of the inexplicable, mercurial, fickle, and inimitable

Irons, for when all is set aside the Boleyn Ground; the London Stadium; the players, the owners; even we, the fans, will abide. We have always been and will always be there. We will not 'fade and die', even though fortune might 'always be hiding'.

So, Europe awaits next season, or some season, and the romantic escapade will be rekindled. New games will be played, different clubs encountered, and fresh heroes will arise from the fray. One day, our Women's side will sally forth for the first time in a major European tournament, which will be glorious, but the feelings for them will hardly differ from those we might have for any team in 'our' shirt.

Such adventures have shown me there is a world beyond my world. These other worlds, I now realise, are part of my world—and also that my world belongs to others. Visiting other cultures and places firstly reminds us of the commonality of humanity. It helps us look into our own identity—what it is to be 'us'. 'Over there' is a cultural mirror of 'over here'. While you might have a different hat to me, or a beard that I do not have, or I might not eat something you eat—how can we generate hate or go to war over such trifles? In Jonathan Swift's *Gulliver's Travels*, the traveller's encounter with the Lilliputians commentates on such insanity: 'Difference in opinions has cost many millions of lives; for instance, whether flesh be bread, or bread be flesh; whether the juice of a certain berry be blood or wine.'

We all need drink. We all need to be fed. We all need to be warm, rested, touched, and—if we are lucky—loved. Without such necessities, no flag, national identity, beard, trinket, repeated incantation, or hat, will save us.

Where do we find the tiny necessities of our existence—the everyday solidarity of 'we-ness'—if not in our shared identity with others? Wherever I have gone in the world following my team, I have found fellow pilgrims—folk not like me who are, in fact, just like me.

I have talked of football with locals during the dark days of an Icelandic winter and the sunlit nights of the Antarctic. I have chatted about a young man's family fidelity for Juventus in Malta, and, in the mid-1990s, to a shop-assistant in China about David Beckham. This same young man asked me in broken English; 'Where you from?' I said 'West Ham.' He raised a finger and replied: 'Ah, Bobby Moore!'

In my late twenties, I found myself trekking on the edge of the Namibian desert wearing a very old, battered West Ham shirt. I had not seen anyone for a day or so, but at one point, far in the distance I saw a dot. This grew gradually into a blob and ultimately a person. As we walked towards one another, eventually I saw this was a man about my age—and he was wearing a red Leyton Orient shirt! As we passed one another, we exchanged smiles and nods. I turned once or twice to watch him fade into the landscape. No words were necessary.

Football joins us. In it we can be one—be it a 'Gooner' or a 'Spud', a 'Ger' or a 'Bhoy', an 'O' or 'Magpie', an 'Eagle of Lisbon' or even a 'Lion'. Of course, on a match day I am somewhere deep down still that boy who once sang in the same defiance and solidarity of all the other lonely lads on West Ham's North Bank: 'We're the boys in claret and blue, who the fuckin' hell are you?' I have also stood in tears at Celtic Park tears singing 'The Fields of Athenry'. I had much the same reaction listening to '*Nkosi Sikelel' iAfrika*' at Ellis Park, Johannesburg. Emotion is hard not to share when it is generously offered. The hope for and the extended hand of comradery is something we humans all naturally reach out for.

For me—to quote the fabled and profound words of that cockney anthem that has seen East Londoners through malnutrition, exploitation, war, and oppression—'that's what it's all about!'

EPILOGUE: AND INTO THE FUTURE

The 2015–16 season was West Ham's fourth in the Premier League since their promotion in the 2011–12 season. It was the Hammers' twentieth Premier League campaign and the last to be fought out playing home games at the Boleyn Ground.

West Ham finished the season in seventh place with sixty-two points—a record number for the team in the Premier League. This was enough for the club to qualify for the 2016–17 UEFA Europa League, given Manchester United's record-equalling twelfth FA cup final victory and the fact they had already qualified for the Europa League by finishing fifth in the Premier League. The Europa League place reserved for the FA Cup winners was passed to the Hammers; Slaven Bilic's side joined United and Southampton as England's representatives in the competition.

West Ham entered the competition in the third qualifying round. After playing a couple of games in the USA against American clubs, the Irons started a three-match schedule in Austria.

The first game pitted the East Londoners against FC Slovácko, a side that had finished eighth in the Czech First League.

FC Slovácko (CZE)	Stadion Rohrbach	19/07/2016	D 2–2	Civić 85', 89' Noble 37', Fletcher 52'
West Ham United: Darren Randolph (Raphael Spiegel 71'), Samme Byram, Reece Burke, Declan Rice (Antonio Martinez 74'), Lewis Page (Michail Antonio 46'), Mark Noble (Cheikhou Kouyaté 46'), Sofiane Feghouli (Gökhan Töre 46'), Joshe Cullen, Pedro Obiang (Marcus Browne 69'), Martin Samuelsen (Domingos Quina 46'), Enner Valencia (Ashley Fletcher 46'). Substitutes not used: Adrián, Winsone Reid, Aaron Cresswell, Andy Carroll, Michail Antonio, Håvard Nordtveit, Moses Makasi.				
FC Slovácko: Meca, Simko (Omyla 46'), Kosut (Tok 46'), Rada, Reinberk; Sutiulikoski, Danicek; Biolek (Civic 46'), Mavlik, Kerbr; Divis: coach: Stanislav Levý Subs not used: Mlupik, Koro, Ravic, Sadilek, Brecka				

The next day West Ham met Rubin Kazan, a team that had managed tenth spot in the Russian Premier League, and seemingly felt the pace.

Rubin Kazan (RUS)	Arena Krottendorf	20/07/2016	L 3–0	Dević 24', Lestienne 45', Karadeniz 67'
West Ham United: Adrián, Antonio (Cullen 64'), Nordtveit, Burke (Rice 33'), Cresswell (Page 74'), Kouyaté (Browne 74'), Feghouli (Samuelsen 80'), Quina (Obiang 46'), Noble, Tore (Fletcher 74'), Valencia (Martinez 80').				

However, the the tourists finished off their Austrian expedition with a victory over Karlsruher SC from the second tier of German football.

Karlsruher SC (DEU)	Franz Fekete Stadium, Kapfenberg	23/07/2016	W 0–3	Carroll 9', Feghouli 17', Fletcher 80'
West Ham United: Darren Randolph, Winstone Reid, Aaron Cresswell, Håvard Nordtveit, Sofiane Feghouli, Cheikhou Kouyaté, Andy Carroll, Enner Valencia, Mark Noble, Gökhan Töre, Michail Antonio				

West Ham hosted Juventus at their new home for the Betway Cup on 7 August. A couple of goals from Andy Carroll either side of the half-time break cancelled out the first half efforts of Argentinian international Paulo Dybala and Croasian Mario Mandžukić (who, at the time of publication, has played for his country seventy-four on occasions). However, it was *Le Zebre* (The Zebras) that took the victory with Simone Zaza's net. The sixteen-times capped lad from Policoro struck five minutes from time.

Betway Cup 2016				
Juventus (ITA) Ref: Anthony Taylor	London Stadium, att: 53,914	07/08/2016	L 2–3	Carroll 34', 52' *Dybala 18', Mandžukić 21', Zaza 85'*
West Ham United: Adrián; Michail Antonio (Dimitri Payet 74'), Angelo Ogbonna (Reece Oxford 45'), Winstone Reid (James Collins 45'), Sam Byram (Page 85'); Håvard Nordtveit, Mark Noble (Domingos Quina 60'), Josh Cullen (Browne 82'), Sofiane Feghouli (Reece Burke 45'), Andy Carroll (Ashley Fletcher 54'), Enner Valencia (Martin Samuelsen 74'). Subs not used: Raphael Spiegel. Manager: Slaven Bilic.				
Juventus: Juventus: Buffon (Neto 45'), Alves (Untersee 59'), Benatia (Barzagli 58'), Rugani (Chiellini 58'), Alex Sandro (Kastanos 86'); Pereyra (Zaza 69'), Lemina (Marrone 78'), Pjanić (Macek 78'), Asamoah (Hernanes 68'); Dybala (Pjaca 58'), Mandžukić (Higuaín 45'). Subs not used: Loria. Manager: Massimiliano Allegri.				

However, before the visit of the Italian giants, West Ham had taken their first steps on the European trail with a Europa League qualifying tie against the Slovenian side, NK Domžale. The first leg was played in Slovenia just five days after the Karlsruher fixture, with Slovenian international Matic Črnic twice on target for the home side. The second leg of the tie on 4 August was West Ham's first game at the London Stadium and attracted the club's biggest ever home crowd up to that date, who were not disappointed by the result.

UFEA Europa League 2016–17				
NK Domžale (SVN) Ref: Mete Kalkavan	Stožice Stadium, Ljubljana, att: 8,458	Third qualifying round, 1st leg 28/07/2016	L 2–1	Črnic 11', pen, 49' Noble 18' pen

NK Domžale: Maraval, Brachi, Dobrovoljc, Horic, Balkovec, Morel (Repas 77'), Alvir, Horvat, Majer (Vetrih 86'), Matic Črnic (Xavier Júnior 90+1'), Mance. Subs not used: Milić, Vuk, Širok, Blažič.

West Ham United: Adrián, Michail Antonio (Domingos Quina 81'), Håvard Nordtveit, Winstone Reid, Sam Byram, Sofiane Feghouli, Cheikhou Kouyaté, Mark Noble, Pedro Obiang, Enner Valencia, Andy Carroll. Subs not used: Darren Randolph, Ashley Fletcher, Reece Burke, Reece Oxford, Lewis Page, Josh Cullen. Manager: Slaven Bilić.

NK Domžale (SVN) Ref: Fredy Fautrel	London Staduim, att: 53,914	Third qualifying round, 2nd leg 04/08/2016 (W 4–2)	W 3–0	Kouyaté 8', 25', Feghouli 81'

West Ham United: Darren Randolph, Håvard Nordtveit, Winstone Reid, Cheikhou Kouyaté (Pedro Obiang 79') Andy Carroll (Ashely Fletcher 90'), Sofiane Feghouli (Domingos Quina 88'), Enner Valencia, Reece Oxford, Mark Noble, Michail Antonio, Sam Byram. Substitutes not used: Adrián, Reece Burke, Lewis Page, Josh Cullen. Manager: Slaven Bilić.

NK Domžale: Maraval, Horic, Horvat (Husmani 62'), Brachi, Dobrovoljc, Majer (Xavier Júnior 77'), Balkovec, Mance (Bratanovic 68'), Matic Črnic, Alvir, Morel. Substitutes not used: Milić, Vetrih, Repas, Blažič.

It may be relatively hard to believe, but the play-off round draw for the Europa League once more pitted West Ham against Astra Giurgiu. The Albanian international Kristi Vangjeli put the home side back on level pegging just seven minutes from time.

A week later, Astra came to East London. Filipe Teixeira, a thirty-five-year-old Portuguese player who had been with West Brom between 2007 and 2010, scored the only goal of the game to see that the Hammers went no further in Europe that term.

Astra Giurgiu (ROM) Ref: Artur Soares (POR)	Stadionul Marin Anastasovici, att: 3,360	Play-off round, 1st leg 18/8/16	D 1–1	Alibec 83' Noble 45' pen

Astra Giurgiu: Silviu Lung, Geraldo Alves, Fabrício Silva Dornellas, Takayuki Seto, Junior Maranhão, Florin Lovin, Daniel Niculae, Cristian Săpunaru, Alexandru Ioniţă (Daniel Florea 85') , Kristi Vangjeli (Denis Alibec 58') , Filipe Teixeira (Silviu Balaure 90+4').
Subs not used: George Gavrilaş, Cristian Oroş, Boubacar Mansaly, Alexandru Stan. Coach: Marius Şumudică.

West Ham United: Darren Randolf, Enner Valencia (Andy Carroll, 63), Pedro Obiang, Mark Noble, Gökhan Töre, (Marcus Browne 75), Angelo Ogbonna, Sam Byram, Johnathan Calleri (Collins 63), Michail Antonio, Reece Burke, Reece Oxford. Subs not used: Adrián, Winstone Reid, Ashley Fletcher. Manager: Slaven Bilić.

Astra Giurgiu (ROM) Ref: Manuel Gräfe (DEU)	London Stadium, att: 56,932	Play-off round, 1st leg 25/08/2016 (L 1-2)	L 0–1	Filipe Teixeira 45'

West Ham United: Darren Randolph, Reece Burke (James Collins 88'), Håvard Nordtveit (Enner Valencia 46'), Angelo Ogbonna, Winston Reid (c), Sam Byram, Cheikhou Kouyaté, Gökhan Töre, Pedro Obiang, Michail Antonio, Jonathan Calleri (Ashley Fletcher 61')
Substitutes not used: Adrián, Reece Oxford, Marcus Browne, Grady Diangana. Manager: Slaven Bilić.

Astra Giurgiu: Silviu Lung, Fabricio Silva Dornellas, Junior Morais (c),Cristian Sapunaru, Geraldo Alves, Alexandru Ionita (Alexandru Stan 75'), Florin Lovin (Daniel Florea 88'), Takayuki Seto, Filipe Teixeira, Denis Alibec, Daniel Niculae (Cristian Oros 58'). Subs not used: George Gavrilas, Silviu Balaure, Romario Moise, Madalin Raileanu. Coach: Marius Şumudică.

Astra managed to qualify from their group behind Italian big boys, Roma. At the time of writing, the Romanians await a round of thirty-two meeting with Ghent. I hope they win; the game is a week or so in the future from my keyboard, but what is the shape of things to come for West Ham and British football generally?

The days when the Hammers could field a winning first team of eleven cockneys, or the time when Celtic could send a team made up entirely of boys from Glasgow out to become champions of Europe have long gone. Indeed, I very much doubt we will ever see the likes of such things again. Today, top teams are rarely made up of players characteristic of the area of the club's geographic location, but those whose talent represents what money the club has to spend. For the most part, these journeymen are transiants with more loyalty to their agents than those willing them to perform in their name.

The Irons of the 1960s came from a time and place where kids attended football matches to observe and often, athough not entirely consciously, learn. I watched Arsenal's fabled Charlie George as a youth player at Upton Park. He is about five years older than me, and although it still irks me to say it he was a massively impressive talent; I knew I could not be him, but I had friends who thought they could and so they sought to emulate in the parks and streets of East London what they had seen him do.

I personally was more in the mode of West Ham's John Charles and as such, a few Charlie George impressionists had to learn to deal with my impersonation of Charlo's 'muscular' response. I also came up against nascent George Bests, Dennis Laws, and one lad who appeared to be an avatar of Alan Hudson—complete with the '70s King's Road haircut courtesy of his apprentice hairdresser sister. This was the way Islington-born George honed his craft, and how Canning Town boy Charlo started on the road to becoming the first black player to wear the three lions over his heart. This is also how the old-fashioned craft apprentices learned their trades, long years of watching, practicing, experimenting, and learning by doing.

Like my mates and I, Charlie and Ron had learned by watching, immitating, and playing in what Ray Oldenburg called the 'third place'; an informal, social atmosphere. Oldenburg saw 'third spaces' as possessing the following hallmarks:

1. Free or inexpensive

2. Highly accessible: proximate for many (walking distance)

3. Involve regulars – those who habitually congregate there

4. Welcoming and comfortable

5. Both new friends and old should be found there

The football 'third places' were roads, playgrounds, and almost any open space (in my youth, this included bombsites from the Second World War). In these locations, there were no critical parents, over-keen coaches, or other superfluous judges passing on their pearls of wisdom. Of course, there was the odd 'pass it you silly fool' kind of thing—or something a little stronger—but this sort of critique was often passed straight back with a hearty cry of 'bollocks!' and forgotten almost as soon as it was uttered.

By and large, we in the modern era do not have these venues or the facility of access at pocket-money prices to the excitement and romance of the first-class game. I saw Bobby Moore, Geoff Hurst, and Martin Peters play week in, week out against the likes of Bobby Charlton, Colin Bell, and Roger Hunt for less than what would be paid today for a newspaper.

This being the case, we in Britain are not producing quality players in the numbers we once did; we have a football skills shortage in much the same way as we have in many other industries. We import mercenaries from every corner of the planet at a tremendous cost, which is passed on to the punter. Many of the best of these 'soldiers of fortune' started their playing days on the streets and in the open spaces under African and South American skies, unfettered by a fixation for expensive reproduction kits, boots, and over-schooled adult instructors from the football counterpart of what Ivan Illich called the 'Disabling Professions'.

However, just as we have a transitory football workforce, great numbers of fans are almsot equally 'temporary'. East Londoners who have never and will never see the inside of Anfield sit in their living rooms singing 'You'll never walk alone' as the Liverpool Reds strut their stuff on pay-per-view. Folk who have been born, brought up and live in Bristol refer to 'us' when speaking of Manchester City. These are truly fans, but they have little resemblence in terms of fidelity to those of us who have had our connection to the badge and club passed down for generations. These 'far-flung-fans' are more consumers of football and will shift their loyalty like they might change supermarkets as soon as the shirt they have bought becomes more associated with failure than success. This is an incarnation of what the Marxists call 'commodity fetishism'; you will never walk alone as long as you keep winning, and I can con myself into believing that I have something over on Bournemouth born and bred Bert the Blue.

For all this, the shirt is still claret and blue; the crossed hammers remain; and bubbles continue to fly so high. I have never been anything but a Hammer; I was born that way with it in my DNA. As my family say, 'it's the way me muvva put me 'at on.' My mum sang 'Bubbles' to me in my cradle, I sang it to my son (to his annoyance right, into his teenage years). I have never wanted to be any thing else; it is who I am. It makes no difference at all whether we win or lose. I am West Ham until I die—and after.

BIBLIOGRAPHY

Belton, B., *Days of Iron: The Story of West Ham United in the Fifties* (Derby: JMD Media, 2013)

Belton, B., *Johnny the One*, (Stroud: Tempus, 2004)

Belton, B., *The Battle of Montevideo* (Stroud: The History Press, 2008)

Belton, B., *The Black Hammers* (London: Pennant, 2006)

Belton, B., *The Men of 64* (Stroud: Tempus, 2005)

Illich, I., Zola, I. K., McKnight, J., Caplan, J., and Shaiken, H., *Disabling Professions* (London: Marion Boyars, 1977)

Oldenburg, R., *The Great Good Place: Cafes, Coffee Shops, Community Centers, Beauty Parlors, General Stores, Bars, Hangouts, and How They Get You Through the Day* (New York: Paragon House)